THEATER
IN THE
AMERICAS

A Series from
Southern
Illinois
University
Press

Scott
Magelssen
Series Editor

Working in the Wings

New Perspectives on Theatre History and Labor

Edited by Elizabeth A. Osborne and
Christine Woodworth

Southern Illinois University Press • Carbondale

Printed in the United States of America

18 17 16 15 4 3 2 1

Library of Congress Cataloging-in-Publication Data
Working in the wings : new perspectives on theatre history and labor / edited by Elizabeth A. Osborne, Christine Woodworth.
pages cm. — (Theater in the Americas.)
Includes bibliographical references and index.
ISBN 978-0-8093-3420-9 (paperback)
ISBN 0-8093-3420-8 (paperback)
ISBN 978-0-8093-3421-6 (ebook)
1. Theater—United States—History. 2. Theater—Production and direction—United States—History. I. Osborne, Elizabeth A., 1977– editor. II. Woodworth, Christine, editor.
PN2221.W67 2015
792.0973—dc23 2014039263

The paper used in this publication meets the minimum requirements of American National Standard for Information Sciences—Permanence of Paper for Printed Library Materials, ANSI Z39.48-1992. ♾

To our families,
who taught us how to work and feel the effects of our work most deeply,
and to all the other workers in the wings

Contents

Illustrations and Table

Illustrations

Table

Acknowledgments

As with all books, this project would never have survived without the help of many individuals, a number of whom labored without thought of compensation. Our thanks to all, and our apologies to anyone we inadvertently miss.

Indispensable to this project has been the steadfast devotion of the individuals who worked so diligently over the past few years to make the Mid-America Theatre Conference a home to high-quality theatre scholarship: Ann Haugo, Scott Magelssen, John Fletcher, and Peter Campbell. The excellent 2012 Theatre History Symposium was the starting point for this volume, and we send a collective shout-out to all those who presented that year. Thank you to our many fabulous MATC colleagues, including Megan Lewis, Rob Shimko, Sara Freeman, Lisa Jackson-Schebetta, Kris Messer, and the illustrious Heather Nathans, for expanding the ways that we think about theatre, history, and labor.

We extend our gratitude to those at Southern Illinois University Press, especially Kristine Priddy, Bob Schanke, Scott Magelssen, Wayne Larsen, Julie Bush, the editorial board, and the anonymous outside peer reviewer. We deeply appreciate your guidance and enthusiasm for this project.

We also appreciate the support of institutional colleagues along the way. To Mary Karen Dahl, Daniel Sack, Kris Salata, Nia Witherspoon, George McConnell, and Cameron Jackson at Florida State University, Jim Fisher and Ann Dils at the University of North Carolina at Greensboro, and Pat Collins, Heather May, and Chris Hatch at Hobart and William Smith Colleges, we are grateful for your unending patience, suggestions, and encouragement. Academic labor relies on grants and other funding sources.

We would like to especially thank Hobart and William Smith Colleges, the University of North Carolina at Greensboro, Florida State University, and all those institutions that supported our authors in their work. And for her heroic work on the proofs and index, a huge thank you to Beth's graduate assistant, Shelby Lunderman.

The work reflected in these essays would not be possible without the labor of a great many librarians—heroes to all theatre historians. We extend our thanks to the library and research staff at the following collections: the Manuscripts and Archives Division at the New York Public Library, the Billy Rose Theatre Division at the New York Public Library, the Library of Congress, Special Collections and Archives at George Mason University, the Walter P. Reuther Library at Wayne State University, St. Augustine Historical Society Research Library, the Channing Pollock Theatre Collection at Howard University, the New York Historical Society, the Curtis Theatre Collection at the University of Pittsburgh, the Paul Bierley Collection in the Center for American Music and Sousa Archives at the University of Illinois, City Museum of New York, and the United States Institute for Theatre Technology.

A huge thank you must also go to our dedicated essay contributors for working so hard to make deadlines, secure permissions, and reply to unending queries and comments on their scholarship. Your work is fabulous—the book would be nowhere without it!

Finally, as most theatre people and scholars know, our work extends well into daily life at home. We are grateful for our families and friends who allowed us to debate ideas over dinner, cared for children so we could write, and held our hands during the darkest days. Jack, Mary Ann, Connor, Joe, Lisa, and David, we love you. While it may be invisible to the reader, your labor will be forever inscribed in our hearts. Thank you.

—Beth and Chris

Working in the Wings

Introduction: The Work of Play in Performance

Elizabeth A. Osborne and Christine Woodworth

> In everyday life, "if" is a fiction, in the theatre "if" is an experiment. In everyday life, "if" is an evasion, in the theatre "if" is the truth. When we are persuaded to believe in this truth, then the theatre and life are one. This is a high aim. It sounds like hard work. To play needs much work. But when we experience work as play, then it is not work anymore. A play is play.
>
> —Peter Brook, *The Empty Space*

> All work and no play makes Jack a dull boy.
>
> —anonymous proverb

It was the opening night of Augustin Daly's famous melodrama *Under the Gaslight*, August 12, 1867. The play's climactic moment features the debut of one of melodrama's best-known spectacles—a character is bound to the railroad tracks and saved at the last moment from instant and horrible death by the romantic lead. In this case, though, a one-armed male soldier was bound to the tracks. Just as the female lead burst from the shed to save him, the spectacle collapsed. As Daly's brother recounted in his biography of the playwright and impresario:

> The intensely wrought feelings of the spectators found vent in almost hysterical laughter when the "railroad train" parted in the middle and disclosed the flying legs of the human motor who was propelling the first half of the express. Had the effect of the scene depended not upon the suspense and emotion created by the whole situation, but upon the

> machinery, the piece had been irretrievably lost; but the real sensation was beyond chance of accident.[1]

The "chance of accident" that resulted in the failure of the much-anticipated train effect, now typically relegated to the status of amusing anecdote, has often been situated as a mere footnote in the narrative surrounding the historic significance of Daly's play. The revelation of the operator's legs is often glossed over in favor of the contentious, international legal battle that ensued between Daly and Dion Boucicault, whose play *After Dark, a Drama of London Life* bore a striking resemblance to Daly's melodrama.[2] Yet the very failure of the train effect provokes some vexing questions for theatre scholars: Who was the man in the train? Who or what failed on that fateful evening? Why not investigate this failure further?

Theatre has long been an art form of subterfuge, concealment, and illusion, and practicing artists often actively hide the work in the wings in order to foster a sense of theatrical magic. Oftentimes, the only opportunities to glimpse the mysteries behind the curtain arise from failures, such as the one that occurred on the opening night of Daly's *Under the Gaslight*. Even radical deviations from realism and naturalism, whether inspired by classical tragedies, Renaissance verse plays, or the theories of Bertolt Brecht, intentionally mask elements of their process from the audience. Traditionally, the theatre practitioner presents the finished product rather than the work in progress. Even those contemporary companies that focus on showing their process do much of the actual work out of sight. The legacy of shrouding the work of artists and craftsmen in order to foster a deceptively seamless or even an intentionally ruptured night at the theatre has created enormous challenges for theatre and performance scholars hoping to document the creative process—the specific people and acts required to realize a work of theatrical art. In what ways can we measure if that work *works*? How might that theatrical event be documented, preserved, and interpreted over time? How do we theorize the work of play when it has been intentionally or unintentionally hidden from view? What is missing from the current conversation about theatrical work? In short, what does it mean to work, and to create work, in the theatre?

In the wake of the economic downturn and global recession following the 2007 bursting of the real estate bubble, discussions of work preoccupied the world. The public discourse has been dominated by employment statistics, labor concerns of the unemployed or underemployed, and the work-life balance for those who allegedly work too much (or too little), making it clear that work shapes our individual and collective identities. Indeed, in this contemporary world, who we are and how we fit within social structures is largely defined by the work we do—whether or not that work is actually paid labor. To this point, studies of work have constellated around labor practices, workers' rights, and the ways in which work—in concept and practice—reverberates through the public imaginary. In theatre studies, much writing has been done on the intersections of specific labor movements with theatre. Yet within the performing arts, definitions of work also transcend the person or practice and focus on the product—the work of art—generated by the collaborative act of creation. In what ways might a fresh examination of labor—spanning a range of time periods—offer insights into the cultural myths that permeate the public imagination regarding the topic of work? With this collection of essays, we intend to explore these many timely questions and issues, using theatre as a lens through which to consider, challenge, and revise our understanding of work.

How an individual and a culture define *work* determines how they value (or devalue) the act of labor and, in turn, the people who perform that labor. Theatrical work has historically been marginalized compared with other, more profit-generating industries. Yet the theatre—and the labor it requires to create its work—has persisted for thousands of years, unfettered by differences in culture and continent. Indeed, the theory of play, which brings together fields as diverse as child development, anthropology, neuroscience, technology, and sociology to assess the function of imagination and game playing in human development, has gained remarkable traction in the worlds of finance, engineering, and product development. Prominent employers from within Fortune 500 companies have identified the value of time spent in creative exploration in terms of employee productivity. In one example, Microsoft testing director Ross Smith asserted, "Using productivity games and play in the workplace is a successful technique to build organizational trust and, by extension, create a culture of innovation."[3] While this is certainly an important and worthwhile realization, it is one that many theatre scholars and professionals are already well aware of: theatre is both work and play. As is quoted in the epigraph, Peter Brook suggests in *The Empty Space* that the hard work of the "if" warrants scrutiny and celebration not as an alternative to or as a bolster in support of more traditional conceptions of labor but as work in its own right. As Brook so wisely writes, "It sounds like hard work. To play needs much work."[4] For many the theatre is an escape from the drudgeries of daily toil. For the artists and craftsmen called to this field, theatre making is not a distraction from labor but is, in fact, legitimate labor in its own right.

Theatre and performance work does not exist in a vacuum, and recent writing, such as Shannon Jackson's *Social Works: Performing Art, Supporting*

Publics, illustrates how public works of art serve as nexuses between the artists who labor over their creation, the institutions that present that work, and the public that witnesses them. She argues for a new paradigm for exploring art's connection to the "social sphere" in order to posit new understandings of "the paradoxes of Art and its Support."[5] Jackson's notion of support includes that which enables the creation of art from institutional and ideological veins and encompasses how art, in turn, supports those infrastructures and ideas. Similarly, we seek to examine the relationship between theatre and work, borrowing from Jackson's understanding that "performance both activates and depends upon a relational system, a contingency that makes it a prime venue for reflecting on the social and for exposing the dependencies of convivial and expressive spheres."[6] Jackson's study illustrates the "relational system" of public art, revealing the interdependencies that are often hidden from view. The tendency to conceal these interdependencies parallels the ways in which much of the work of theatre is intentionally disappeared for the sake of illusion. Just as the symbioses between artists and institutions are integral for the survival of each, the work in the wings and the work behind the footlights cannot exist independent of each other.

Theatre can be one of the most public of all the arts, drawing legions to witness its work unfold. Yet beneath the surface of any theatrical production lurks a subterranean world of artists and craftsmen whose labor has been deliberately obscured from view. *Working in the Wings* aims to bring the same level of public and scholarly attention to the carefully hidden work of the theatre. By exposing what is concealed, this collection reveals the artists, craftspeople, and laborers who create the illusions set before audiences. More than that, though, we aim to delve into both the representation of work in performance and the visibility of labor—as an act, a process, and a creative product. Indeed, labor itself serves as one of the ghosts of the theatre. Marvin Carlson argues that theatre is "a cultural activity deeply involved with memory and haunted by repetition. Moreover, as an ongoing social institution it almost invariably reinforces this involvement and haunting by bringing together on repeated occasions and in the same spaces the same bodies (onstage and in the audience) and the same physical material."[7] While this repetition—ghosting—fosters active remembering, at times it is at the expense of particular individuals or groups that have been intentionally forgotten. This collection seeks to remember differently by exploring the ways that a fresh examination of American theatrical labor across a range of time periods offers insights into the cultural myths that permeate the public imagination surrounding, and as a result of, those moments that connect work and theatre.

In a parallel act of forgotten concealment, scholars themselves are often accustomed to occupying the hidden substrate of labor that goes into the creation of a scholarly product. Whether in Research-I universities or in community colleges, scholarly research is habitually relegated to those stolen moments between committee meetings, grading, course preparation, student advising, rehearsals, and community outreach. More often, research happens over holidays, during vacations, and in the wee hours of the morning as faculty juggle increasing demands on their time and ever-shrinking research and travel budgets. With this academic reality in mind, this collection also seeks to foreground the work of the theatre historian, challenging the methodological legacies that perpetuate the tradition of obscuring academic research and writing. Thomas Postlewait highlights these methodological challenges in his 2004 essay "Constructing Events in Theatre History: A Matter of Credibility." Yet he connects historiographic concerns, such as the constitution of effective evidence, the ways in which organizing categories reveal assumptions and biases, and the struggle to place theatrical events within particular contexts, directly to the scholar's individual act of scholarship and reputation. He writes, "Our sources provide the credible witnesses to the events we attempt to construct, but each of us who works as a historian is also a witness to history. In our scholarship, our historical narratives, we perform our own acts of witnessing. Our credibility, like that of the statements we draw upon, is always on the line."[8] Indeed, our scholarly bodies of work are generated by our scholarly bodies. The act of recognizing that research and writing are part of our labors—physically, emotionally, creatively, and intellectually—and the fact that these labors have both cost and payoff for our minds and bodies are imperative to our continuation as scholars. Likewise, our labor has ramifications for the field, contributing to the overall valuing or devaluing of particular artists and creations. To put it simply, work has a price.

Fieldwork: A Survey

The critical examination of "work" as a concept, practice, and social institution has historically been the purview of social scientists, cultural historians, and critical theorists who seek to understand how work defines and in turn is defined by social contexts. Recent publications within sociology underscore this legacy, including Tony Watson's *Sociology, Work, and Organization* and Stephen Sweet and Peter F. Meiksins's *Changing Contours of Work: Jobs and Opportunities in the New Economy.* Both of these texts have become staples in large sociology courses, illustrating the preponderance of work as foundational to social systems. Current social theorists trace this conceptual framework back to the Enlightenment theories of John Locke and his contemporaries while acknowledging the radical ideological shift in definitions of work following the writings of Karl Marx. In his book *Work*, sociologist Steven Peter Vallas notes this change in this line of thinking: "Humans are doubly creative: we not only transform the external world though our labor; in so doing, we also transform ourselves. It is in this sense that work constitutes an especially formative influence at both the individual and the collective level of analysis."[9] In other words, work becomes an active, creative, and generative force that literally makes—and shapes—the world.

In recent years, scholars in fields as diverse as labor studies, business, political science, and history have also authored studies on work, further expanding and complicating what is now a largely interdisciplinary field. Yet despite the volume of scholarship focused on exploring, analyzing, and realizing the concept of work, it is difficult to settle on a clear and comprehensive definition of what constitutes work, who is able to perform that work, and how work reverberates through life. Clearly, before delving into this topic further, an exploration of terms incorporating the wealth of scholarship from diverse fields is in order. Despite the variety of perspectives, a number of common threads emerge that illustrate the difficulties inherent in offering a fixed and stable definition of work. Labor studies scholar John W. Budd puts forward a sweepingly broad approach in *The Thought of Work*, even as he argues that such an approach requires boundaries. He contends that "a meaningful definition of work [. . .] needs to lie somewhere between the overly narrow focus on paid employment and the excessively broad inclusion of all human activity" and ultimately defines work as "purposeful human activity involving physical or mental exertion that is not undertaken solely for pleasure and that has economic or symbolic value."[10] At first glance, a study of paid employment exclusively may seem much tidier in that the boundaries of "work" could be drawn at the paycheck. However, such a definition ignores the vast connotations of work that exist in all facets of society. Even defining work as that which is paid is far from straightforward and confined. Instead, monetarily compensated labor presents a host of fraught issues: labor unions and workers' rights, perceptions of work legitimacy, pay equity, the reliance on unpaid (or underpaid) labor, benefits and health care, a living wage, and much more. Certainly, Budd's assertion that work can be defined through "economic or symbolic value" opens up the field of study while simultaneously complicating that field through its very expansiveness. If symbolic value determines work, what then *is* work?

Government scholar Russell Muirhead similarly addresses the vexing task of defining work in his book *Just Work*:

> Work is endlessly differentiated. How could it be that the nineteenth-century domestic servant, the assembly-line worker, and the corporate consultant have anything in common? There are as many experiences of work as there are workers, as many kinds of work as there are jobs. Work [. . .] reflects a historically contingent division of labor, while on the other [hand], its every instance suggests the infinite expanse of the human mind and spirit.[11]

While it is clear that definitions of work are "endlessly differentiated," recent work scholarship across disciplines underscores the innumerable ways that work shapes daily life, identities, and cultures.[12] A broader study—and a more amorphous understanding of the concept of "work"—encompasses paid and unpaid labor, the application of embodied effort over time in the creation of a product or service (and, indeed, the product itself), and the ways in which labor constitutes countless identities. This extraordinary vastness reveals new possibilities for considerations of work across time, space, and discipline. The omnipresence, yet imprecision, of "work" as a cultural signifier illustrates the complexities of weaving a coherent work narrative and underscores precisely why a collection dedicated to theatre and performance work is necessary.

Other tropes that have emerged in the field of work studies and that connect directly to theatrical work include the ways that work shapes public imaginaries and individual identities; the permeability or erasure of the boundaries between work and life; the connection between work and economic, social, or political power; the ways that labor is embodied and, in turn, how particular types of labor are inscribed on the bodies of workers over time; and the value ascribed to certain kinds of work over others. Budd describes the border between work and life as "nebulous," while Vallas asserts that "the boundary between 'work' [. . .] and 'non-work' has become an increasingly difficult line to draw in recent years."[13] The seeming nebulousness, porosity, or erasure of the boundary between work and nonwork or between work and life raises the critical question of who determines what constitutes work and how that work is valued. Budd argues that "cultural norms define what is valued as work or who is deemed a worker across time and space."[14] Historically, divisions of inclusion/exclusion, citizenship/alienation, enfranchisement/disenfranchisement, and stability/instability have fallen out across lines of gender, race, class, and disability. As business scholars Sharon C. Bolton and Maeve Houlihan contend, "Work matters because it is rarely only that; it is about esteem and disrespect, status and subordination, opportunity and cost, commitment and alienation. If we listen to people talk about their work we are reminded that work and workplaces are fields of struggle where interests can both coincide and clash, and personhood is both attacked and maintained." Bolton and Houlihan further note, "Thinking in terms of work matters recognizes that work has both material and subjective dimensions rooted as it is in a moral economy; a world where the *social* and the economic are immutably symbiotic and interdependent."[15]

It is perhaps this interdependence that complicates analyses of work, as Vallas seems to suggest in his claim that the "sociology of work coexists uneasily alongside parallel literatures devoted to the study of organizations, occupations, labor markets, professions, and economic networks."[16] Part of this "unease" may stem from the embodied nature of work. Marjorie L. DeVault contends, "We all live physical lives, located in particular material settings, with limitations imposed by our human bodies and all their frailties. People use their bodies in work and work always takes a physical toll, though quite differently in different kinds of work. [. . .] It may seem obvious that workers live in bodies but employers and policymakers have often acted as if they didn't."[17] DeVault then offers a paradigm for institutional ethnography that includes "attention to work processes," "texts and textualizations," and "mapping social relations" as a means to better explain and contextualize formations of work and workers.[18] Yet, as Vallas points out, texts and textualizations are not always reliable artifacts of work, in that "there is a hidden underside of workplace life, often invisible to authority figures, where informal norms and practices are established that often stand at odds with formal expectations."[19] The concealed underbelly of work is not always simply a mode of resistance, however. Much labor—in every era and culture—is made deliberately invisible, often because of cultural norms that value one form of work over another.

Shifting to a more direct consideration, in theatre and performance studies the issue of work is both visible and invisible. Intersections of work and theatre—or of workers in the theatre—are most plentiful in historical studies that center on unions, strikes, and the workers that take center stage in these real-life dramas. For example, cultural histories such as Susan Duffy's *American Labor on Stage*, Kirk W. Fuoss's *Striking Performances/Performing Strikes*, and the extensive literature surrounding the Federal Theatre Project explore the worker struggles and uprisings that characterized the Great Depression (1929–39) in the United States.[20] Often linked to leftist or progressive political agendas, similar explosions of research surround other historical moments that witnessed large-scale worker rebellion and revolution: the Communists' League of Workers' Theatres; mass spectacles in Germany prior to the rise of the Nazi Party and World War II; British workers' theatre in the 1920s; radical street theatre of the 1960s; and the infamous Russian "mass action," the Storming of the Winter Palace. Scholarship also circulates around specific theatre companies and artists dedicated to social change and the working class, including the San Francisco Mime Troupe; El Teatro Campesino; the Berliner Ensemble; Augusto Boal's Theatre of the Oppressed; and the Jamaican women's rights collective, Sistren Theatre.[21] The wealth of scholarship that operates at the intersection of the laborer and theatre brings visibility to the ways that workers fight for recognition and social change in their places of employment, communities, and societies. Indeed, by choosing these historical moments and performances as the subjects of interrogation, scholars bring public attention to the issues at stake in a way that effectively mirrors the purpose of the original performance. Such choices return the historic workers, the issues those workers faced, and the drive for social change to the forefront of the contemporary conversation, thus recovering these actions and performances from the realm of the invisible, the forgotten. Just as important to scholars of theatre and performance, such examinations consider how theatre becomes one tool in the arsenal for performing that struggle, gaining recognition, and enacting change.

While it may seem that the exploration of work and performance is well documented, there are many points that remain invisible in the current scholarly conversation. The choice to highlight particular eras such as the Great Depression omits those historical moments in which workers' theatres struggled to make themselves heard or played to a more confined, niche audience. Moreover, these decisions run the risk of privileging certain performance activity and thus silencing other voices. Theatre created by and for workers or working-class audiences frequently carries theatrical stigmas that parallel those of popular or amateur entertainments. Just as melodramas, vaudeville, pageants, and community theatre were dismissed for many years as unworthy of scholarly attention, so too have the aesthetic and social merits of workers' performances frequently gone unremarked. And yet, like the eruption of high-quality scholarship on popular entertainments in the past thirty years, recent scholarship has begun the long process of recovering the worker in a wide range of cultures, historical moments, and geographies, even as it makes use of a wide range of methodologies. This important work documents the role of theatre in the recent Canadian labor movement, explores the many uses of activist theatre in South Africa, considers how theatre has "played" in Australia's labor movement, and complicates the ways that the concept of work offers insights into the functioning of medieval Christian communities via the York Cycle.[22] Such explorations expand previous conceptions of work beyond the power of agitprop pieces like *Waiting for Lefty* and offer new possibilities for ways of thinking about theatre history and performance's potential influence on the wider world.

Another important consideration at the intersection of work and theatre centers on the workers of the theatre itself—writers, actors, directors, designers, choreographers, managers, stage technicians, run crew, builders, marketers, and producers—who contribute to and create the work that manifests on stage for an audience.[23] While performance tradition foregrounds the visibility of actors and directors for audiences and scholarly traditions often privilege the written text—and many excellent books and articles regarding the work of the playwright, actor, and director already exist[24]—the individuals necessarily located "behind" the illusion often remain in the proverbial shadows. Hidden backstage, the workers who build sets, ensure an actress makes her costume change, operate the fly lines, or manage the plethora of minor (and major) performance-night traumas have a real, immediate, and lasting impact on the performance that an audience experiences on any given evening. Though these efforts can be challenging to document and/or locate in historical ephemera, they illuminate the process of creating work for the stage. As Christin Essin argues in her 2011 article "An Aesthetic of Backstage Labor," the backstage performance is often every bit as choreographed as the onstage performance, and the use of tools, technology, physical strength, skill, and creativity is part of a "functional *and* aesthetic practice" (emphasis in original) that conveys meaning.[25] This facet of work and performance sheds light on the actual work of the people who create theatre itself. Whether those individuals are veteran professionals, first-time community theatre volunteers, or somewhere in between, their contribution to theatre has all too frequently remained "backstage" in the scholarly conversation. In a curious contrast to scholarly writing, popular literature on the stage frequently delves into these backstage activities. Numerous newspaper and magazine articles purport to reveal the proverbial magician's secrets of the theatre through photo exposés of backstage activities and interviews with designers, theatre technicians, and other theatre workers.[26] The burgeoning scholarly interest in these otherwise invisible theatre workers promises to twine together these threads of popular discourse and scholarly historiography in productive ways.

These discussions about the oft-ignored theatre worker and the ways in which politics, class, and workers often burst onto the stage offer important insights into some of the ways that the larger concepts of work and theatre collide. And yet, while they remain vital considerations, they also omit many of the more theoretical ways that work permeates self-identity at a foundational level, thus blurring boundaries between public and private, social expectations and self. The consideration of work as both an abstract and formative concept reveals the possibility that theatre may be, to borrow an idea that appears in Elizabeth Reitz Mullenix's essay later in this volume and serves as one of the major section themes, the "work of the public mind." This characterization of theatre operating within an imagined space of individual, community, and nation formation opens numerous scholarly possibilities. Though certainly more abstract, these prospects offer new and fruitful ways of considering the complex web of relationships that influence, build upon, and sustain concepts of performance, history, and labor.

This Volume at Work: A Reader's Guide

In *The Problem with Work*, Kathi Weeks challenges her readers to think about why work holds such a treasured and troubled place in contemporary society—why, she wonders, is it "normal" that work takes such a physical, psychological, and emotional toll on the bodies and minds of the workers? Focusing her study in the United States, Weeks troubles not only the widespread acceptance of this system but also the tendency to elevate work to a position of immense power in individual private lives. As she succinctly posits, "What is perplexing is less the acceptance of the present reality that one must work to live than the willingness to live for work." In many ways, Weeks's analysis makes manifest the proverb "All work and no play makes Jack a dull boy." Within her framework, it would seem that Jack has likely accepted the cultural assumption that work plays a foundational role in his life and has, in fact, chosen to live as a dedicated workaholic. Though Weeks writes from the perspective of a political theorist, she explicitly discusses popular culture's part in the reinscribing of this characterization of work on the public psyche, bemoaning the "lack of interest in representing the daily grind of work routines in various forms of popular culture [and] the tendency among cultural critics to focus on the animation and meaningfulness of commodities rather than the eclipse of laboring activity that Marx identifies as the source of their fetishization."[27]

In some ways, this book picks up where Weeks ends, confronting the myriad resonances of work in the theatre and considering how theatre—as that most public of art forms—might serve as a nexus for demonstrating and interrogating such concerns. *Working in the Wings* considers theatre from act to artifact in order to reveal the obscured or concealed facets of theatrical working conditions, the creative work and the processes of creation, the ways in which theatrical work constitutes overarching cultural narratives, and ways that historically marginalized workers resist or defy confining perceptions. Taken together, these essays further expand the significance of theatrical work, destabilizing fixed notions of theatrical work as complete yet ephemeral. By examining the process of theatre making from the perspectives of the artists themselves, the relationships between artist and audience, artist and historic context, become all the more richly textured. Demystifying the elements of production that have historically been obscured reveals the hierarchies of labor at play as well as the human effort exerted to create art. Ultimately, this results in the recovery of lost or devalued creative collaborators and a revaluing of their contributions. Revealing and revaluing the hidden work of theatrical production enables a fresh examination of the consumption of theatrical art by audiences and publics. Several contributors address how this interplay constructs both individual and social identities. In a related vein, this collection foregrounds the work of the theatre historian, highlighting the perils and pleasures of delving into neglected terrain. The artifacts under consideration in this collection range from traditional archival materials, such as performance texts and architectural structures, to less tangible remains, delving into the complexities of the working process that elude or preclude the leaving behind of material traces.

The essays that follow use theatrical performances to foreground both labor and laborer in a variety of ways. Whether the focus is on the challenges of documenting the work of longtime creative partnerships, on reconstructing the work of the Federal Theatre Project's massive outdoor Caravan Theatre, or on the active physical labor of designing or constructing stage scenery, we aim to celebrate the heretofore uncelebrated. In addition to recovering these laborers and their labors, the authors included in this collection interrogate the ways that we conceptualize this volatile topic. As demonstrated by the widespread joblessness and economic turmoil of the "Second Great Contraction"—a term formulated by Kenneth Rogoff and Carmen Reinhart to describe the economic recession of the early twenty-first century—work plays a vital role in the economic future, but it is far more than that. Work, and the confidence that stable, well-paying work engenders, is integral to the conception of self and the national imaginary.[28] Indeed, work—and the lack of it—has become such a contentious and charged issue in the contemporary United States (and in much of the contemporary world) that we wonder if the nation has lost its ability to think about work critically, to question our assumptions and our approaches. This book seeks to do exactly that, using theatre as a way to experience performances of work and to stimulate discussions about these fundamental issues.

The essays in this volume are united by the call to expand the boundaries of preconceptions about work, theatre, and history and to incorporate methodologies and theories from fields as diverse as theatre history, cultural history, historiography, work studies, architecture, legal studies, economics, and literary analysis. To this end, the collected essays in *Working in the Wings* are variously concerned with the labor and laborers involved in the creation of theatre, and they encompass a swath of historic moments and theatrical forms ranging from union theatres in the factories of Detroit to African Americans dancing the cakewalk in Florida's resort hotels, from the complex cultural labor of Chicago's Columbian Exposition (1893) to Rinde Eckert's Obie Award–winning piece, *And God Created Great Whales* (2000).

With the dual goals of interrogating the intersections of work and theatre and of expanding how we, as scholars, conceive of the concepts of work and theatre, we have organized this volume around four often overlapping thematic concepts: working conditions; inscription, erasure, and recovery—palimpsests of labor; myth, memory, and manifestation—the work of the public mind; and the creative work / the work of creation. Each section includes in-depth exploration of major questions and themes. Working independently, the individual sections offer different ways of thinking about labor connected to theatre and performance conceptually. Studies of backstage laborers, of the working class finding a voice through performances of their lives, or of unemployed artists and craftsmen finding livelihoods—and audiences—represent those workers or groups whose untold stories require a bit of digging in the archives. Yet the potential for meaningful research that operates at the intersections of work and theatre extends far beyond these explorations, and the second and third sections of the volume explore these issues. In what ways might theatre become the public stage wherein the construction of American identity and nationhood collide with the conceptual importance of work? How might the myths, memories, and ambitions of the nation work and play on and off American stages, and how does theatrical performance refute and reinscribe these concepts? By examining such questions across different sections using complementary methodologies, this volume takes a historiographical stance, exploring why certain figures have been erased or displaced from historical narratives and the resulting archival and theoretical challenges of resituating them in the histories of theatre. Additionally, this collection looks at the confluence of these tropes through examinations of the oft-hidden processes of creating art and its interconnectedness to cultural narratives of labor. *Working in the*

Wings goes on to raise questions about the need to reconsider the historiographic work of theatre historians themselves. This thematic organization operates as a map of where the field has been by expanding upon known frameworks even as it presses onward into unknown territories.

The first part, "Working Conditions," delves into the physical terrain of worker concerns, collaborations, conditions, and perceptions. This attention to the immediate material conditions of the worker leads to a consideration of the ways that work shapes, influences, and dictates worker identities. By pairing these dual concerns, this section highlights the intentionally hidden theatre laborers, bringing them into focus in their historical moment and seeking connections to theatre and cultural history. It begins with Chrystyna Dail's essay, an articulate case study that integrates careful archival research with cultural history to explore the multifaceted political, economic, and racial implications of work for an often-silenced generation of laborers in the post–World War II era. Sara Freeman then analyzes the collaboration of director Les Waters and designer Annie Smart, husband-and-wife theatrical artists, and suggests historiographical approaches for considering theatrical job descriptions, gender relations, and duration in creative and marital partnership. In his essay, Tom Robson mines the J. R. Clancy catalogs of the late nineteenth-century stage for their use of technology and technician marketing and suggests ways of ensuring that stage technicians take on a more prominent place in theatre history. Finally, in her essay on the socially significant "day jobs" of two early twentieth-century actresses, Christine Woodworth directs us to reconsider the ways we think about the lives of theatre workers outside the theatre itself. Collected together, the essays in "Working Conditions" examine the challenges of writing about the manifestations of labor in regard to theatre praxis and interrogate the ways in which existing methodologies reinscribe the very histories that scholars strive to contest.

The second part, "Inscription, Erasure, and Recovery: Palimpsests of Labor," details those workers whose contributions are often intentionally erased from the archival record. Whether their work is overwritten in the hopes of stealing or reassigning credit, intentionally hidden as a history the majority wants to forget, or simply prioritized as something of so little importance that it vanishes or is rewritten to make it more palatable, these workers have earned their places in theatre history through unrewarded, often backbreaking labors. These essays rely on the careful assembly of historical records from a wide range of sources, which the scholar then integrates back into theatre and performance history. Dorothy Chansky examines one such population in her work, comparing representations of female domesticity in two pieces, Sarah Ruhl's *The Clean House* and Martha Rosler's *Semiotics of the Kitchen*, and connecting class, gender, and identity with the complex politics of domestic labor in the late twentieth century. With his essay, Max Shulman deepens the discussion by examining how the disfigured, misshapen, world-weary bodies of vaudevillians and clowns served as markers of the working class, mirrored the performance of race and ethnicity, and made manifest the spiritual and psychic concerns of the industrial period. Elizabeth A. Osborne goes on to highlight the frequently forgotten popular entertainments of the only national theatre to exist in the history of the United States. Through an examination of the Caravan Theatre's free summer performances and other community theatre work, she interrogates and revises the public identity of the Federal Theatre Project. Concluding this section, Jerry Dickey refocuses attention on the background, training, and innovation of the African American waiters and dancers who transformed the cakewalk—the first social dance in U.S. history to be shared by whites and blacks—into the most popular event in the weekly calendars of exclusive East Coast resort hotels at the turn of the twentieth century. Each essay explores the ways that individuals and groups that are often marginalized by their race, class, gender, or geography used theatrical work and performance to claim their identities and resist limiting narratives. They rewrite the histories that have been occluded.

Part three takes a step back to consider theatre as "Myth, Memory, and Manifestation: The Work of the Public Mind." In this section, essays press against defined boundaries as theatrical performances meld with the public imagination to take on the work of identity and nation formation. In their varied historical encounters with theatre history and performance, these essays encourage a reconsideration of theatre as a larger framing force that both influences and creates the popular imaginary. In so doing, theatre becomes an idea that circulates through the population, a "work of the public mind" that connects works of art with larger ideological narratives of cultural, political, and historical identity. Beginning this section is Elizabeth Reitz Mullenix's essay drawing together Dion Boucicault's famous melodrama *The Octoroon*, the public execution of radical abolitionist John Brown, and the play's potential influence on Republican politics on the eve of the physically and ideologically destructive Civil War. AnnMarie T. Saunders continues this explication of the points of convergence between theatre, labor, and the public mind as she considers the first efforts to construct a theatre on the unstable foundations of the U.S. capital and the manifold challenges revealed as a young nation strove to balance lofty ideals with harsh reality. Wrapping up this section is Rosemarie K. Bank's nuanced explication of

Chicago's Columbian Exposition. Bank focuses on the cultural workers, drawing parallels between the nineteenth-century trope of painting protesting and striking workers as savages with the Exposition's "show Indians" and suggesting the inability of such constructs to contain the diversity and brotherhood of labor that was, even then, constructing and embracing the idea of a "savage" American legacy and future. While each essay maintains a foundational connection to theatre history, Mullenix, Saunders, and Bank use that history to propel their work beyond the physical theatre building or individual creative work. They pursue the formative power of theatre as a way to shape, destroy, and inspire the "public mind."

The final part, "The Creative Work / The Work of Creation," draws together elements from each of the previous divisions, incorporating the embodiment of history and the theatrical performance and making visible the very work of creation even as it examines the creative work itself. This section unites the physical, intellectual, and emotional processes of creating theatrical works with the historiographical interrogation of the product itself, dealing with issues of embodiment, communal identity, the creation and interpretation of historical records, and the traumas that serve as catalysts for such creative work. Melissa Rynn Porterfield explores the collision of Pittsburgh's working-class identity and Shakespeare. Through a careful examination of the Three Rivers Shakespeare Company's strategic use of the rhetoric of work in its marketing strategies, Porterfield suggests that finding an audience is indeed an integral—and artistic—factor in every creative work. Tracey Elaine Chessum's essay on composer John Philip Sousa reveals the connections between Sousa, his comic opera *The Free Lance* (1906), and the virtues of the nineteenth-century relationship between work and American masculinity. In a collision of ideologies between masculinity and artistic rights, *The Free Lance* became the vehicle for taking one of the first debates regarding intellectual property rights directly to the American people. Last, focusing on the work of creation itself, Jonathan Chambers documents Rinde Eckert's struggle to create a performance piece based on Herman Melville's literary giant *Moby-Dick*. The work and cost of creation become the literal subjects as Eckert's character fights to finish his opus before his failing memory vanishes forever, even as the performance itself is endowed with literary and theatrical beauty. In their attention to both the artistic work and the creative artists who produced that work, Porterfield, Chessum, and Chambers delve into the complex issues of creative and intellectual rights, inspired creations, and the challenges of negotiating fundamentally conflicting identities over time.

These four primary sections serve as a structure for this volume, building on one another as they explore different, and often ignored, facets of labor in the theatrical world. The first section's focus on physical conditions and worker needs paves the way for the second section's emphasis on those labors and laborers that frequently slip through the scholarly cracks. The third part pursues the hidden labor that takes place even further behind the scenes. In this case, Mullenix, Saunders, and Bank attend to the role that theatre and cultural performance play in the formation of national identity and ideology, observing the manifestation of multiple myths through their work. The fourth and final part serves to draw together many of the questions that have resounded through the previous sections. Whether harnessing the power of local identity to shape an ad campaign, identifying the fundamental ideological disconnect between a nation that prized the individual's contribution while robbing that person of his or her wages, or investigating the bodily trauma that creation exacts on the creator, this section returns to those issues that populate the book even as they raise more questions about theatrical workers, the creative work itself, and theatre's potential for influencing individuals, communities, and the nation.

While these section divisions serve to structure this volume, we recognize that they are artificially imposed themes and questions. This collection can be read in multiple ways, and we have installed several features to help readers make the most of the volume as time permits. For those who choose to read the volume cover-to-cover or in parts, we suggest making use of the brief section introductions, where we have pulled together major themes and questions. For those drawn to a particular essay, we encourage the perusal of other essays in the section or looking for potential connections across the volume. For example, Chrystyna Dail's exploration of the UAW Union Theatre in Detroit parallels the Federal Theatre Project's focus on the working class in Elizabeth A. Osborne's essay, as well as Melissa Rynn Porterfield's discussion of Attilio "Buck" Favorini's battle to engage Pittsburgh's working class with the city's new Shakespeare festival. Sara Freeman and Rosemarie Bank both challenge historiographic models to engage differently through their respective examinations of the reverberations of intimate partnerships and cultural workers. Max Shulman, Christine Woodworth, and Jerry Dickey all deal in some way with the lives of theatrical workers outside the theatre. Elizabeth Reitz Mullenix, Chrystyna Dail, and Tracey Elaine Chessum integrate cultural history and close textual analysis. These connections—thematic, theoretical, and methodological—are only a few of many that exist across and through this collection. We encourage readers to confront the collection as a whole or to consider the ways that single essays connect to other pieces in the collection.

While each case study is uniquely situated within its historic context, common themes across seemingly disparate topics resonate through *Working in the Wings*: recovering the worker's visibility and identifying workers with the theatre they create; exploring how the forgotten and, in some cases, deliberately obscured histories of workers can be returned to the scholarly conversation; expanding the ways in which theatre can become the "work of the public mind" through its influence on the popular imagination; and delving into the myriad intersections between the creative work itself—the artifact—and the often repetitive, sometimes destructive, and altogether exhilarating work that creation demands of its creator. Taken as a whole, *Working in the Wings* aims to expand and deepen familiar territory, map uncharted terrains, and transcend the concept of work with respect to theatre, performance, and history.

Notes

1. Joseph Francis Daly, *The Life of Augustin Daly* (New York: Macmillan, 1917), 75.
2. Seldon Faulker, "The Great Train Scene Robbery," *Quarterly Journal of Speech* 50, no. 1 (1964): 24–28.
3. "How Play and Games Transform the Culture of Work: An Interview with Ross Smith," *American Journal of Play* 5, no. 1 (2012): 6–7.
4. Peter Brook, *The Empty Space*, 1st American ed. (New York: Atheneum, 1968), 140–41.
5. Shannon Jackson, *Social Works: Performing Art, Supporting Publics* (New York: Routledge, 2011), 29.
6. Ibid., 14–15, 30.
7. Marvin Carlson, *The Haunted Stage: The Theatre as Memory Machine* (Ann Arbor: University of Michigan Press, 2001), 11.
8. Thomas Postlewait, "Constructing Events in Theatre History: A Matter of Credibility," in *Theatrical Events: Borders, Dynamics, Frames*, ed. Vicky Ann Cremona, Peter Eversmann, Hans van Maanen, Willmar Sauter, and John Tulloch (New York: Rodopi, 2004), 48.
9. Steven Peter Vallas, *Work: A Critique*, Key Concepts (Malden, Mass.: Polity Press, 2012), 7.
10. John W. Budd, *The Thought of Work* (Ithaca, New York: ILR Press, 2011), 2.
11. Russell Muirhead, *Just Work* (Cambridge, Mass.: Harvard University Press, 2004), 4.
12. Vallas, *Work*, 3.
13. Ibid.; Budd, *Thought of Work*, 3.
14. Budd, *Thought of Work*, 2.
15. Sharon C. Bolton and Maeve Houlihan, eds., *Work Matters: Critical Reflections on Contemporary Work*, Critical Perspectives on Work and Employment (New York: Palgrave Macmillan, 2009), 2.

16. Vallas, *Work*, 3.
17. Marjorie L. DeVault, *People at Work: Life, Power, and Social Inclusion in the New Economy* (New York: New York University Press, 2008), 2.
18. Ibid., 5–9.
19. Vallas, *Work*, 6.
20. Colette A. Hyman, *Staging Strikes: Workers' Theatre and the American Labor Movement*, Critical Perspectives on the Past (Philadelphia: Temple University Press, 1997); Elizabeth A. Osborne, *Staging the People: Community and Identity in the Federal Theatre Project*, Palgrave Studies in Theatre and Performance History (New York: Palgrave, 2011); Susan Duffy, *American Labor on Stage: Dramatic Interpretations of the Steel and Textile Industries in the 1930s*, Contributions in Drama and Theatre Studies (Westport, Conn.: Greenwood Press, 1996); Kirk W. Fuoss, *Striking Performances/Performing Strikes* (Jackson: University Press of Mississippi, 1997). Many articles and essays address these topics and concerns as well.
21. See, for example, Helen Allison, *Sistren Song: Popular Theatre in Jamaica* (London: War on Want, 1986); Lizbeth Goodman, *Contemporary Feminist Theatres: To Each Her Own*, Gender and Performance (New York: Routledge, 1993); James Harding and Cindy Rosenthal, *Restaging the Sixties: Radical Theaters and Their Legacies* (Ann Arbor: University of Michigan Press, 2007); Christopher Innes, *Erwin Piscator's Political Theatre: The Development of Modern German Drama* (Cambridge: Cambridge University Press, 1972); Claudia Orenstein, *Festive Revolutions: The Politics of Popular Theater and the San Francisco Mime Troupe*, Performance Studies (Jackson: University Press of Mississippi, 1998); Louis L. Snyder, *Great Turning Points in History* (New York: Van Nostrand Reinhold, 1971); Eugene Van Erven, *Radical People's Theatre* (Bloomington: Indiana University Press, 1988); R. G. Davis, *The San Francisco Mime Troupe: The First Ten Years* (Palo Alto, Calif.: Ramparts Press, 1975).
22. Chris Hillier, *Melbourne Workers Theatre: Theatre from the Shop Floor* (Melbourne: Melbourne Workers Theatre, 1990); Glenn D'Cruz, ed., *Class Act: Melbourne Workers Theatre 1987–2007* (Carlton North, Victoria, Aus.: Vulgar Press, 2007); Sharon A. Cook, Lorna R. McLean, and Kate O'Rourke, *Framing Our Past: Canadian Women's History in the Twentieth Century* (Montreal: Ithaca Press, 2001); Alan D. Filewod and David Watt, *Workers' Playtime: Theatre and the Labour Movement since 1970* (Sydney: Currency Press, 2001).
23. Though not mentioned here, we do not intend to exclude the work that audience members must often do to fulfill their own roles as vital members of the theatrical performance. However, since this effort is not the focus

of this volume, we will avoid delving into it further. For more information, see Susan Bennett, *Theatre Audiences: A Theory of Production and Reception* (New York: Routledge, 1997) and Richard Butsch, *The Citizen Audience: Crowds, Publics, and Individuals* (New York: Routledge, 2007).

24. A range of possibilities include Anne Bogart, *A Director Prepares: Seven Essays on Art and Theatre* (New York: Routledge, 2001); Brenda Murphy, *Tennessee Williams and Elia Kazan: A Collaboration in the Theatre* (Cambridge: Cambridge University Press, 1992); Richard Schickel, *Elia Kazan: A Biography* (New York: HarperCollins, 2005); David Richard Jones, *Great Directors at Work: Stanislavsky, Brecht, Kazan, Brook* (Los Angeles: University of California Press, 1986); and Toby Cole and Helen Krich Chinoy, eds., *Directing the Play: A Source Book of Stagecraft* (Indianapolis: Bobbs-Merrill, 1953).
25. Christin Essin, "An Aesthetic of Backstage Labor," *Theatre Topics* 21, no. 1 (2011): 35.
26. Articles featuring backstage workers frequently appear in major magazines and newspapers such as the *Washington Post*, the *New York Times*, the *Los Angeles Times*, *Variety*, *Time*, *People*, and many more. See, for example, Maurice Zolotow, "She Keeps the Glitter in Broadway Shows," *Saturday Evening Post*, February 2, 1952, 34, 81–84; "Go Backstage and Back in Time to Broadway," *New York Times Book Review*, September 24, 2006, 24; and Andrew L. Yarrow, "Grand Tours: A Guide to Getting Behind the Scene," *New York Times*, February 28, 1986, C1.
27. Kathi Weeks, *The Problem with Work: Feminism, Marxism, Antiwork Politics, and Postwork Imaginaries* (Durham, N.C.: Duke University Press, 2011), 2.
28. Kenneth Rogoff and Carmen Reinhart coined the term "Second Great Contraction" in their in-depth study of the world economy based on more than eight hundred years of empirical data, *This Time Is Different: Eight Centuries of Financial Folly* (Princeton, N.J.: Princeton University Press, 2009). They consciously followed in the footsteps of Milton Friedman and Anna Jacobson Schwartz's groundbreaking study of the Great Depression, *The Great Contraction, 1929–1933*, arguing that early twenty-first century economic conditions parallel those seen only once before in the United States—during the Great Depression. Bill Javetski and Tim Koller, "Understanding the Second Great Contraction: An Interview with Kenneth Rogoff," *McKinsey Quarterly* (October 2011), http://www.mckinsey.com/insights/economic_studies/understanding_the_second_great_contraction_an_interview_with_kenneth_rogoff (accessed July 20, 2012).

Part One
Working Conditions

Conceiving of theatrical work as multilayered, the first section of this volume considers work in its most basic form, beginning with the acts of laborers—artists and craftspeople—who work behind the scenes to bring a performance to fruition. How might expectations regarding work (and the laborers who perform that work) influence the historical identities ascribed to workers? How might existing epistemologies and methodologies reinscribe the very histories that scholars strive to challenge when writing about workers, work, and working-class theatre? This first section offers ways of thinking about these questions, ranging from Chrystyna Dail's insightful analysis of the controversial union theatre performance of *Discrimination for Everybody!* to Tom Robson's careful archival exhumation of nineteenth-century theatre technicians. Sara Freeman and Christine Woodworth similarly challenge the ways scholars frequently approach the creative artist through their work by exploring the fundamental role that intimate partnerships and day jobs play in the lives and work of the people who create theatre. Whether an artist finds himself or herself employed as an activist or in the midst of a long-term romantic relationship with another theatre professional, Woodworth and Freeman demonstrate that these seemingly outside forces reverberate through the creative work. The range of approaches offers a glimpse of the many potential paths scholars may travel in similar explorations of workers and working conditions.

1. Driving Race Work: The UAW, Detroit, and *Discrimination for Everybody!*

Chrystyna Dail

Drawing a connection between Edward Mabley's *Discrimination for Everybody!* and Elmer Rice's *The Adding Machine* is inevitable. Their shared leitmotif—incessant typing—aurally elucidates each playwright's materialist critique of his specific cultural moment. Yet much had changed in U.S. economic and labor policy during the quarter century separating the two pieces. By the time adding machine–underscored *Discrimination for Everybody!* emerged on the theatrical scene in Detroit, Michigan, in 1949, industrialization was conventional. The play's first Detroit audiences—automotive and other labor union workers—were the recipients and embodiments of decades of discoveries and experiments in scientific management theory. But despite considerable advances in labor management since the 1920s, the need for significant developments in racial, ethnic, and gender equality in the workforce remained. Starkly contrasting with *The Adding Machine*, Mabley's play willingly accepts industrialization as standard practice and instead capitalizes on its adding machine soundscape to promote a uniquely post–World War II outcome filtered through an economic lens: namely, the creation of a dramatized environment in which to advocate for equality and civil rights—race work—in one of the most racially volatile cities in the United States.

The advocacy for workplace equality central to *Discrimination for Everybody!* was not an isolated incident in 1949 but instead a top-down U.S. affair. President Harry S. Truman took a firm stance on the need to eradicate discrimination in employment, education, and voting rights in the 1948 State of the Union address, challenging Congress to establish "a Fair Employment Practices Commission to prevent unfair discrimination in employment."[1]

Not surprisingly in an election year, there was little traction gained on any of Truman's civil rights goals. Upon reelection Truman again emphasized his support for civil rights. For race workers across the United States—multiracial coalitions of activists determined to promote racial equality above all other social inequities—the establishment of a permanent and federally directed Fair Employment Practices Commission (FEPC) was long overdue. In light of its absence, some unions, businesses, and even states had by 1949 created their own antidiscriminatory employment commissions. The United Automobile Workers (UAW), one of the largest labor unions in the country, established a Fair Practices Department in 1944. National in scope, the department operated out of union headquarters in Detroit because it was the home of both the national headquarters and the majority of racially integrated plants.[2] Wartime saw manufacturing employment explode in Detroit by 40 percent and the hiring of black workers increase by 103 percent.[3] UAW leaders used the wartime employment and economic surge in Detroit to their advantage and "strongly backed civil rights, particularly the FEPC, which spoke directly to the tie between racial discrimination and economic injustice," believing workplace equality was fundamental to overall economic democratization in the United States.[4]

During the late 1940s, the UAW used theatrical performances to educate its audiences about a variety of political issues and to advocate for social change. The UAW Union Theatre, established by and for labor union members, produced over thirty performances in three years, extolling the virtues of UAW political agendas. The most popular performance in the UAW Union Theatre's repertoire was Edward Mabley's satirical examination of U.S. economic and social problems born out of racism and bigotry. Backed by UAW leadership and race workers in Detroit, the preeminent theatre critic John Gassner reviewed it as "one of the few effective short propaganda pieces on group relations presently available."[5] Through analysis of *Discrimination for Everybody!*, this essay elucidates how the UAW Union Theatre brought national debates surrounding civil rights and fair employment practices to Detroit labor union audiences through the medium of live performance.

The UAW Union Theatre was the Detroit-based performance outlet of the most powerful union in the Congress of Industrial Organizations (CIO). During the Great Depression and World War II, the UAW was touted as "one of the most racially egalitarian leaderships among the CIO unions."[6] Debates regarding racial inequality in the automotive industry gained prominence in the city. The violent strikes and riots that occurred in the summer of 1943 and garnered national attention initiated Detroit's race debate. During the

Detroit Packard "hate strikes," twenty-five thousand white workers walked out of plants protesting the hiring or promotion of black workers. The UAW leadership, however, continued enforcing its policy of nondiscrimination by continually defending black workers. The relationship between black labor and the UAW so improved following the 1943 race riots that large numbers of black workers joined the labor union. When Walter Reuther became president of the UAW in 1946, he supported the belief that racial equality was paramount not only for maintaining growth and order in the union but also for acquiring a new national economic policy that would counteract what he regarded as the long-standing monopoly capital model in the United States. The UAW's advocacy of civil rights, and its theatrical performances offered in support of those rights, sent a critical message to industry and government leaders that the issue of racial equality in the United States could not be ignored if the country wanted to remain fiscally viable. In their search for social change, Walter Reuther and playwright Edward Mabley attacked leaders where it hurt most—in their wallets.

What is significant about *Discrimination for Everybody!*, separating it from other equal rights performances of the 1940s, is that the play focuses on the social and economic struggles not only of black Americans but also of Latinos, Asian Americans, and Jews. Embracing a mixed economy or Keynesian perspective, Mabley suggests that racial equality will lead to improved economic standards for everyone. Thus, although the play highlights the humanitarian outcomes of equality, it additionally celebrates the capitalistic pursuit of private property and goods. One act in length, the play emphasizes the effects of discrimination in both private and government sectors and projects the forthcoming economic, creative, and intellectual outcomes of discrimination in the United States if a fair employment policy fails to become a unified national mandate. *Discrimination for Everybody!* therefore addresses differing opportunities for attaining economic stability as a manifestation of local and national political structure inequalities rather than as inevitable outcomes of racial difference.

The setting for *Discrimination for Everybody!*, like that of many labor union agitprop plays, is a town hall–style meeting in which the theatre company plants actors or "stooges" among a predominantly union audience. On the stage behind a long folding table and speaking in hushed tones are board members of the SPCD, or, as the audience discovers when the meeting is called to order, the Society for the Prevention of Cruelty to Discriminators. A meeting has been called to find out how much the monthly dues will increase for the SPCD in order to maintain its high level of discriminatory practices. The chairman of the SPCD Membership Committee, Mrs. Matilda

Hoyt, welcomes the "guests" to the meeting and in doing so sets in motion the satirical premise of the play:

> At last the country has an organization set up to protect the interests of those who are *really* hurt by discrimination—those who practice it. Now, we don't want anyone to think that discrimina*tees* aren't welcome in our organization. Today's discrimina*tee* may be tomorrow's discrimina*tor*, and yesterday's discriminator may be today's discriminatee, as history shows. Or, as often happens, one may be a discriminator and a discriminatee at the same time. [. . .] So everyone is welcome. The S.P.C.D. is completely democratic, with a goal of one hundred and forty million members. Our aim is to help everyone, whenever he practices discrimination, because believe me, he's going to need it.[7]

As the piece progresses, a variety of citizens air their discrimination grievances. SPCD treasurer Mr. Thornton, feverishly typing away on his adding machine, tallies the costs of discrimination in terms of increased dues for society members following each of the complaints. The first case brought to the attention of the SPCD is that of Jose, the fifteen-year-old son of Mexican immigrants who was recently arrested for stealing a car with a group of gang members and is now being sent to reform school for a year. Jose's parents are campesinos (migrant farm workers), and therefore the family spends much of the year following fruit and sugar beet harvests in various parts of the country (Texas, Idaho, Michigan, and Colorado are named). Jose and his siblings regularly miss school or stop attending altogether to help with the harvests, especially because their mother is tubercular and often unable to work. When an SPCD member asks if Jose's mother's illness is "traceable in any way to discrimination," a physician from the public clinic replies, "Well, it's due to the conditions she's forced to live under, and those conditions are the result of discrimination."[8] The physician explains that many immigrants live in overcrowded tenements with poor—if any—sanitation, leading to "diphtheria, scarlet fever, polio—some diseases even run ten times as high. [. . .] It should be pointed out, too, that contagious diseases don't stop at the railroad tracks. They endanger everybody."[9] The clinic physician is followed by a long line of city government officials such as the treasurer, a social worker, a truant officer, a police detective, a school superintendant, a judge, and even a local fireman, relaying to the SPCD board the high financial cost of discriminating against immigrants and their families. Thornton adds into the dues all the costs to city officials (and therefore taxpayers) associated with issues of ethnic and racial discrimination in public elementary and high schools, housing, the court system, and medicine. Before leaving the stage, the city treasurer reminds the SPCD board that discrimination is not just a situation faced by Mexican immigrants: "And don't forget, the same thing can happen in *any* group we set apart—Negro, Puerto Rican, Filipino, and so on."[10]

The issues facing Jose and his family—unequal access to steady work and adequate housing as well as the interconnected hemorrhaging social problems and costs—also confronted a significant population of Detroit audiences during the 1940s. Recognizing that inequality extended far beyond awarding or denying an individual a job due to race or ethnicity, the Mayor's Interracial Committee—which originated following the 1943 race riots—restructured itself in 1944 in order to allow for the directors of education, parks and recreation, welfare, police, health, and housing to serve as members. This was done because many race workers felt the committee was slow in facilitating changes regarding racism and discrimination in Detroit's public services. By the time the UAW Union Theatre added *Discrimination for Everybody!* to its repertoire, "a quarter-million Detroiters lived in substandard housing, many without toilets or running water."[11] Appointing directors of public services to the Mayor's Interracial Committee may not have instigated rapid change, but it "placed certain city departments in a position where their heads at least were forced to learn something of the realities of interracial tensions and of how such tensions might be eased."[12]

Following a critique of how social services are unable to curb the mounting wave of U.S. discrimination, the SPCD focuses next on the hiring practices of a local manufacturing plant. The characters in this scene include the plant president, a union leader, and the pastor of a local black church. Pastor Morton introduces the dialectic of this scene, stating, "I'm not putting it [hiring practices] on the basis of fairness, gentlemen. We've had racial discrimination for a long time, and it's never been fair. Everybody knows that. What I'm saying is that it's a mistake from a *practical* point of view."[13] Pastor Morton explains to the others that when they discriminate against black workers in their area, they are not only adding to regional poverty but also damaging their own financial prosperity. Positioning a black pastor as *raisonneur* for this scene was culturally significant to both the UAW and Detroit during the 1940s. Black pastors harnessed substantial political power in the city. Church was often a secondary meeting place for black UAW activists outside of the labor union halls, and pastors steered their congregations in choosing to join (or not) unions and other activist groups.[14]

The pastor's impassioned appeal is the dramatic expression of a situation that was playing out in almost every major northern metropolitan city in the United States following World War II. As labor historian Robert H. Zieger astutely explains, "The postwar deterioration of the great industrial cities left hundreds of thousands of blacks segregated in crumbling ghettoes, imprisoned by formal and informal codes of discrimination that relegated them to the poorest housing, the most overcrowded schools, and declining and marginal jobs."[15] Pastor Morton challenges the union leader's pathetic justification for why his "hands are tied" from hiring black laborers: "When you exclude Negroes you create a mass of cheap labor that presses down on your own wage scales every time there's a business setback. You limit the effectiveness of your union."[16] Turning next to the plant president, Morton maintains:

> And look what it costs you manufacturers, Mr. Gaines. There are thirteen million colored people in this country. By leaving most of them in a lower standard of living, you cut down your own market. You pass up one potential customer in every ten, and that's poor business. My people want clothes, and cars, and refrigerators the same as the rest, but they can't buy them when they're not given a chance to make a good living.[17]

Once Pastor Morton has completed his testimony on behalf of the unemployed black workers in Detroit, Mr. Thornton is asked to add into SPCD dues the cost of economic discrimination against blacks in the United States.

Mabley complicates the debate further by introducing in the next scene the costs involved in counseling against educating and hiring motivated minority students. First, Abram Goldstein, a young Jewish man who has high academic scores and is a war veteran, rises from the audience and asks the college administrator at the SPCD head table why he was not admitted to the local state university. The president of the SPCD requests Mr. Thornton add into dues the costs of discrimination in college education, to which Thornton, exasperated, quips, "You want me to put a dollar estimate on Albert Einstein? Or Marian Anderson?"[18] An engineering professor at the university in question then stands up and takes another audience member to task for failing to hire his brilliant Chinese engineering graduate student, George Ching, for a supervisory position at his company. The human resources manager replies, "Professor, you know the answer to that. We can't use a Chinese in a supervisory job, over other men. He wouldn't fit into the office either."[19]

Why Ching would be controversial in the office is not made explicit; however, this scene highlights the possibility of three major discriminatory hiring practices prevalent in 1949. First, it is intimated that Ching is an immigrant, an assumption often made regarding Asian—especially Chinese—workers. Second, assuming that Ching is an immigrant, there is a possibility that he is also a communist. And third, Ching is not white, and 1940s historical precedent in Detroit illustrates that white workers went on strike or turned violent when racial minorities were placed in managerial positions. Ultimately the audience is left wondering why Ching was not hired; the human resources manager responds, "Professor, you understand—I liked the boy, but—well, you know how these things are," and Thornton must add to the dues the cost of wasted skills.[20] The plight of Goldstein and Ching brings into question not only anti-Semitism in 1940s higher education and potential political or racial discrimination but also problems facing all World War II veterans attempting to use promised GI Bill funding. Federal government findings mirrored the play's stance on discrimination facing returning war veterans and minorities. The final report issued by the FEPC before its 1946 dissolution described "prevalent discriminatory practices against returning service men of minority groups [. . . who] were having trouble getting into school, getting GI loans and obtaining skilled jobs. These difficulties were being encountered not alone by Negroes, but also by Jews, Mexican-Americans and Nisei."[21] The inclusion of material so specific to the cultural moment signals that the UAW Union Theatre performed *Discrimination for Everybody!* not as frivolous entertainment for union members but as a call to action by race workers regarding wide-sweeping discrimination in U.S. society.

Thornton adds in the costs to the federal government for missed international industrial growth opportunities and for the lives of U.S. citizens lost during wartime due to perceived American xenophobia. He then promptly passes out. When asked how to revive the treasurer, the physician rises from the audience and suggests whispering in Thornton's ear, "No more dues. We're not going to foot the bill for discrimination any more," thus calling for the elimination of discrimination and segregation from American life.[22] An alternative ending to the play has the physician recommending that society devote its best interests to the list of President Truman's four motions included in the Report of the President's Committee on Civil Rights:

1. In general, the elimination of segregation from American life
2. For employment, the enactment of a federal Fair Employment Practice Act prohibiting all forms of discrimination in private employment
3. For education, enactment by the state legislatures of fair employment practice laws for public and private educational institutions, prohibiting discrimination in the admission and treatment of students
4. For housing, the enactment by the states of laws outlawing restrictive covenants[23]

In customary agitprop style, the SPCD—and presumably the audience—approves the physician's motion. The mock meeting is adjourned, thus concluding the play.

Discrimination for Everybody!, because it is so clearly grounded in its historical moment, serves as an evocative case study of how union theatres during the 1940s served their members as well as the greater community. Like the working-class population of Detroit itself, UAW Union Theatre audiences were exceptionally diverse in terms of race, religion, and ethnicity. Detroit's diversity in the late 1940s stemmed from a combination of native-born inhabitants, immigrant workers of European descent, the post–World War I northern migration of white and black southern workers, and the massive influx of industrial workers during World War II.[24] Detroit emerged as a quintessential U.S. melting pot city during World War II, yet the disparate cultural flavors of this population paella were not melding favorably. Thus Edward Mabley's *Discrimination for Everybody!*, illustrating the economic dangers a city faces when unable to alleviate discriminatory practices, signaled a serendipitous performance opportunity for Detroit. Mabley sent UAW Fair Practices Department codirector William Oliver his script in February 1949, stating, "I'd be very grateful for your suggestions about getting [*Discrimination for Everybody!*] into the hands of labor groups that might be interested in producing it. As you will see, it can be done very simply, making few demands either in staging or acting. It can, in fact, be done in any large room, without a stage."[25] Oliver immediately saw the script's potential for advocating civil rights and a permanent FEPC, forwarding it to Joanne Stern of the UAW Union Theatre the very next day.

Joanne Stern was the organizational force behind the UAW Union Theatre throughout its existence. She was chairman of and a performer with the group while simultaneously holding a position in the Mayor's Interracial Committee office. In 1945, Detroit mayor Edward Jeffries appointed an experienced social service executive, George Schermer, as director of the Interracial Committee.[26] Schermer advocated moving beyond the black/white divide in committee policy and instead focusing on the "tensions [. . .] buried deep in the economic and cultural fabric of the community. The program, therefore, cannot be limited to a direct attack on Negro-white tensions. It must be a broad and comprehensive program."[27] Schermer, much like playwright Edward Mabley and UAW president Walter Reuther, saw discrimination as a direct outgrowth of economic disparity. Schermer implemented action-based initiatives focused on educating Detroit citizens regarding discrimination through every possible outlet, including the arts.[28] Not surprisingly, it was under Schermer's tenure as director of the Mayor's

Interracial Committee, while Joanne Stern was employed there, that the UAW Union Theatre emerged.

The UAW Union Theatre collaborated with and received funding from the Mayor's Interracial Committee as well as from the UAW Fair Practices Department. It is therefore logical that the group chose to focus on civil rights in many of its productions, hoping to bring actionable change to Detroit. A pro–civil rights perspective was also in keeping with the UAW Union Theatre's original mission, which included "helping to reflect the background and the climate in which the labor movement philosophy operates"; "publicizing the current issues in which union people are interested"; and "serving as a cultural tool for the general growth and education of laboring people so that they may better learn to understand and to appreciate their present and potential role in society."[29] The mission statement and publications of the company further stressed that the group be made up entirely of labor union personnel, even if this meant risking the artistic merit of its productions.[30] The UAW Union Theatre clearly prioritized education, political advocacy, and social change above theatrical artistry. For example, as Joanne Stern wrote to William Oliver regarding *Discrimination for Everybody!*, "Altho [*sic*] I don't think it's the best play in the world from a dramatic standpoint, I think probably we can make a pretty good presentation with it from a fair practices point of view."[31]

While educating UAW labor union members about current social problems was a vital function of the UAW Union Theatre, another goal was establishing cross-union membership to address concerns throughout Detroit's diverse labor union population. Meeting minutes of April 1948 indicate that under Stern's leadership, the group was achieving that goal.[32] Additionally in 1948, Eleanor Wolf was elected to the UAW Union Theatre's board. Wolf served as executive secretary of the Michigan Labor Committee to Combat Intolerance, a group dedicated to ending intergroup prejudice.[33] As the UAW Union Theatre's meeting minutes illustrate, beginning in 1948 it was engaging participants, sponsorship, and advice not only from Detroit UAW locals but also from a growing number of other Detroit labor unions, the mayor's office, and state government officials, many of whom could be considered significant to race work in the city and metropolitan area.

Despite the popularity and prescient message of *Discrimination for Everybody!*, it was one of the UAW Union Theatre's final performances; the company folded following Stern's departure from Detroit in the late spring of 1949.[34] But even had Stern remained chairman of the group, its days were more than likely numbered. Many of the hopes for strong federal antidiscrimination policies faded away amid the conservative haze settling over the United States in 1949. Truman's civil rights initiative faced blockage by Dixiecrat and Republican senators, and it died in committee as skillful politicians began linking civil rights advocacy with communism.[35] As early as 1947, a federal loyalty review board member queried, "Of course the fact that a person believes in racial equality doesn't *prove* that he's a communist, but it certainly makes you look twice, doesn't it?"[36] Red-baiting was already strong in 1946 when the UAW Union Theatre emerged, and it reached a fever pitch in 1950 when Senator Joseph McCarthy made his infamous declaration in Wheeling, West Virginia, of significant communist infiltration in the State Department. By 1951 President Truman abandoned hope not only for passage of a civil rights package but for the remainder of his Fair Deal agenda as well.[37]

Politically savvy UAW president Walter Reuther ably navigated the conservative political turn despite his clear distaste for right-wing politics. Perhaps this was due most directly to his insistence on purging communist factions from the CIO following the passage of the Taft-Hartley Act.[38] When anticommunist fervor ratcheted up across the country, labor unions—including the UAW—mirrored Capitol Hill politicking. With hope for an FEPC eviscerated and the prevalent political linking of communism with civil rights, a labor union theatre group openly supportive of racial equality was doomed. As historian Kevin Boyle astutely concludes, "The resulting miasma of anger and fear not only destroyed the UAW's hopes of building on the Fair Deal. It also led Reuther to back away from the moral and political core of his ideology, to retreat from what was best in his personality and philosophy—his profound commitment to social change and economic justice—and to embrace what was worst."[39] The UAW Union Theatre became collateral damage following Reuther's retreat from activist race work, and *Discrimination for Everybody!* joined the ranks of a seemingly endless supply of popular agitprop plays turned dated dramatic literature pariahs within a year or two of publication.

Due to the brevity of its three-year duration, the UAW Union Theatre's influence in theatre history may at first appear insignificant. Yet in connecting its race work to the web of pro–civil rights theatre groups operating during the early Cold War, such as Stage for Action and People's Drama, Inc., as well as to the sociological and political debates surrounding the surging economic crisis facing urban manufacturing cities during the postwar years, it becomes clear that it was responding to vital issues. UAW Union Theatre's live performances offered audiences perspectives on social problems directly influencing their everyday lives and did so in a way that was not only educational and entertaining but motivational as well. Social and political historian Thomas J. Sugrue evaluates grassroots activism in

Detroit in this way: "The fate of the city is the consequence of the unequal distribution of power and resources [. . . and] the actions of the poor can be fully understood only in the context of the larger structures that limit their choices and constrain their options."[40] The UAW Union Theatre consisted of a small group of race workers who keenly understood the potential implications of a federally mandated FEPC for their city. Through *Discrimination for Everybody!*, they actively resisted Detroit segregation policies (both overt and de facto). Using performance as their medium, they agitated for equal access to employment, housing, public services, and the basic needs presumably granted to everyone.

Notes

1. Harry S. Truman, "The Text of President Truman's Message on Civil Rights," *New York Times*, February 3, 1948, 22.
2. UAW Fair Practices and Anti-Discrimination Department, box 55, folder 84, Walter P. Reuther Library, Wayne State University (hereafter UAW Fair Practices). General Motors, Ford, and Chrysler "concentrated their production in the industrial Midwest. Though the manufacturers maintained plants throughout the United States, 80 percent of their employees worked in Ohio, Indiana, Illinois, Wisconsin, and Michigan." See Kevin Boyle, *The UAW and the Heyday of American Liberalism: 1945–1968* (Ithaca: Cornell University Press, 1995), 12.
3. Thomas J. Sugrue, *The Origins of the Urban Crisis: Race and Inequality in Postwar Detroit* (Princeton, N.J.: Princeton University Press, 1996), 27.
4. Boyle, *UAW*, 47.
5. John Gassner, *Human Relations in the Theatre* (New York: Anti-defamation League of B'nai B'rith, 1949), 40; The UAW Union Theatre was not the only labor union finding relevance in *Discrimination for Everybody!* The New York Central Dramatics Group of the ILGWU (International Ladies' Garment Workers' Union) closed out its 1949 season with the play as well. See General Executive Board, "Report to the ILGWU," vol. 24 (1950), 235, ILGWU Publications, box 70, folder 19, Kheel Center for Labor-Management Documentation and Archives, Cornell University.
6. August Meier and Elliott Rudwick, *Black Detroit and the Rise of the UAW* (Oxford: Oxford University Press, 1979), 4; Christopher H. Johnson, *Maurice Sugar: Law, Labor, and the Left in Detroit, 1912–1950* (Detroit: Wayne State University Press, 1988), 11.
7. Edward Mabley, *Discrimination for Everybody!* (New York: Samuel French, 1948), 10. According to the U.S. Census Bureau, the national population in 1948 was 146,631,302.

8. Mabley, *Discrimination*, 13.
9. Ibid., 13–14.
10. Ibid., 15.
11. Boyle, *UAW*, 66.
12. Alfred McClung Lee and Norman Daymond Humphrey, "The Interracial Committee of the City of Detroit," *Journal of Educational Sociology* 19, no. 5 (January 1946): 284.
13. Mabley, *Discrimination*, 17.
14. David M. Lewis-Colman, *Race against Liberalism: Black Workers and the UAW in Detroit* (Champaign: University of Illinois Press, 2008), 31.
15. Robert H. Zieger, *American Workers, American Unions* (Baltimore: Johns Hopkins University Press, 1994), 144.
16. Mabley, *Discrimination*, 18.
17. Ibid.
18. Ibid., 21.
19. Ibid., 22.
20. Ibid.
21. "Nisei" was a term used for the children of Japanese immigrants who were born and educated in the United States. Jay Walz, "FEPC's Life Ends with No Hope Held for Early Revival: Final Committee Report Says Job Discrimination against Minorities is Increasing," *New York Times*, July 1, 1946, 1.
22. Mabley, *Discrimination*, 24.
23. Ibid., 25. For the entire Report of the President's Committee on Civil Rights, see Harry S. Truman, "Text of President Truman's Message on Civil Rights."
24. Boyle, *UAW*, 14.
25. UAW Fair Practices, box 27, folder 4.
26. George Schermer was a renowned housing rights activist and in 1979 was the principal author and project manager for HUD's major study on widespread discrimination in the U.S. real estate market.
27. Lee and Humphrey, "Interracial Committee of the City of Detroit," 284–85.
28. Nina Mjagkij, *Organizing Black America: An Encyclopedia of African American Associations* (New York: Routledge, 2001), 189.
29. UAW Union Theater, unprocessed collection, Walter P. Reuther Library, Wayne State University (hereafter UAW Union Theater).
30. Ibid.
31. UAW Fair Practices, box 55, folder 84.
32. Sponsorship of the group included the original three—the UAW Education and Recreation Departments and Workers Educational Service of

the University of Michigan—as well as Locals 7, 49, 306, and 600 of the UAW-CIO, the Communication Workers of America, two United Public Workers locals, one Retail Workers' local, and a local from the Michigan Federation of Teachers.

33. UAW Union Theater.
34. Ibid.
35. The term "Dixiecrat" emerged during the 1948 presidential election to describe members of the States' Rights Democrats—especially Frank M. Dixon, Fielding L. Wright, and presidential candidate Strom Thurmond—who were especially resistant to any promotion of civil rights laws. The Dixiecrat platform in 1948 called for "the segregation of the races and the racial integrity of each race"; see David McCullough, *Truman* (Touchstone: New York, 1992), 645.
36. Quoted in Stephen M. Feldman, *Free Expression and Democracy in America* (Chicago: University of Chicago Press, 2008), 434–35.
37. Boyle, *UAW*, 68–74.
38. Reuther was openly against the majority of the Taft-Hartley Act, which undercut labor unions' ability for collective bargaining and banned them from funding political campaigns using union monies; however, he endorsed its requirement that all labor union members sign an anti-communist affidavit.
39. Boyle, *UAW*, 82.
40. Sugrue, *Origins of the Urban Crisis*, 14.

2. Working Together: The Partnership of Les Waters and Annie Smart

Sara Freeman

If pivotal moments of theatrical storytelling come from collaborative interchange, as Allen Kuharski suggests in *Dramaturgy in American Theatre: A Sourcebook*, then theatre historians need to examine how different types of exchange produce specific theatrical works.[1] To accomplish this, historians might observe, recover, and imagine conversations between collaborators; track changes over time about how collaborative relationships are understood; and draw on materials specific to distinct types of jobs in theatrical production. In order to consider the collaboration between a director and a designer, like Les Waters and Annie Smart, images matter alongside scripts, narrative descriptions of rehearsal and performance, and reviews. The collaboration between a director and designer results in a set of insights expressed by the set, costumes, lights, and performance behavior: these things are simultaneously an outcome, a visual and an aural world, and an inscription of the process it took to produce that ephemera. But collaborations also occur outside the theatre, in the personal lives of artists. Artistic collaborations between committed partners bear the marks of both professional and personal exchanges, and personal relationships between theatrical artists are extraordinarily common. How might theatre historians begin to document these multiple, competing contributions to artistic creation?

I began to wrestle with historiographical concerns around writing about the work of director-designer collaborations when interviewing Les Waters and Annie Smart about their work together staging the premieres of three Caryl Churchill plays between 1982 and 1994 (*Fen*, 1982; *Mouthful of Birds*, 1986; and *The Skriker*, 1994) with Joint Stock, the Royal Court Theatre, and the National Theatre in England.[2] Longtime theatrical collaborators, they are also romantic partners and parents. Together since the late 1970s, they officially married in 1995 to allow their whole family to immigrate to the United States.[3] Waters and Smart, who built their careers in British alternative theatre, relocated when Waters took a position leading the MFA directing program at University of California, San Diego (UCSD). He then spent eight years at Berkeley Repertory Theatre as associate artistic director and was appointed by the Actors Theatre of Louisville as the third artistic director in the company's history in 2011. In her career, Smart designs both costumes and sets. She taught in the MFA design program at UCSD and lectures on costume design at University of California, Berkeley. Waters and Smart work apart almost as often as they work together, though their mutual work forms the backbone of their careers. They share more than thirty years together as partners, parents, and collaborating artists. Their partnership thus entails both creative collaboration and domestic labor, making them a revealing case study for historical questions about work in theatre.

For a "creative couple" like Waters and Smart, there are public and private dimensions to the give-and-take of ideas in the process of staging a show, and historical writing may trouble the privacy that scholars often accord to romantic partners.[4] This essay thinks through questions about partners like Waters and Smart and the challenges of and possible approaches to writing them into history in a way that matters to labor history and women's history as well as to theatre history. Waters and Smart make no secret of their personal relationship, but their partnership receives no direct analysis in journalism beyond acknowledging its existence, and no specific scholarship about Waters and Smart exists. Waters and Smart present a compelling case of coupled collaborators whose work sits on the continuum of work life and home life. Seeking to know about the whole range of dynamic interaction shaping important theatrical pieces is less an intrusion on privacy and more an attempt to do justice to the holistic dramaturgical labor of theatrical creation. It is also a contribution to the framing of gender in theatre, exploring how the work of romantic partners can be written about as a result of dynamic dialogue with each other rather than as a zero-sum game of attribution.

Psychologist Vera John-Steiner describes both cognitive and emotional dimensions in her study of "joined lives and shared work" in creative couples. John-Steiner spends her conclusion to *Creative Collaboration* providing a strong refutation of biases that narrate achievement in terms of individuality. Instead, she offers a model for understanding shared work drawn from the premise that "human beings come into being and mature in relation to others."[5] In the case of Waters and Smart, their early work on

Caryl Churchill's plays proved instrumental not only in the formation of each artist's individual identity but also in their ability to engage in creative collaborations. There is a recurrent thread of insanity in the Churchill plays that Smart strongly identified as motivating her work and that also captivated and fused the couple together. Yet each of them worked out his or her individual artistic identity through the pieces. "*Fen* was my first really visible work," Smart noted in our interview, and both agreed with Waters's assessment that *Fen* took off and became a turning point in their individual careers. Smart delved deeper into the Joint Stock process after *Fen*, while Waters worked with a broader range of theatres. When they came together again for *Mouthful of Birds* and *The Skriker*, they were drawn to different elements of Churchill's plays. Smart felt a link between the imagery and the formal concerns of all the projects, while Waters identified Churchill's writing as his primary attraction. Yet together they took on the challenges of the shows' formal experiments and took big artistic risks. Differentiating himself from Smart yet embracing the shared project of the Churchill shows, Waters reflected that his experience with *The Skriker* demanded a greater willingness to relax control as a director than he had developed at the time. Embracing John-Steiner's conclusions regarding the ability of relationships to help one mature, Waters felt he would be much more suited to that work now, given how his collaborative habits developed in relationship with designers and writers.

Interestingly, John-Steiner's approach to discussing intimate creative collaboration rarely uses marriage as a metaphor for what it is like to work together.[6] In contrast, in discussions of collaborations between artists who are not actually romantically partnered, the marriage metaphor frequently arises, although its use reveals as much about attitudes toward marriage at a given point in time as it does about artistic work. Take for example the following idea of what constitutes a good collaboration as expressed by Ronald Hayman in a 1980 article about playwrights and directors: "The best [artistic] partnerships, then, like the best marriages, are those in which the interdependence is limited and invisible."[7] This ideologically loaded statement masks the immense labor required for interdependence to remain invisible, echoing ideas about the separation between public and private spheres that have underpinned patriarchal privilege. Hayman's phrasing shows a distinct bias toward "independence" as superior to "interdependence," which is hard to reconcile with more egalitarian early twenty-first century notions about marriage. In recent contexts, marriage can suit as a metaphor for theatre work because it implies the jointure of individuals under shared values; contemporary marriage's paradoxical legal and symbolic rendering of two-into-one-who-are-still-two signifies deeply because artistic collaboration similarly fuses collaborators into a corporate body while they also maintain their individuality.

For theatre history, both topics—the artistic collaboration and the personal partnership—suggest important questions. The first is about terminology, which can be used to separate the labor of theatrical collaboration from the emotional relationship or can wrap them together. Phrases like "creative couple" or "intimate collaborators" meld the influences of several sources. "Partner" signifies in ways creative, personal, and commercial, highlighting many senses of collaboration. For this study, the distinctions lie between romantic partnerships, artistic partnerships that do not include romantic intimacy (acknowledging that theatrical collaboration often produces its own unique intimacy), and hybrids that incorporate both personal and artistic partnerships. Little hope exists of keeping the categories perfectly distinct, but the virtue lies, for this case, in a dominant sense of partnership that folds together the intimate and the artistic to better address all dimensions of work affecting a theatrical production.

Parsing this terminology emphasizes a second set of conceptual questions about the function of individuals working in relation to one another, which also produces historiographical questions: How can observers and historians document artistic work that emerges from within a relationship? What type of work is a relationship itself and how is that documented? What criteria should be used to attribute and evaluate accomplishment? What disciplinary guidelines should be followed when narrating intertwined personal and professional lives across different specializations? For instance, designer Jo Mielziner receives important treatment in scholarship, but the way much scholarly work is framed around the Tennessee Williams/Elia Kazan dyad rather than on the creative triad that includes Mielziner illustrates how easy it is to elide the work of designers in documentation of collaborative processes.[8] This essay aims to refigure that emphasis by moving Annie Smart into full circulation with Les Waters in histories of collaborative processes on British and American new writing. This is where dramaturgy—a word for the "working of actions" necessary for all collaborating artists to undertake while bringing a play to production—becomes a key methodological concept and the dimensions of scenographic collaboration take on increased weight.[9] Important director-designer collaborations pepper theatre history: David Garrick and Philip De Loutherbourg; Charles Kemble and J. R. Planché; Konstantin Stanislavski and Viktor Simov; Bertolt Brecht and Caspar Neher; Tyrone Guthrie and Tanya Moiseiwitsch. Naming the dramaturgical aspect of these collaborations focuses attention on the generative aspects of meaning making accomplished by and through the shared work of a director and designer in conversation with a text and writer.[10]

This role of scenography and/as dramaturgy transfers to dynamics in Waters and Smart's partnership. Playwright Jordan Harrison initially made this connection between scenography and dramaturgy for me. He said his experience working with Waters and Smart on a staging of *Finn in the Underworld* (2005) made him conclude that "Annie Smart is one of the best dramaturgs I have ever worked with."[11] Harrison explained that the questions Smart asked him during the production process not only clarified things she needed to solve to create costumes but also brought him new insight about the structure of his play. For Harrison, Smart provided both the impetus and the space to consider different ways of thinking about his play, and she and Waters seem to occupy a similar role for each other. Director-designer collaborations in theatre history are rarely foregrounded as an object of study in their own right; textbooks note they exist, but few studies give as close attention to mise-en-scène as they do to play text. When they do, the designer may not be framed with the same centrality as the director and the writer. Is Simov as mythical a name in theatrical study as Chekhov and Stanislavski? Do we expect all theatre students to know his name?

Previous scholars have explored artistic and personal partnerships in various ways. Brecht scholarship is one example, including John Fuegi's controversial vindication of the dramaturgical and compositional work done by Brecht's pivotal lovers and the decision in *The Cambridge Introduction to Scenography* to treat Brecht/Neher as a dyad when the rest of the book focuses on individuals.[12] Conspicuous and consequential partnerships must become core considerations in theatre history, and a method for analyzing their work is vital. The best available model concerns director Stephen Daldry and designer Ian MacNeil. Their romantic relationship figures explicitly into Wendy Lesser's study of Daldry's work, which contains detailed discussions of how Daldry and MacNeil negotiate working together as partners.[13]

Lesser frames Daldry's interaction with designers in terms of nurturing—of "feeding the designer" in developmental stages—which leads to what MacNeil describes as mutual influence on the shape of production even prior to discoveries in rehearsal. Lesser likewise tracks Daldry's and MacNeil's characterization of how their domestic life feels the impact of the shows they work on together through a quote from an interview with the *Independent*: "It's not just 'Let's do a show,' it's 'Let's tear the relationship apart and rebuild it while we do a show.' If it works, it's fantastic. If it goes wrong, it's awful." Lesser posits that some of Daldry's decisions about when to collaborate with MacNeil stem from decisions about what balance to preserve at home.[14] Still,

Lesser's thrust remains an assessment of Daldry's accomplishments, even as she contextualizes his work within modes of collaboration.

Waters's and Smart's creative processes are similarly intertwined, and this deserves nuanced scholarly attention beyond the initial treatment presented in this chapter. Waters lists Smart as one of his "heroes," and she notes the trust he gives his collaborators: this speaks to their interwoven processes in production and exploration in the rehearsal room.[15] They share a co-immersion in a set of materials, texts, and institutions, and they trade mutual aesthetic influence. Their artistic work cannot make sense if their partnership is not acknowledged, because in each other they have the most persistent audience, respondent, and supporter. Yet Waters and Smart function fully as complete artists in their own right: their partnership in no way makes them less than whole or elides their individuality. They both possess strong individual careers and collaborate with some of the most prominent artists in the field.[16] Across Smart's career, Waters has directed roughly one-third of the productions she has designed. Waters has worked with Smart for about one-fourth of the total productions he has directed.

While Waters and Smart certainly warrant individual assessments, evaluating them together reveals as much, and perhaps more. This approach is particularly valuable since their early collaboration in British alternative theatre meant they often worked together in rooms where design and staging decisions unfolded and texts developed as a result of discoveries in workshops, as with the process that created *Mouthful of Birds*. In that process, Churchill composed text as the ensemble developed and explored Ian Spink's choreography. The initial approach, said Waters and Smart in our interview, was that, character by character, "everyone got a scene." Then, in the end, the scenes that became the show were assembled into order in consultation with the collaborative team. Waters and Smart work in more traditionally organized ways as well, and therefore their interchanges of influence can flow several directions. On *The Skriker*, for example, Smart constructed a set model before rehearsals, even though the show required nearly constant movement and physical transformation by the actors. As Smart explained, prior to the start of rehearsals she "gave them a space [she] figured would serve all the different things they were likely to come up with."[17] The set made a space that contained and focused the collaborative invention for both partners and demonstrated the equality of exchange between Waters and Smart as director and designer. Smart made a space for Waters's staging, just as his directorial approach made a space for Smart's guidance and framing.

As John-Steiner's model predicts, when Waters and Smart work together there is a breadth of material and venue that they experience consistently with no one else. Across eighteen months in 1986–87, for instance, Smart and Waters opened or prepared four widely divergent shows: Federico Garcia Lorca's *The House of Bernarda Alba* (Guthrie Theatre, Minneapolis); Caryl Churchill and David Lan's *Mouthful of Birds* (Joint Stock tour, England); Anne Devlin's *Ourselves Alone* (Arena Stage, Washington, D.C.); and *The School for Scandal* (Theatre Royal, Bristol). Between 2007 and 2011, Waters and Smart had another such virtuoso run as they went from premiering a musical adaptation of Virginia Woolf's *To the Lighthouse* to investigating George Bernard Shaw's *Heartbreak House*, both at Berkeley Rep; they then staged the premiere of Charles Mee's *Cardenio* (American Repertory Theatre, Cambridge, Massachusetts), launched *In the Next Room* (Berkeley Rep) and transferred it to Broadway, dug into Naomi Iizuka's *Concerning Strange Devices from the Distant West* (Berkeley Rep), and capped 2011 with Chekhov's *Three Sisters* (Yale Rep). Their work gained momentum across these five years, and reviews indicate that the design and directing became more ferocious as the arc crested.

Reconstruction from reviews and pictures suggest that the signature feel and look of their work together lies in the frisson of Smart's designs—which often superimpose interior and exterior spaces or allow for the layering of multiple realities in the space—with directorial choices that treat nonrealistic content with intimacy and realistic content with a boldness often reserved only for fantasy. This dynamic can especially be seen in Smart's designs for *Fen*, with its potato field in the middle of a worker's house, and for *Mouthful of Birds*, for which Smart designed a mobile, multilevel structure that created the frame of a crowded council estate of apartments yet also made room for Dionysian possession rituals like the "fruit ballet" in the center of the stage. In more recent work, facets of these juxtapositions were again at play in *To the Lighthouse*, with its expressionistic, dialogue-free sequence about time passing, during which fog, shadows, and beams of light play over the stage as "the garden tries to enter through a window."[18] Waters is renowned for probing the text and for listening to its rhythms and the responses of his collaborators.[19] Smart makes stage space unfold and flow. Arts critic Chloe Veltman summed up the effect of their 2007 production of Shaw's *Heartbreak House* as "spacious but taut," with a "harmonious" and "airy" blue-tinged set contrasting with "spine-chilling" pacing and a performance ethos that drove home the play's implicit critique for Berkeley's privileged audience.[20] In Smart's spaces, Waters activates the actors to produce that sense of ideas sparkling in the air to which Veltman so strongly responded as a reviewer.

This short, reconstructive "reading through" of Waters and Smart's collaborations serves multiple functions for the purposes of this essay. It recalls

John-Steiner's notion of individuals maturing through relationships as well as Smart's and Waters's mutual abilities to create dramaturgical space for each other. It also helps make visible the contributions of both Waters and Smart as artists, countering gender and work role hierarchies that make it more habitual to document the work of one partner or the other. Meanwhile, it points up that egalitarian contemporary relationships still deal with the real effects of power, historical privilege, and experience disparities. So, for instance, aside from her administrative work with Joint Stock during the 1980s in England and her tenure as head of the master's program in fine arts at Wimbledon School of Arts (cut short by their relocation to the United States), Smart has rarely taken visible positions of artistic administration as Waters had at Berkeley Rep and now inhabits at the Actors Theatre of Louisville.[21] This reflects the status of directors as designated leaders of productions and institutions in twentieth- and twenty-first-century theatre as well as patriarchal traditions about men as leaders.

While Waters and Smart demonstrate an equality of exchange in both their artistic collaboration and their marriage, the timeline of their work and family life shows the pair moving for Waters's positions. Indeed, the impact of child-rearing produces patterns in Smart's résumé different from those in Waters's. After 1988, when their first child was born, there were years when Smart designed only one or two shows. Their second child was born in 1991 and the third in 1996.[22] Overall, until the children were all older, the pace and geographical spread of Smart's theatre projects stayed more restrained except when she worked with Waters.[23] Certainly, some balance of professional and family life must be negotiated no matter what gender dynamic is at play within a relationship, regardless of how much the partners break from or replicate traditional gender roles. Smart frames the interplay of closeness and space in their relationship this way:

> We give each other a lot of room. I think that's the way we survive, by being incredibly respectful of each other's spheres. It makes us quite an odd couple. We're very separate because we're together a lot. We're together at work and together at home. He goes away for weeks to do shows, and when he comes back I say, "How was it?" and he gives me a good moan about it, and that's about as far as it goes.[24]

As Smart notes, couples that work together often need to mark out a space that differentiates work from home in order to maintain individuality and set the relationship apart from work. Smart's quote also implies that this room is a facet of the trust and respect they show for each other while working, while her sense of their being an "odd couple" provokes the contextual question, How are they odd, and in relationship to which internal or external standards? Finally, Smart's description of "being incredibly respectful of each other's spheres" returns to my earlier discussion of dramaturgy as the act of creating space for one another; in this, Smart and Waters have created space for each other in their personal relationship and in their creative collaborations.

Though a few reviews acknowledge Waters and Smart's relationship, none discuss the design and directing of shows with respect to their long-term collaboration. Feature articles and interviews with Waters and Smart across the last fifteen years, however, demonstrate both individuals commenting on the important presence, resonance, and impact of their children in their lives.[25] In 2010 Waters talked about being drawn to working on his first musical, an adaptation of Matthew Sweet's CD *Girlfriend*, because it was about teenagers and "I live in a world of teenagers. My kids have been going through their teenage years and I remember being a teenager and feeling that all my nerves were no longer inside my body."[26] In 1998 Smart commented about missing the freedom to take on more travel and projects yet in some ways not wanting "to have that option, while [the children] are so young."[27] That Smart travels more widely and frequently when she is working with Waters suggests a type of economy-of-scale in the work life / home life and may be one of the benefits, in fact, of working together for a couple with children.

The issues to consider about Waters and Smart—partnered theatre artists who work together—break down into sets of questions about intimacy and marriage and also about working together while being married. In terms of being married, analysis turns on the sort of family created by the partnership and on the social and personal expectations for spousal and family roles, however traditionally or nontraditionally defined: the presence of children or other family dependents, the meaning and legal status of marriage in a given time period, social and personal expectations about marital partnerships, ideas about the role of sex and sexuality and how partnership channels those parts of identity, and the availability of role models about such relationships. So far, I have chosen to treat the questions the same (though the answers will not necessarily be similar) whether the couples under consideration are same-sex partners, like Daldry and MacNeil, or opposite-sex partners, as long as they are in a long-term, committed relationship. These concerns all frame how to write pairings into history.

Questions about working together further suggest detailing aspects of equity and credit: Do the partners have the same last name? How is the relationship noted or not noted publicly? Who receives credit for what work? They also require a consideration of how the pair gets represented in any existing documents: Who is the most visible figure? Are photos of both available? Who is talked about more in reviews? Finally, it means exploring approaches to art: Do they have similar or different aesthetic philosophies about theatre? Do they narrate a shared approach or philosophy of theatre, or do they acknowledge major differences? These questions encourage a direct tussle with the determining aspects of work life and home life; if that information becomes part of the conversation, historians have pushed deeper into both theatre production and the context in which it is created.

Waters and Smart fascinate because of how they negotiate connection, independence, and space over a long term. They work together and apart. They have kept their own last names. They have made decisions to advance their individual careers yet also embrace their status as a unit and work to keep their family geographically united. As spouses and parents they reflect a mindset informed by both alternative political and artistic views and by the middle-class and upper-middle-class demographic of university-educated Brits and Americans to which they belong and to whom their theatre has largely been addressed. When they work, they both receive direct credit for their artistic contributions. The legacies of women's invisibility and historical valorization of directors over designers means that on his own, Waters receives far more press coverage than Smart. Yet her accomplishments are distinctly discussed in reviews, and she is interviewed on her own by journalists. She escapes the designation of "hidden partner" within this creative duo; she inhabits neither the position of muse to his artistry nor sidekick to his front man, and both individuals strive to give each other space in the theatre and at home.

Thinking through these questions, some of the dynamics of Waters and Smart's partnership can be thrown into relief by comparison with other creative pairs whose partnerships have also been elided. Besides Daldry and MacNeil, two other key examples of designer-director dyads are George Devine and Jocelyn Herbert at the Royal Court in the 1960s and Declan Donnellan and Nick Ormerod, whose company, Cheek by Jowl, founded in 1981, forms their mutual home base. Each pair emerged within a shared period and geography of British theatre, partaking in a similar, though evolving, landscape of cultural expectations about theatrical collaboration and marital partnership.

Devine and Herbert's work together took place during the peak years of Devine's tenure as artistic director of the English Stage Company at the Royal Court Theatre; at the Court, Herbert designed sets, lights, costumes, and masks, notably for Arnold Wesker's *The Kitchen* (1959) and Samuel Beckett's *Happy Days* (1962).[28] Her minimalist, lighting-driven style matched Devine's insistence on the primacy of the writer's work. Their personal relationship was semisecret—both were married to others—and was one of several liaisons, like the one between Keith Johnstone and Ann Jellicoe or the one between William Gaskill and Desmond O'Donovan, that animated the energies of production and collaboration at the English Stage Company across this period.[29]

Devine and Herbert contrast strongly with Waters and Smart. Waters and Smart's romantic partnership, more long-lasting than that of Devine and Herbert, began before their artistic collaborations and also tracks across multiple institutions and even continents, whereas Devine and Herbert began their illicit relationship while working and collaborated only at the Royal Court. Yet Devine and Herbert's example points to the importance of not expecting the facets of intimate and artistic partnerships to fall into contained boxes. Indeed, the most revealing observations from historians may come from recording the ebb and flow of the work in tandem with the ebb and flow of the relationship: that is one way of dealing with secrecy, duration, and work milieu regarding shared lives and artistry.

Donnellan and Ormerod offer another example of a partnership with both personal and professional facets. Like Waters and Smart, they met at university and worked on student productions together. After their personal partnership connected, they decided to start a company together.[30] Cheek by Jowl's all-male production of *As You Like It* (1991) quickly exemplified the eclectic, dynamic, queer aesthetic of their work. The partnership of these two men—their marriage and their artistic collaboration—dictates their almost total preference for working with each other, though occasionally Donnellan works with another designer and Ormerod designs for another director.[31] Waters and Smart have never run a company together nor spoken of the desire to do so, but they seem to integrate into each other's theatrical institutions with ease.

The contrast between these two sets of partners highlights the persistent questions of autonomy and interconnectedness, what John-Steiner calls fusion and separation, suggesting that describing a continuum of shared-work will benefit historical analysis. On one end of the spectrum are romantic partners who work predominantly together. On the opposing side rest those engaged in an intimate partnership but without a working artistic relationship. In this relationship map, Donnellan and Ormerod would fall farther on the continuum toward total integration while Waters and Smart might sit more in the middle, but both are recognizable configurations of partnership and neither is an anomaly.

Finally, these comparisons highlight important questions about how two artists influence each other aesthetically. Herbert's minimalism both responded to key aesthetic ideas at the Royal Court and called forth aspects of Devine's staging. The comparisons also raise questions about documenting the outcomes of that interchange and influence—Donnellan and Ormerod both stress how much they hate scene changes, so analytic attention might focus on their strategies for eliminating them, as seen in their overlapping transitions for the London premieres of Tony Kushner's *Millennium Approaches* (1992) and *Perestroika* (1993) at the National Theatre.[32] Waters's and Smart's influences on each other and their shared aesthetic vision continue to evolve but consistently center on shared approaches for the staging of new writing and the pursuit of high-impact production effects, creating what a Berkley Rep program feature about Waters and Smart's collaboration calls "a palpable vitality in the life of a play."[33] However, the type of information that records how personal relationships affect artistic collaboration in a way that differs from unpartnered collaborators is both challenging to obtain and has not consistently been documented or discussed by theatre artists, reviewers, or historians, as is the case still for Waters and Smart, beyond the observations I have begun to collect.

Pursuing historiographical questions about the work of partnered artists implicates the dynamics of expected theatrical job descriptions, gender relations, and duration in creative and marital partnerships. The significance of intimacy and gender in creative partnerships crosses biological, social, and aesthetic aspects of identity and work. Marriage as a metaphor for collaboration both reveals and obfuscates: marriage, especially a companionate and largely egalitarian marriage as practiced by Waters and Smart, details something about the real labor of collaboration. Such labor may allow both partners independence and interconnection, but it does not remove challenging decisions of priority, as Smart's decision to leave Wimbledon for the move to the United States confirms. In collaboration and marriage, conflict can be productive and power differentials matter, even as they constantly shift as partners take on different roles over time.

As artists and as spouses, Waters and Smart make a difference to each other's work; given the negotiation of intimacy and creativity that I observed while interviewing them, the question is, what sort of difference? The difference has to do with a pursuit of shared meaning making and a sense of creative space around it, or what Pamela Howard defines as the dimension of scenography that allows the "literary mind and visual mind" to work together.[34] This description resonates with discourse about dramaturgy as a process concerned with the relationship between creators and the union of approaches to storytelling and performance composition. As Jane Ann Crum and Geoff Proehl suggest, what the dramaturg does specifically is make room—conceptually, emotionally, and intellectually—for the staging process.[35] I posit, for future research, that in a richly scenographic and dramaturgical way, Smart and Waters together make room for a staging process conceptually, emotionally, intellectually, *and* materially.

Waters and Smart suggest two moves theatre historians can make to help document and narrate the work of creative and marital partners. The first necessary move in dealing with the labor of partnered theatre artists is to acknowledge that the personal relationship exists and to chart its impact. This initial step often proves to be the hardest: it can seem respectful to ignore or gloss over artists' personal lives, and it is hard to articulate how work and marriage interact. Moreover, in spite of extensive occurrences of married or romantically partnered theatre artists across history, the dominant known models are couples formed by a director and an actor, a playwright and an actor, or two performers. These relationships carry more muse-artist iconography with them and signify about the erotic power of performance in ways that further complicate questions of autonomy and togetherness. With directors and designers, neither artist inhabits the glamour of the performance moment directly; their work together happens in the shared process of getting the performance ready rather than in guiding performance behavior, providing material to perform, or reacting to each other for others to watch. Next, theatre historians can continue to pursue conceptual models about autonomy and togetherness and to seek writing strategies that allow a plural subject to be the central unit of analysis without eliding each partner's self in the process of collaboration.

Acknowledging and truly factoring in serious personal and artistic partnerships might offer new insights into areas of theatre history, revealing specific economic structures, historical periods, or social contexts where partnerships flourish or disappear. Such awareness might further suggest patterns in the nature of working conditions and in the style of work where partnership is possible, desirable, or unwanted. Historical evaluations might reveal the impact of partnered artists on major trends and achievements. Insights might be developed about collaborative processes because of the dynamics laid bare when partnerships factor into the account.

In that spirit, when at work, the difference Waters and Smart make to each other is a dramaturgical one, and *that* specific creative exchange has been given even more space by their marital exchange. Waters and Smart's work together elucidates nonidealized aspects of theatrical collaboration, reveals tradeoffs related to the labor of raising children while also doing theatre work, and prompts a continued theorization of the work of designers in theatre. When the dramaturgical elements of partnership can be given historiographical treatment, theatre history will recover some of the gendered and interpersonal dynamics that are hard to document but that often make artistic production work.[36]

Notes

1. Allen Kuharski, "Joseph Chaikin and the Presence of the Dramaturg," in *Dramaturgy in American Theatre: A Sourcebook*, ed. Susan Jonas, Geoffrey Proehl, and Michael Lupu (New York: Harcourt Brace, 1997), 144–58.
2. Les Waters and Annie Smart, interview with Sara Freeman, January 30, 2010, Berkeley, Calif. (hereafter Waters and Smart interview).
3. Robert Hurwitt, "Berkeley Rep's Les Waters Dives into New Work," *San Francisco Gate*, April 11, 2010, http://www.sfgate.com/performance/article/Berkeley-Rep-s-Les-Waters-dives-into-new-work-3192843.php (accessed July 30, 2013).
4. The term "creative couple" blends the terminology of Vera John-Steiner in *Creative Collaboration* (New York: Oxford University Press, 2002) and Joshua Wolf Shenk in his series on creative pairs in *Slate* across September 2010, http://www.slate.com/articles/life/creative_pairs/2010/09/html.
5. John-Steiner, *Creative Collaboration*, 11–35, 192–96, 187–204, 76.
6. See, for example, Whitney Chadwick and Isabelle de Courtivron, eds., *Significant Others: Creativity and Intimate Partnerships* (London: Thames and Hudson, 1996). Geoff Proehl considers romantic metaphors related to dramaturgical collaboration in "The Images before Us," in *Dramaturgy in American Theatre*, ed. Jonas, Proehl, and Lupu, 134.
7. Ronald Hayman, "Double Acts," *Sunday Times Magazine*, March 2, 1980, 21.
8. Brenda Murphy's important close study of Williams and Kazan focuses on authorship through the "symphony" and "cinema" models. Brenda Murphy, *Tennessee Williams and Elia Kazan: A Collaboration in the Theatre* (Cambridge: Cambridge University Press, 1992), xii–xiii.
9. Eugenio Barba, "The Nature of Dramaturgy: Describing Actions at Work," *New Theatre Quarterly* 1, no. 1 (1985): 75.
10. See Pamela Howard, *What Is Scenography?* (London: Routledge, 2002), 124. See also Joslin McKinney and Philip Butterworth, *The Cambridge Introduction to Scenography* (Cambridge: Cambridge University Press, 2009), which treats Mielziner and Neher under the idea of a "dramaturgical scenography" (5, 55).
11. Interview with Sara Freeman, November 30, 2009, Eugene, Ore. In *American Theatre*, Harrison also went on record about Waters's dramaturgical sensibility, expressing surprise and thankfulness at how deeply Waters engaged with the text during rehearsals. See Chloe Veltman, "Les Waters: Explorer with an Ear," *American Theatre* 24, no. 10 (December 2007): 43.

12. John Fuegi, *Brecht & Co.*, 2nd ed. (New York: Grove Press, 2002), 194–202, 374–81, 421–50; McKinney and Butterworth, *Cambridge Introduction*, 44–51.
13. Wendy Lesser, *A Director Calls* (Berkeley: University of California Press, 1997).
14. Ibid., 224–25.
15. "Twenty Questions," *American Theatre* 18, no. 8 (October 2001): 136; Sam Hurwitt, "Encore: Annie Smart," *Theatre Bay Area* 33, no. 8 (August 2008): 60.
16. Smart works with directors like Bill Gaskill, David Leveaux, Tony Taccone, Kurt Beattie, and Jonathan Moscone. Waters works regularly with David Zinn, Meg Neville, Scott Bradley, and Antje Ellermann. Since production teams often have more than one designer, designers who work regularly with Waters also work regularly with Smart.
17. Waters and Smart interview.
18. Adele Ealing Shank, "To the Lighthouse," *Theatre Forum* 33 (2007): 60–61.
19. Veltman, "Explorer with an Ear," 43.
20. Chloe Veltman, "House of the Rising Gun," *San Francisco Weekly*, September 19, 2007, http://www.sfweekly.com/2007–09–19/culture/house-of-the-rising-gun/ (accessed July 30, 2013).
21. Diane Haithman, "Who's Afraid of Henrik Ibsen?," *Los Angeles Times*, May 24, 1998, http://articles.latimes.come/1998/may/24/entertainment/ca-52985 (accessed July 30, 2013).
22. Ibid., 2.
23. See Annie Smart professional website, "Annie Smart, Theatre Design," http://anniesmartdesign.net/shows.html.
24. Sam Hurwitt, "Encore: Annie Smart," *Theatre Bay Area* 33, no. 8 (August 2008): 60.
25. I have consulted fifteen reviews about the shows between 2007 and 2011; no other searches have produced reviews addressing their partnership. Examples of features and interviews include "Twenty Questions" and the articles by Robert Hurwitt, Sam Hurwittt, Haithman, and Veltman.
26. Robert Hurwitt, "Berkeley Rep's Les Waters."
27. Haithman, "Who's Afraid of Henrik Ibsen?," 2.
28. On Herbert, see Cathy Courtney, ed., *Jocelyn Herbert: A Theatre Workbook* (London: Art Books International, 1993). For Devine, see Philip Robert, *The Royal Court Theater and the Modern Stage* (London: Cambridge University Press, 1999); the entry in Samuel L. Leiter, *The Great Stage Directors: 100 Distinguished Careers of the Theatre* (New York: Facts on File, 1994), 90–93; and Irving Wardle, *The Theatres of George Devine* (London: Eyre Methuen, 1979).

29. See Harriet Devine, *Being George Devine's Daughter* (London: Barkus Books, 2006), 83–85. George Devine's wife, Sophie Harris, was also a theatrical designer, one-third of the pioneering design team Motley. Regarding the other couples, see William Gaskill, *A Sense of Direction* (London: Faber and Faber, 1988); O'Donovan's 2011 obituary (http://www.guardian.co.uk/stage/2011/jan/24/desmond-o-donovan); and the introduction to Jellicoe's collected plays, *"The Knack" and "The Sport of My Mad Mother"* (London: Faber and Faber, 1985).
30. Nick Curtis, "How We Met: Declan Donnellan and Nick Ormerod," *Independent* online, January 16, 1994, http://www.independent.co.uk/arts-entertainment/how-we-met-declan-donnellan-and-nick-ormerod-1400506.html (accessed September 1, 2013).
31. Ibid. See also the interview with Donnellan and Ormerod (the only pair to be interviewed in a book about directors) in *In Contact with the Gods? Directors Talk Theatre*, ed. Maria Delgado and Paul Heritage (Manchester: Manchester University Press, 1996), 79–92.
32. I saw these productions in the spring of 1994 and was astonished by the seamless blend of action that still maintained absolute clarity about where each scene took place. See also Vincent Canby in the *New York Times* comparing the New York and London productions of the cycle, "Sunday View: Two Angels," January 30, 1994, http://www.nytimes.com/1994/01/30/theater/sunday-view-two-angels-two-journeys-in-london-and-new-york.html?pagewanted=all&src=pm (accessed June 30, 2013).
33. "The Mysteries of *Irma Vep* Revealed," http://www.berkeleyrep.org/season/0304/iv_program.asp. See also the "Twenty Questions" in *American Theatre* where Waters finishes the prompt, "It isn't theatre if . . ." with "it's not bigger than us," 136.
34. Howard, *What Is Scenography?*, 125–26.
35. Jane Ann Crum, "Toward a Dramaturgical Sensibility," in *Dramaturgy in American Theatre*, ed. Jonas, Proehl, and Lupu, 70–77; Geoffrey Proehl, "The Images Before Us: Metaphors for the Role of Dramaturg in American Theater," in ibid., 124–36.
36. Research for this article was generously supported by a Junior Professorship Development Grant from the University of Oregon and a Martin Nelson Summer Research Grant at the University of Puget Sound. Thanks to both Hayley Hilmes and Andrew Fox for assistance as research scholarship students at the University of Puget Sound.

3. Advertising and the Commercial Spirit: Cataloging Nineteenth-Century Scenic Studio Practices

Tom Robson

Richard Marston, a nineteenth-century English scenic designer who worked in the United States, lamented the changes he saw in scenic art during his time. According to an account of his words in Orville K. Larson's *Scene Design in the American Theatre, 1915–1960*, Marston identified a shift away from individual artists working closely on specific productions and toward a mass-produced "factory system" of American stage design in the period.[1] Recognizing an emerging system wherein carpenters and painters could quickly build, paint, and ship a small repertory of standardized designs nationwide, Marston attributed these changes to the industry's reprioritization from art to profit. He complained, "The overwhelming influence of the commercial spirit is crushing scenic art in the theatre and fostering scenic factories the products of which will be in turn superseded by wallpaper. The removal of scenic painting from the sphere of art to manufacturing is demoralizing to the artist who pursues it."[2] While I would not presume to speak to whether or not a specific laborer felt demoralized, Marston's complaint suggests a significant shift in scenic design as the nineteenth century drew to a close: the rise of the independent scenic studio unaffiliated with a specific theatre or producer and primarily concerned with the creation of scenery for profit.

Marston's comments reveal a clear personal privileging of certain types of work, establishing a hierarchy that prioritizes artistic creation above factory reproduction. He also elevates the creative work of the artist-designer above the replicative work of the craftsman-technician. Ironically, as Nick Hunt and Susan Melrose point out, the Greek word *techne*, the root word for both "technology" and "technique," "is usually translated as *either art or craft*" (emphasis added).[3] In other words, if we, as scholars, accept Marston's artificial stratification between theatrical artists and technicians, we also accept two oppositional meanings from the same root word. On the surface this is a linguistic issue, but out of language grows meaning, and perhaps this linguistic schism reflects a larger historical shift in understanding the work of the craftsman. This would make the wider community of scholars—myself included—equally culpable with the Marstons of the world in diminishing the work of the theatre technician.

The difficulty of giving scholarly attention to unseen labor has challenged theatre historians for some time. In a 1965 speech to the Fourth International Congress on Theatre Research, Alois Nagler set forth a list of questions needing to be answered about the nineteenth-century theatre, all having to do with stagecraft, technology, and theatrical production.[4] While many of the questions Nagler posed have been addressed in the intervening fifty years, a number of the material conditions of the late nineteenth-century stage still suffer from a paucity of critical attention. If audience members and critics prize the visible act of performance, scholars prize the legible historical artifact.[5] As historians know, the availability of evidence often dictates their ability to recover the past. Happily, a newly digitized archival source now permits historians to recover the work of the late nineteenth-century scenic studio artist-technician.

In her own recovery of theatrical technicians, Christin Essin connects historical neglect of the technical theatre worker with the producer's marginalization of these collaborators, saying, "Producers [. . .] overlook the technicians, whose investment of time and labor regularly outweighs that of their collaborators. Scholars are also guilty of this oversight, giving only secondary consideration to the labor needed to make theatre artistry happen."[6] Despite linguistically reaffirming the divide between "labor" and "theatre artistry," Essin takes a significant step toward a greater understanding of the artistry of craft. With this insight Essin attempts a reconfiguration of the way we view the relationship between theatrical labor and historical study. First, she establishes the investment of time as a measuring unit of a worker's value to a production. By pointing out that a scenic carpenter spends more time laboring on a given project than that project's designer, she makes an implicit argument for that carpenter's equal, if not greater, worth. This relationship between invested time and value upends the traditional valuation of contributors, which relies on their recognition by audience members in production. Yet the essence of backstage labor's dramatic effectiveness lies in its invisibility. While the fruits of the technician's labor—the tangible costumes, sets, props, and such—may be seen, the Western theatre typically masks the labor needed to create these visible pieces. The viewer witnesses the actors onstage, sweating and exerting themselves, while only the inanimate final product of the craftsman signifies his or her labor.[7] This essay demonstrates one way to recover that labor.

In 1882 John Clancy, a stagehand from Syracuse, New York, found himself displeased with the selection and availability of stage equipment, so he began to build his own; three years later, seeing the need for a company to provide such technology to theatres nationwide, he founded the J. R. Clancy Company.[8] Now in operation for more than 130 years, the Clancy Company continues operation as a provider of technical theatre equipment to this day and recently donated a collection of materials to the United States Institute for Theatre Technology (USITT). USITT, in turn, digitized many of these materials, including nearly a century's worth of equipment catalogs, from the first issue in 1886 through 1999.[9] Providing a wealth of information, these catalogs contain comments from Clancy himself, illustrations of equipment, pricing, explanations of use in scenic construction, descriptions of materials used, billing and shipping procedures, and advertisements. These catalogs prove particularly valuable to the theatre historian looking to explore theatre technicians, as they offer new insights into scenic construction, stage equipment, and business practices for these theatre artists.

For the purposes of this essay, I am especially concerned with the advertisements found in the back of the catalogs, as they reveal aspects of the technical theatre industry of the period. In Clancy's first five catalogs, from 1886 to 1891, the company included several pages of advertisements in the catalog's closing pages.[10] In this space, scenic artists, stage machinists, and scene shops could promote their services to a nationwide customer base in an attempt to draw business. Since I hope to begin reconstructing the processes—the work—of these technicians, I have found it helpful to shift from asking historiographical questions of "why" to asking questions of "how." The questions, then, to ask regarding the Clancy catalogs might be as follows. How do these catalogs reveal scenic practices of the late nineteenth century? How did scenic studios operate in a national theatrical environment? How do these catalogs disrupt traditional narratives of late nineteenth-century theatre history?

The last of these questions can begin to be answered by the catalog advertisements, which provide intriguing evidence in the debate about the level of theatrical centralization in the period. Both Jack Poggi and Alfred L. Bernheim have posited that American theatre centralized itself in New York in the 1870s, while Rosemarie K. Bank and others have challenged this narrative.[11] The data from the catalogs comes down firmly in favor of a decentralized theatrical industry. Seventy-six scenic studios advertised in the back pages of this six-year run of the Clancy catalogs, representing twenty-four different cities.[12] New York City was the most heavily represented, with fifteen advertisements across the five catalogs, but several other cities showed heavy representation as well. Table 3.1 highlights those locations outside New York City with three or more advertisements in Clancy's catalogs, providing a sense of the geographic diversity of the scenic industry.[13] These data reflect advertisements by geography, not by studio. For example, Leon Lempert of Rochester, New York, advertised in multiple catalogs; the chart counts each of those ads as a separate data point. As the table shows, the greatest geographic concentration was located in the northeast region (Rochester, Philadelphia, Buffalo, and Boston), but a strong midwestern presence remained as well. Additionally, advertisers stretched into the South, with single ads from studios in Memphis and New Orleans, and into the West, with two from San Francisco.

By placing advertisements in a national catalog, these scenic studios, spread as they were throughout the country, existed to supply more than just their own local markets. Mary C. Henderson mentions the 1875 founding of the Armbruster Scenic Studio in Columbus, Ohio, which "supplied generic sets of scenery [. . .] to managers, stars, traveling minstrel shows, and hundreds of theatres, both professional and amateur, throughout the country."[14] Henderson highlights the studios' abilities to supply wares to producers regardless of geography and argues that the significant improvements in American infrastructure during the nineteenth century, specifically the growth of rail travel, permitted it. While Poggi points to the railroads as a reason for

Table 3.1. Geographic locations of scenic studios most commonly found in the Clancy catalogs between 1886 and 1991

City	*No. of Advertisements*
Rochester, New York	8
Kansas City, Missouri	6
Columbia, South Carolina	5
Philadelphia, Pennsylvania	5
Cincinnati, Ohio	5
Buffalo, New York	4
Chicago, Illinois	4
Boston, Massachusetts	3
Toledo, Ohio	3

theatrical centralization, I would suggest that the sudden interconnectivity of the United States actually permitted decentralization for theatrical technicians. While the enhancement of transportation might potentially have led to a small number of studios serving theatres nationwide—a form of centralization—the catalogs do not suggest this. Rather, they show dozens of studios spread throughout the country. Greater efficiency in transportation created the possibility of constructing a set in one location, then performing on it somewhere altogether different. While this idea might initially raise logistical concerns, the years covered by the Clancy catalog advertisements saw major changes to freight rail transportation in the United States. During the period from the end of the Civil War to the beginning of the twentieth century, freight rail improved in speed, volume, efficiency, and construction while also lowering prices.[15] To accommodate this greater size, engineers continually redesigned boxcars for greater stability and resilience, strengthening walls, popularizing the combination wood/sheet metal roof to prevent leaks that could damage merchandise, and transitioning from the use of wood to the use of metal for much of boxcar construction.[16] In concert with these innovations, the cost of rail transport dropped steadily between 1877 and 1887, making it more cost-effective to transport scenery long distance. These dramatic improvements in the functionality and coverage of freight rail, combined with the accompanying drop in prices, permitted studios to ship mass-produced scenery nationwide in a cost-effective way.

The Clancy catalogs themselves also provide an additional window into the relationship between scenic studios and freight rail transportation. Though the catalogs supplied different merchandise from what the studios that advertised in their pages sold, their shipping practices were suggestive of others in the theatrical industry of the period. In the "Terms" section that spelled out shipping and billing procedures at the front of the catalogs, Clancy offered purchasers the choice of having their goods shipped "by express or freight" but recommended, "Large orders should always be shipped by freight."[17] Clancy here emphasized the significance of freight rail shipping to his business practice and, by extension, to the business practices of the scenic studios advertising in his closing pages; if Clancy insisted on using freight rail to deliver large orders, it is reasonable to suppose that studios shipping full sets and drops would have taken advantage of the same system.

Clancy's "Terms" section also provides evidence of the ability to ship scenic goods great distances. In explaining his payment terms for cash-on-delivery orders, Clancy divided his customers into two categories: those within three hundred miles and those farther away than three hundred miles.[18] This acknowledgment of customers more than three hundred miles away demonstrates the expansiveness of Clancy's geographic reach, even in the company's early years, and also suggests a theatrical industry willing to order goods over great distances. Clancy's reference to a market for his merchandise more than three hundred miles away—merchandise for which he would still accept cash-on-delivery orders, no less—points to an industry for which geography was no longer one of the primary determining factors in selecting business partners. This lack of concern with geographical distance is reflected in the advertisements. The scenic artists "Moses & Lauderback," advertising in the 1890 catalog, indicated that they would supply cost estimates "to all Parts of the World" from their Chicago studio.[19] With few concerns about delivering goods throughout the country, Moses and Lauderback were free to solicit business from producers nationwide, and while there is no evidence to suggest that they—or their competitors—shipped beyond the continental United States, the catalogs certainly do show that they sought business from beyond their local communities. Yet even with all of the improvements in railroad shipping, Clancy noted the possible travails of freight shipping and provided his company with legal cover in the event of damage, saying, "After goods leave our depots in regular form, they will be considered in the possession of the parties ordering, and we will not guarantee any loss that may occur."[20]

Concerns about damage to scenery aside, the growth of freight rail transportation and the accompanying decentralization of the scenic industry also affected other aspects of the business practices of scenic studios, and these changes can be seen by examining the advertisements in the Clancy catalogs. Scenic design scholar Orville Larson points to the nineteenth century as the period in which theatre underwent a shift toward the more decidedly commercial and argues that this change played into the rise of the designer. The shift toward greater commercialism in the theatre also resulted in the independent scenic studio and its craftsmen. As the designer rose in stature, as producers placed increasing emphasis on the scenic investiture of their productions, and as transportation methods evolved, the role of scenic studios in the larger theatrical industry began to shift as well. During this period, producers began soliciting bids for the construction of their scenery, creating competition among studios to see who could deliver the lowest possible prices for their services. Fourteen of the advertisements in the back of the catalogs between 1886 and 1891 specifically mention providing estimates to producers, and, according to Larson, producers frequently made their selections "with little regard for the artistic quality of the finished product."[21]

The advertisements in the back pages of Clancy's catalogs reflect this increased competition for business, with multiple studios emphasizing their abilities to balance cost with artistry. L. R. Close & Company announced in its 1887 ad that it performed "Artistic Work at Low Prices!"[22] Harry G. Carter's 1889 and 1890 listings declared, "Charges reasonable."[23] Harley Merry & Sons' 1890 ad stated, "Being Importers of Canvas and Colors, we are enabled to give greater value for money than any other Scenic Firm in America."[24] In 1891, W. F. Wise and Company highlighted its remote location in Tyrone, Pennsylvania, saying, "Being located in the country our expenses are low. Our customers benefit by it."[25] In each of these cases the studios demonstrated their value to producers through their ability to deliver high quality merchandise at good prices, and Wise even directly addressed the issue of remote geography as an asset.[26]

An analysis of the Clancy catalog archive further shows the tactics used by scenic studios to appeal to producers. Studios used their ads to frame themselves, highlighting their assets and making conscious choices regarding their methods of self-presentation. If the first of the most common approaches to self-presentation was emphasizing value, the second seemed to be emphasizing an advertiser's ability to provide multiple services on a single contract. Of the seventy-six total advertisements in the five years of the Clancy catalog's era of advertising, fifteen of them specifically mentioned a combination of scenic painting and stage machinery. These advertisements made no distinction between the techniques of painting required for painted drops and the techniques of engineering required for mechanical effects. Both advanced skill sets fell under their purview, demonstrating the breadth of their abilities and further troubling the artist-craftsman binary posited by people like Marston. Among the most common listings was the term "Scenic Artist and Stage Machinist" or some derivation thereof, indicating the studio's facility with both painting and the creation of stage effects, a necessary production element for any producer wishing to present most nineteenth-century melodramas. O. L. Story of Boston, in the 1887 catalog, labeled himself with the headline "Scenic Artist" but immediately followed it with the statement, "Contracts taken for Scenery and all kinds of Stage Mechanism[s] for Halls, Theatres, etc."[27] Story here used the layout of the advertisement—leading with a large type, all capital letters, and italicized font that described him as a "Scenic Artist" and following with a slightly smaller, nonitalicized reference to his ability to provide stage machinery—to draw the reader's eye in and then explain the many services he could offer. Rep Logle of Toledo adopted a similar approach in 1890, using a large headline to label himself "Scenic Artist and Stage Machinist" and following with the description "Scenery and Equipments [*sic*] for Stages of Theatres, Halls, Etc."[28] As these examples show, advertisements frequently united artistry and technical expertise, suggesting that treating these skills as separate and distinct in contemporary scholarship leaves one with an incomplete picture of theatre practice in the nineteenth century.

This emphasis on stage machinery and effects made a great deal of sense for advertisers in the 1880s and 1890s, not long after the massive success of *The Black Crook* in 1866. Brooks McNamara attributes the success of *The Black Crook* to its heavy use of spectacle and asserts that "hundreds of plays were written solely as vehicles for magic, special effects, or elaborately trapped settings" as a result.[29] In a post–*Black Crook* theatrical world, producers looked for ways to replicate that production's immense appeal, making a scenic studio proficient in stage machinery all the more valuable. Yet the success of *The Black Crook* rested on more than just its machinery. Critics also pointed to its spectacular lighting effects, especially its use of calcium lights.[30]

Some advertisers in Clancy's catalog reflected this increased emphasis on lighting, suggesting another version of the one-stop-shopping approach taken by the stage machinists. Theatrical troupes of many stripes, if they could afford the expense, sought the use of calcium lights because of their greater ability to thrill audiences.[31] Knowing that producers placed such high value on these lights, George Collins—advertising in Clancy's 1889 catalog—wisely boasted, "I Carry My Own Calcium Apparatus."[32] Collins framed himself as a multitalented technical theatre craftsman, billing himself "Property King, Stage Carpenter, and Calcium Operator." L. R. Close & Company in the 1886 catalog announced, "Full detail plans for building *and lighting* stages free of charge where we supply scenery."[33] Close & Company adopted a similar approach to Collins's, indicating the company's multiple skill sets, but its mention of lighting technology was placed less prominently than in Collins's ad, positioned almost as a special added feature. Only Close & Company and Collins specifically connected lighting with scenic construction and painting in the five Clancy catalogs, but a number of advertisements highlighting effects and accessories suggest that other studios were dabbling in this work as well. Indeed, one of the biggest revelations of the catalogs is the way these studios emphasized their ability to contribute to theatrical presentation in as many ways as possible, making them an invaluable part of the artistic process.

In a 1951 *Educational Theatre Journal* essay, J. Wendell Johnson wrote, "The men who devised the traps and machines, the waterfalls, the apparitions, and the thundercarts deserve to be remembered, if not honored, with the poets. [. . .] As long as we have a theatre which demands illusion, poet and carpenter must work together."[34] History, however, has all too often overlooked the work of the carpenter. Possibly stemming from the insidious divide that prioritizes one form of *techne* over another or from the genuine historiographical challenge of finding and processing surviving evidence, scholars have largely mirrored Marston's privileging of certain theatrical workers over others, yet the evidence found in the Clancy catalogs suggests that such a binary is both false and misleading. Indeed, these catalogs demonstrate that the individuals who built sets, provided effects, painted backdrops, and expanded their reach into lighting saw little or no distinction between those who built and those who designed. These theatre professionals made it their business to practice in both fields, building skill sets that incorporated carpentry, artistic painting, designing machinery, and running lights.

Marston's disdain for studios producing large amounts of scenery without regard for originality preserves the position of theatre worker of value for a rarefied elite. Larson also quotes scenic artist Homer C. Emens, who complained of these scenic studios, "Everything is done in a hurry and the rush forbids the best results."[35] Yet Emens did not hesitate to place himself in the company of these scenic factories, advertising in Clancy's 1886 catalog. Emens & Coatcher's ad bears a striking resemblance to those of the company's competitors. Emens and his partner Coatcher employed the catchall title "Scenic Artist," listed the location of their studio, and cited the companies for which they had worked. If we analyze solely the content and layout of the advertisement, Emens & Coatcher appear no different from any other studio, yet Emens clearly attempted to distinguish his own studio from the rushed work of his competitors.

If the Clancy catalog advertisements reveal a highly competitive and nationalized scenic industry, with studios seeking every edge they could find when marketing themselves, then Emens's complaint about scenic studios may well have been just another marketing strategy. While some used advertisements to positively promote their own work, Emens's use of negative advertising attempted to run down the quality of his competitors' work. In 1889, Rep Logle similarly cautioned, "Don't have your stage ruined by inexperienced persons."[36] While slightly less adamant than the Emens quotation cited by Larson, Logle used the threat of inferior work performed by others as a means of making his studio stand out. If one considers Emens's critique of scenic studios through this lens of self-interest, why not apply the same critical analysis to the Marston quotation with which I began this essay? On one level, Marston certainly acknowledged a widespread change in scenic practices during the period, a change that is documented by many scholars of nineteenth-century theatre. At the same time, Marston's claims about artistic quality must be treated with some skepticism, as the advertisements in the Clancy catalogs suggest a very strong possibility of self-preservation and promotion in his words. As with Emens and Logle, if Marston could convince producers that these scenic studios delivered inferior work, he stood to gain more business for himself.

The emergence of the Clancy catalog archive as a resource for historians permits a continuation of the study of the period begun by others. This wealth of new evidence leads to a deeper understanding of the period, challenging some previous assertions, supporting others, and offering a host of new questions for study. An examination of these catalogs and the advertisements within offer insights into the ways that independent scenic studios operated in this crucial period. We see how they promoted their work, how they separated themselves from others, and how they relied on technological and aesthetic developments to further their business. Moreover, we begin to see how we can start to fill in something of a scholarly lacuna. My essay here has only begun to scratch the surface of what this exciting new archive can add to the scholarly conversation surrounding theatre technicians, builders, and the nineteenth-century stage, suggesting possibilities for further research. Indeed, the J. R. Clancy catalogs provide a previously unavailable way of making the unseen seen, of tangibly interacting with the labor of the nineteenth-century technician.

Notes

1. Orville K. Larson, *Scene Design in the American Theatre, 1915–1960* (Fayetteville: University of Arkansas Press, 1989), 13.
2. Ibid., 17.
3. Nick Hunt and Susan Melrose, "*Techne*, Technology, Technician: The Creative Practices of the Mastercraftsperson," *Performance Research* 10, no. 4 (2005): 70.
4. Vera Mowry Roberts, "New Viewpoints on Nineteenth Century Scene Design," *Educational Theatre Journal* 18, no. 1 (March 1966): 46, http://www.jstor.org/stable/3205118.
5. For excellent coverage of the early and mid-nineteenth century, see Rosemarie K. Bank, *Theatre Culture in America, 1825–1860* (Cambridge: Cambridge University Press, 1997); David Grimsted, *Melodrama Unveiled: American Theater and Culture, 1800–1850* (Berkeley: University of California Press, 1987); and Bruce A. McConachie, *Melodramatic Formations: American Theatre and Society* (Iowa City: University of Iowa Press, 1992). For detail on late nineteenth-century performers and managers, see Kim Marra, *Strange Duets: Impresarios and Actresses in the American Theatre, 1865–1914* (Iowa City: University of Iowa Press, 2006); Garff Wilson, *A History of American Acting* (Bloomington: Indiana University Press,

1966); Tracy C. Davis, *Actresses as Working Women: Their Social Identity in Victorian Culture* (London: Routledge, 1991); Alfred L. Bernheim, *The Business of the Theatre* (New York: Actors Equity Association, 1932); and Jack Poggi, *Theater in America: The Impact of Economic Forces 1870–1965* (Ithaca: Cornell University Press, 1966).

6. Christin Essin, "An Aesthetic of Backstage Labor," *Theatre Topics* 21, no. 1 (March 2011): 35, doi:10.1353/tt.2011.0012.
7. As a possible sign that contemporary theatre practice might be shifting away from this, consider the 2011 Playwrights' Horizons production of Jordan Harrison's *Maple and Vine*, directed by Anne Kauffman. In this production, which featured numerous onstage scene changes of fully realized locations "performed" by a run crew of four in dim lighting, the run crew received the final bow during curtain call, upending the traditional convention of ignoring the presence of the stagehand during ovations. If contemporary theatre practice is beginning to give greater acknowledgment to technical labor, the time is ripe for theatre scholarship to do the same.
8. The J. R. Clancy Company, "History: Over 125 Years of Innovation and Quality," http://www.jrclancy.com/abouthistory.asp (accessed September 30, 2013).
9. Because this is currently an unprocessed and closed collection, it lacks an official finding aid and is somewhat loosely organized in individual files online. Researchers interested in exploring it further should contact USITT directly. Due to USITT usage requirements, URLs are unavailable. Hereafter, citations referring to this collection will include name of document, year of publication, page number, and "USITT."
10. Clancy did not publish a full catalog in 1888, opting instead to distribute two partial catalogs, including his major goods. These partial catalogs are not included in the USITT collection, but Clancy makes reference to them in his welcome note in the 1889 catalog. The catalogs ceased to include these closing advertisements in 1892.
11. Poggi, *Theater in America*; Bernheim, *Business of the Theatre*; Rosemarie K. Bank, "A Reconsideration of the Death of the Nineteenth-Century American Repertory Companies and the Rise of the Combination," *Essays in Theatre* 5 (November 1986): 61–75.
12. In both the 1890 and 1891 catalogs a handful of studios listed themselves with multiple locations. In an effort to represent the geographical diversity of these advertisers with the highest accuracy, I have counted each location separately in my data analysis.
13. I have chosen to highlight those regions with three or more advertisements, as I believe that three indicates enough of a trend to draw conclusions.

14. Mary C. Henderson, "Scenography, Stagecraft, and Architecture," in *The Cambridge History of American Theatre, Volume 2: 1870–1945*, ed. Don B. Wilmeth and Christopher Bigsby (Cambridge: Cambridge University Press, 1999), 497.
15. In 1880 the United States had 93,671 miles of rail line across the country; a decade later it had 159,271 miles (Slason Thompson, *A Short History of American Railways, Covering Ten Decades* [Chicago: Bureau of Railway News and Statistics, 1925], 229). Between 1870 and 1900, boxcar capacity grew from ten tons to fifty tons, and its cubic volume doubled from one thousand cubic feet to two thousand (John H. White, Jr., *The American Railroad Freight Car: From the Wood-Car Era to the Coming of Steel* [Baltimore: Johns Hopkins University Press, 1993], 192). David Marple, "Technological Innovation and Organizational Survival: A Population Ecology Study of Nineteenth-Century American Railroads," *Sociological Quarterly* 23, no. 1 (Winter 1982): 108, http://www.jstor.org/stable/4106356; Thompson, *Short History*, 229–44; White, *American Railroad Freight Car*, 192–242.
16. White, *American Railroad Freight Car*, 192–242.
17. Clancy catalog, 1891, ii, USITT. Though I am here quoting specifically from the 1891 catalog, some version of this language appears in every catalog discussed in this article.
18. Clancy told customers that he would ship goods COD with payment of a 30 percent deposit on orders within three hundred miles and with payment of a 50 percent deposit on orders from beyond that distance. Ibid., ii.
19. Clancy catalog, 1890, 32, USITT.
20. Ibid., ii.
21. Larson, *Scene Design*, 9–10.
22. Clancy catalog, 1887, 30, USITT.
23. Ibid., 1889, 30; 1890, 31.
24. Ibid., 1890, 29.
25. Ibid., 1891, 33.
26. As the crow flies, Tyrone, Pennsylvania, is roughly 170 miles from Philadelphia and 94 miles from Pittsburgh in central Pennsylvania.
27. Clancy catalog, 1887, 25, USITT.
28. Ibid., 1890, 30.
29. Brooks McNamara, "The Scenography of Popular Entertainment," *Drama Review* 18, no. 1 (March 1974): 20–21, http://www.jstor.org/stable/1144857.
30. Leigh George Odom, "'The Black Crook' at Niblo's Garden," *Drama Review* 26, no. 1 (Spring 1982): 35, http://www.jstor.org/stable/1145443.
31. Brooks McNamara, "The Indian Medicine Show," *Educational Theatre Journal* 23, no. 4 (December 1971): 441, http://www.jstor.org/stable/3205750.

32. Clancy catalog, 1889, 19, USITT.
33. Ibid., 1886, 22.
34. J. Wendell Johnson, “To the Technician: Salute and Invitation,” *Educational Theatre Journal* 3, no. 1 (March 1951): 32, http://www.jstor.org/stable/3203677.
35. Larson, *Scene Design*, 18.
36. Clancy catalog, 1889, 28, USITT. Logle also used the same verbiage in the 1890 catalog.

4. Don't Quit Your Day Job: Situating Extratheatrical Employment in the Performance Archive

Christine Woodworth

In the second act of Edna Ferber and George S. Kaufman's 1936 play, *Stage Door*, playwright Keith Burgess returns from a successful year in Hollywood to lure actress Terry Randall to join him on the West Coast. He indelicately states, "You can't go stumbling around like this forever. You're not working, are you?" When Terry replies in the affirmative, Keith asks, "You are? What in?" Terry answers, "The blouse department of R. H. Macy and Co." Keith is stunned but Terry calmly replies, "I have to live, Keith." His response: "Good God!"[1] One year before *Stage Door* was produced, *Family Circle* featured an article on unusual careers, highlighting Doris Bryant. She had moved to New York City to be an actor. Upon arrival, however, "she discovered that dozens of other girls were pouring into the city by every train with the same idea. And not being very wealthy, her money ran out before she had established herself as a second Bernhardt or even a Katharine Cornell."[2] A lifelong cat lover, Bryant found pet resources lacking, so she opened a cat shop that carried everything from medicine to accessories. She eventually cultivated an international clientele that included customers from the American theatre such as Claire Luce and other prominent actresses.[3]

In the make-or-break world of theatre today, "survival jobs"—often in restaurants or retail, and rarely in the realm of pet care or small business ownership—are standard practice for those looking to break into professional theatre. Countless resources are available for aspiring artists to figure out a way to pay their bills and continue to audition, write, and direct. In fact, day jobs can offer more than a means to paying bills. A recent post on Backstage.com titled "Don't Quit Your Day Job—It Could Help Your Career" suggests that low-pay and even no-pay positions in related industry fields (casting, talent management, clerking at the Drama Book Shop) can improve networking and offer an insider glimpse at those in decision-making positions.[4] Today's "survival jobs" seem to fall within two categories: those that pay the bills but are unrelated to the theatre, and those that are related to theatre but "pay" dividends primarily in networking opportunities. At what point did the day job transition from the apparently shocking necessity endured by Terry Randall to being *de rigueur* for all artists pursuing a career in the theatre? Although that in itself would be a fascinating point of inquiry, this essay will instead offer a consideration of how to situate extratheatrical employment within the performance archive, arguing that it is a critical component of historical narratives in the theatre. Acknowledging survival work can potentially influence how audiences receive theatrical work as well as the ways in which historians situate theatrical work within a broader context, particularly in regard to individual contacts, influential networks, political activism, and celebrity notoriety. Incorporating these facets into studies of theatre artists provokes the question, what is the relationship between the paid and unpaid work completed away from the stage and that which is done onstage?

This essay will explore the work of two women theatre artists who were laboring in and outside the theatre in the midst of critical watershed moments within first-wave feminisms. The extratheatrical work of actresses Neysa McMein and Kitty Marion illustrates the fraught complexities of "survival work" for early twentieth-century women whose notoriety wove together their work in and outside the theatre. Although both women ultimately garnered positions in narratives of theatre history, their work outside the theatre was the principal source of their renown. The publications, memoirs, news clippings, and prison records that primarily illustrate their extratheatrical employment provide historiographical challenges to theatre scholars intent on considering their artistic labor. Yet the support from their "survival jobs," the impact made by this work, and the material traces left behind from this employment afford scholars the opportunity to consider the ways in which extratheatrical employment may be intrinsic to narratives of theatre history.

For several hundred years, the few occupational choices available to women outside the home were limited to service, factory labor, and theatre jobs such as actress, playwright, or manager. Still, as the experiences of Neysa McMein and Kitty Marion illustrate, sometimes work in the theatre was simply not enough to sustain a living. By the end of the nineteenth century, the opportunities for women in the theatre—specifically actresses—had become more complicated. Tracy C. Davis notes in *Actresses as Working Women* that "career pathways multiplied but the constancy of touring, the fluidity of the acting community in touring companies, and the famous competition for employment had an even greater effect on theatrical women than on men because of the implications for restricted variety in casting, disruptions to family life, and the premium on ties to a management giving steady employment."[5] Couple those difficulties with pay inequity and the perils of sexual exploitation for employment gain and it is no wonder that women were often forced to seek additional employment outside the theatre. Female performers who did not attain star status struggled to procure engagements within major cities as well as on regional and provincial theatrical circuits.[6] Talent was not always sufficient in terms of booking a contract. Actresses had to face a gauntlet of challenges put in place by theatrical agents and managers as well as by commercial circuits. Once an actress, singer, or dancer procured an engagement, she often had to arrange and pay for her own travel, accommodations, and costumes. A number of actresses—including Kitty Marion—recorded these challenges in memoirs and autobiographies, archival materials that have become indispensable resources for scholars exploring women's late nineteenth- and early twentieth-century theatrical employment.[7]

The turn of the century also marked a time of social upheaval as women—McMein and Marion among them—began to draw public attention to the gender disparities in the theatre and as the suffrage movement escalated its campaigns in England and the United States. The Victorian "angel in the house" gave way to the dynamic and dangerous New Woman, who quickly transformed into the militant suffragette of the early twentieth century. Identified in the mid-1890s, the New Woman emerged as both an object of scorn and an icon of liberation. Victorian scholar Sally Ledger asserts that "many of the textual configurations of the New Woman were partisan, and were deployed as part of an attempt to undermine the late nineteenth-century women's movement and to limit its influence. A particular class (male and bourgeois) held power at the *fin de siècle*, and the ideological discourses on the New Woman were undoubtedly promoted in order to ridicule and contain renegade women." Ledger goes on to note that the "naming of the New Woman [. . .] was feminism's triumph" in that it allowed for a "reverse discourse" in which "the New Woman began to speak on her own behalf."[8] From the moment of its inception, the New Woman was an unstable designation offering myriad views on education, marriage, motherhood, sexual autonomy, political engagement, and, of course, labor outside the home. In her discussion of Sydney Grundy's satirical comedy *The New Woman*, which lampooned this emergent trope, Viv Gardner asserts that the 1894 production was ironic and powerful in that the caricatured New Woman figures were embodied by actresses who were ostensibly *actual* New Women. "Simply by working," she claims, "they were transgressing the social boundaries that required middle-class women to be dependent on either father, husband or brother. To be working on the stage doubled the offence and alienated the women from 'normal' female society."[9] Given that "doubled" offense of laboring outside the home while being on display publicly in the theatre, Kitty Marion and Neysa McMein's experiences effectively constituted a triple offense: they worked outside the home, worked within the theatre, and actively engaged in the public protests of a variety of social justice campaigns.

It is unknown whether Kitty Marion and Neysa McMein were personally acquainted, but given their mutual involvement in the U.S. suffrage campaign and engagement with artist and activist circles in New York City in the early decades of the twentieth century, it seems possible. What makes Marion and McMein intriguing as a joint case study has to do primarily with the ways in which their careers in professional theatre intersected with extratheatrical employment and protest, with how their legacies and notoriety were established, and with the archival material that describes these enterprises.

The extant documentation of the lives of these extraordinary women offers vexing challenges to historians. Neysa McMein crafted an autobiographical essay for the collection *As I Look at Life*. Evidence of her remarkable career as a painter and illustrator abounds, including dozens of magazine covers, portraits, advertisements, and posters. Stories of McMein are woven throughout letters and memoirs written by the literary and theatrical elite. McMein herself sometimes wrote columns for magazines, including a brief assignment as a film reviewer for *McCall's*. In spite of this, there is much more material written *about* McMein than written *by* her. Kitty Marion, however, crafted an as-yet-unpublished book-length autobiography, which is housed in manuscript form at the New York Public Library with an additional copy held at the Women's Library in London. Piecing together the timeline of Marion's life and career from this document is a daunting challenge as she offers few dates, titles, or names in her reminiscences. Written decades after most of the recounted events actually transpired, it is nearly impossible to determine how subsequent events may have shaped the writing of this text.

The uncertainties within Marion's autobiography and anecdotes about McMein in memoirs of the Algonquin Round Table have given each woman a certain air of mystery as scholars have attempted to separate fact from fiction. In all likelihood, Marion crafted her autobiographical text as a means of generating additional income and also as a mechanism for memorializing her contribution to art and politics. McMein's motivations are less clear. Each woman's account depicts the various facets of her work as well as her personal, professional, and political networks as interwoven components of her life. Marion's narrative illustrates the inseparability of her survival work from her theatrical career, while McMein's writing demonstrates how her work as an actress laid the foundation for her more notable career in painting, which, in turn, influenced the theatre. Such interconnectedness reads as a deliberate rhetorical strategy. As Gardner argues, such autobiographical accounts "offer an opportunity to consider the ways in which the performer/writers employ self-representation, 'autobiographical strategies,' to reposition themselves in the hierarchies and histories of theatre."[10] Neither McMein nor Marion achieved fame in the theatre, which raises questions in regard to the bounds of theatrical employment. While scholars have previously contextualized McMein's work in studies of advertising and art history, and Marion's work on behalf of women's suffrage garners attention in women's studies, to date virtually no scholarship has examined the interrelationship of either woman's work in *and* outside the theatre.[11] How close to the stage does an artist's extratheatrical livelihood need to be positioned in order to claim a career in the theatre worthy of historical inquiry?

Neysa McMein was born in Quincy, Illinois, in 1888 as Marjorie Edna McMein.[12] Although her fame stemmed primarily from her work as a painter and illustrator, it was McMein's early theatrical aspirations that initially brought her to New York City, where she became a regular member of the Algonquin Round Table. As a high school student in Quincy, McMein had appeared in her school's production of *She Stoops to Conquer*, but in spite of her early interest in the stage, McMein's love for art took her to Chicago in 1906 to enroll at the Art Institute.[13] Yet even at the Art Institute, the theatre found its way back into McMein's life. In her autobiographical essay in the collection *As I Look at Life*, McMein relates that she and her fellow art students, "in the Bohemian way of ours, used to gather together and give amateur shows, as frequently as possible."[14] One evening McMein and a friend offered a performance that was an impersonation of Bert Williams, complete with blackface. The performance was supposed to end with McMein pushing her friend down a ramp in a wheelbarrow. However, as she related, "crazed with success and first-night nervousness, I heaped her in the wheelbarrow, trundled it triumphantly off, and missed the incline—clean. We crashed rakishly down a flight of steps, and in record-breaking time had amassed one of the most complete joint collections of bruises, turned ankles, and sprained wrists ever seen in the Middle West."[15] Paul Armstrong happened to be in the audience that night and, in spite of the disastrous end to the performance, offered McMein a role in his play *A Romance of the Underworld*. In a 1931 interview with the *Milwaukee Journal*, McMein noted that although she was making strides in her art career, "I was overcome by a high fever of stageitis [*sic*]. I had to act."[16] Her theatrical career was fairly short-lived, however. The day after the company arrived in New York, McMein was let go. She recollected, "I managed to crash the stage door and no sooner was I inside and of the cast than I hated it. Hating it was my good fortune because I was fired almost immediately. The manager felt the same way about my acting as I did."[17] In his biography of McMein, Brian Gallagher asserts that she found the life of a touring theatre artist less than appealing. Gallagher writes, "Marjorie discovered two things from the succession of one-night stands in dreary, half-full halls, followed by nights in shabby hotel rooms and days on slow, drafty trains: that the life of the traveling player was not for her and that she was not performer enough to sustain that life even if she had wanted it."[18]

During her early years in New York, McMein continued to perform sporadically as a means of supplementing her income. She often appeared as an extra at the Metropolitan Opera and occasionally performed in small roles in plays, largely due to the connections of her friends.[19] During World War I she worked as a troop entertainer for the YMCA.[20] At the same time, McMein's career as a painter and illustrator began to flourish, and she became known for her magazine covers, especially her work with *McCall's*. As Carolyn Kitch points out, "In the work of Neysa McMein, the exclusive cover artist for *McCall's* from 1923 to 1937, the woman of the 1920s was a self-possessed, mature New Woman, depicted as an individual in a modern world."[21] This was hardly surprising given McMein's own status as a New Woman, which she displayed through her lifestyle, work, and political engagement.

McMein actively protested for women's suffrage, and as Gallagher notes, "She walked and rode [. . .] for hundreds of miles in suffrage parades."[22] She created original artwork for use as suffrage propaganda.[23] She also was among the first members of the Lucy Stone League, an organization dedicated to securing the right for women to maintain their own names after marriage.[24] Although McMein married John C. Baragwanath, she was famously known for her independence, publicly maintaining her name and going so far as to leave her husband behind while she honeymooned with playwright Marc Connelly, theatre critic Alexander Woollcott, and musician Jascha Heifetz.[25] As her artwork saw greater demand, McMein enjoyed a respected role in the New York intelligentsia. McMein's studio near Carnegie Hall soon became the secondary meeting place of members of the Algonquin Round Table. Andrew B. Harris asserts that the "epicenter of Broadway banter was the Algonquin Hotel's Round Table, where the wits gathered to either talk up or talk down the shows."[26]

Stuart Y. Silverstein claims that "Neysa's [studio] was the usual Algonk late-afternoon haunt, and likely was New York's leading salon of the time."[27] Drawn by the beautiful artist and her models as well as by McMein's legendary bathtub gin, the famous literary figures of the Algonquin Round Table, in addition to countless actors, musicians, artists, and playwrights, visited McMein's studio. Marc Connelly recounts in his memoir,

> The world in which we moved was small, but it was churning with a dynamic group of young people. [. . .] Neysa's studio on the northeast corner of Sixth Avenue and Fifty-seventh Street was crowded all day by friends who played games and chatted with their start[l]ingly beautiful young hostess as one pretty girl model after another posed for the pastel head drawings that would soon delight the eyes of America on the covers of such periodicals as the *Ladies' Home Journal*, *Cosmopolitan*, *The American* and *The Saturday Evening Post*.[28]

In addition to Connelly and Woollcott, other theatre artists and performers who frequented McMein's salon included Edna Ferber, Robert Benchley, Irving Berlin, Mary Pickford, Robert Sherwood, George S. Kaufman, Charlie Chaplin, Paul Robeson, George Gershwin, Moss Hart, Alfred Lunt, and Lynn Fontanne.[29] One of the most prominent—albeit infrequent—visitors to McMein's studio was Noël Coward, who was one of her closest friends. McMein was instrumental in directing press attention to Coward's work in the United States, as he recounts in his diaries.[30] Many of these figures, including McMein herself, acted in *No Sirree!*, "An Anonymous Entertainment by the Vicious Circle of the Hotel Algonquin," on April 30, 1922.[31]

Neysa McMein's illustration work quickly eclipsed her theatrical career, brought her great renown, and afforded her a more than comfortable living. Although she rarely appeared on the stage once her painting career flourished, she remained closely connected to the theatre and its denizens, providing a space for theatre artists to informally mingle and generate new collaborations.

Across the Atlantic, Kitty Marion found herself in extratheatrical employment that had little to do with her theatrical career. Unlike McMein, who came to identify herself first as an artist and New Woman, Marion continued to refer to herself as an actress, even after she had not appeared onstage in years. Marion had a steady, if unexceptional, career on the music hall and pantomime stage in the late nineteenth and early twentieth centuries. Born in Germany, she moved to England in 1886. She quickly learned English and appeared onstage for the first time in 1889, as a dancer in a Christmas pantomime at the Theatre Royal, Glasgow. Marion recounts, "The opening night was the grand crisis of my life. Although lost in the crowd, I was <u>on</u>

the stage, in paradise."[32] From 1889 until the onset of World War I, Marion worked regularly on the British stage, performing as a singer and dancer in a variety of musical entertainments. When paid engagements were not available, she would sometimes perform for free as a means of exposure, although working without pay often meant relying on the generosity of friends for a place to stay.[33] She details her experiences touring throughout the English provinces in her autobiography, noting the challenges of paying for train travel and finding respectable lodgings on her meager salary.

As her theatrical career evolved, Marion publicly called attention to the threat of sexual exploitation that often accompanied conversations with agents about booking engagements. She eventually joined the Variety Artists Federation and the Actors Association, labor organizations that focused on theatre workers. It was her work in these groups that ultimately led to Marion's involvement in the British suffrage campaign.[34] Marion became one of the most infamous members of the Women's Social and Political Union and the Actresses' Franchise League as she engaged in violent militant activities in her quest for the vote. Her "deeds not words" ranged from selling propaganda in Piccadilly Circus to breaking windows, from committing acts of arson to hunger strikes.[35] A dedicated actor for women's rights, Marion was arrested dozens of times and subjected to violent forcible feedings, yet she never wavered in her commitment to the suffrage cause.[36] In fact, when the Women's Social and Political Union decided to refrain from using militant tactics during World War I, Marion vociferously opposed. Her objection soon became immaterial, though; due to her German birth and countless run-ins with the law, Marion was forced to leave England. She immigrated to New York City, but her militant reputation preceded her, and she could not find gainful employment in the American theatre.

An article printed in the *Pittsburgh Press* on September 10, 1916, titled "How Courageous Kitty Marion Solved Her Hard Luck Problem," details the challenges faced by Marion as she sought employment in the United States:

> Work? queried the managers. Why this market is overcrowded. Militancy? queried the suffragists. But who wants militancy in America? Something else, perhaps. Just wait. We will see. That was in November. Kitty Marion waited, waited patiently until the following May. Money goes quickly on Broadway. One cannot live on the strength of a promise. It takes hard cash to pay for the roof under which to sleep. Where find it? What market needs sellers? Can you guess it, reader? What market in America is never crowded? Kitty Marion put on her apron and became a house maid.[37]

Ironically, the apron that Marion donned was the one that she allegedly made for her role as the German maid in a production of *The Sphinx* in London at the Court Theatre, her final appearance onstage. "I thought it suited the part," Marion told the reporter, "and now I've found that it does to perfection." A photograph of Marion playing the role of the maid in the 1915 production accompanied the article. Marion's real-life job as a housemaid was in a boardinghouse. In the article she recounted the story of one tenant who dropped his cigar ashes on the floor to make sure that she swept daily. When she gave him a piece of her mind for this behavior, he complained to the owner: "What do you keep such a woman in the house for? She ought to be on a soap box at the corner."[38]

A little over a year later, Marion was in fact on a corner soapbox, selling copies of Margaret Sanger's pro–birth control periodical, the *Birth Control Review* (*BCR*), all over New York City, including Times Square, Grand Central Station, Herald Square, and Coney Island. From 1917 until 1930, Marion sold the *BCR*, taking half the proceeds as her salary and becoming such an icon for the pro–birth control movement that Margaret Sanger even noted in her autobiography that many people mistook Marion for her.[39] The image of Marion, bundled up with a satchel of *BCR*s over her shoulder and one in her hand, raised high above her head, became a New York landmark. In fact, at least two different cartoons parodied an anecdote regarding a small child who mistook Marion for the Statue of Liberty.[40]

Marion held that job for thirteen years until new management of the *BCR* decided they no longer wanted to sell the publication in that manner. Following her dismissal from the *BCR*, Marion obtained a Works Progress Administration–funded position, teaching speech improvement to children. Her obituary in the *New York Times* noted, "She never rose high in the theatre, but acquired considerable fame as a 'suffragette.'"[41] The obituary went on to detail some of her more violent escapades within the suffrage movement and her various arrests in New York City for allegedly violating decency laws due to her work with Sanger. She never returned to the stage following her emigration from England. Yet Marion continued to refer to herself as an actress and many publications did as well, long after she took her final bow on the stage.

Neysa McMein and Kitty Marion were public figures known primarily for their social networks and political activism, in and outside the theatre. Certainly their gender, sexuality, and socioeconomic class combined with the historically tumultuous era in a way that affected their labor opportunities. While for a time each was able to earn her livelihood from the theatre, they both sought and held extratheatrical employment as well, and it was primarily this work that led to their notoriety. What are the historiographical limits of theatrical employment when the work either is not explicitly within the theatre or is within the theatre but unpaid? Does the unpaid theatrical labor outweigh the day job in our historical narratives? Does the day job need to be in a related field in order to matter in our understandings of historic practices? Given that artists "have to live," as Terry Randall states in *Stage Door*, what position does the work of survival occupy in the performance archive? Historiographically, questions such as these potentially open up additional bodies of evidence and avenues of inquiry that may enable theatre historians to correlate connections between the theatre and its cultural context. Examinations of extratheatrical employment, interpersonal networks, and political activism can move beyond footnotes of biographical interest to illustrate the immediacy and interconnectedness of the theatre to everyday life. Day jobs, as the examples of Kitty Marion and Neysa McMein illustrate, can move beyond matters of fiscal necessity to facets critical to the formation of personal identity and public persona. Without their "survival jobs" and activist labor, we might not know anything about their work in the theatre. Conversely, their work in the theatre—as inauspicious as it may have been compared with the stardom of other figures in the English and American theatre—was uniquely situated and made all the more fascinating given their employment outside the theatre.

Notes

1. Edna Ferber and George S. Kaufman, *Stage Door* (New York: Dramatists Play Service, 1936), 89–90.
2. Harriet Thorndyke, "They Use Their Heads," *Family Circle*, April 1935, 14.
3. Helen Worden, "New York Pets Lead the Life of Reilly," *Pittsburgh Press*, May 10, 1935, 39.
4. Ronni Reich, "Don't Quit Your Day Job—It Could Help Your Career," *Backstage*, February 19, 2009, http://www.backstage.com/news/dont-quit-your-day-job-it-could-help-your-career/ (accessed February 15, 2012).
5. Tracy C. Davis, *Actresses as Working Women: Their Social Identity in Victorian Culture* (London: Routledge, 1991), 7.
6. Kitty Marion, "Autobiography," p. 52, Kitty Marion Papers, Manuscripts and Archives Division, New York Public Library, Astor, Lenox, and Tilden Foundations. It should be noted that the page numbering of the Marion Papers is in a shambles. Page numbers are skipped, page numbers are duplicated, and certain sections restart the pagination. I have listed the page numbers as marked on each page. However, there are multiple pages

with the same number in vastly different segments of the autobiography. Marion recalls that international touring stars in particular had much better working conditions than the young women who populated the chorus and ballet corps.

7. See Viv Gardner, "The Three Nobodies: Autobiographical Strategies in the Work of Alma Ellerslie, Kitty Marion and Ina Rozant," in *Auto/biography and Identity: Women, Theatre and Performance*, ed. Maggie B. Gale and Viv Gardner (Manchester: Manchester University Press, 2004), 10–38; Jan McDonald, "Lesser Ladies of the Victorian Stage," *Theatre Research International* 13, no. 4 (1988): 234–39; and Jim Davis, "Jessie H. Wilton, Victorian Provincial Actress: Two Historiographical Approaches to Documentation; Part I, 'Tell me whether I am to be starved to death or what . . . ,'" *Theatre History Studies* 12 (1992): 107–24.
8. Sally Ledger, *The New Woman: Fiction and Feminism at the* Fin de siècle (Manchester: Manchester University Press, 1997), 9–10.
9. Viv Gardner, introduction to *The New Woman and Her Sisters: Feminism and Theatre, 1850–1914* (Ann Arbor: University of Michigan Press, 1992), 3.
10. Gardner, "Three Nobodies," 10. Borrowing from the work of Thomas Postlewait, Gardner also explicates the fraught nature of reading autobiographies—those claiming to be both real and fictive—as authentic renderings of events.
11. Brian Gallagher, *Anything Goes: The Jazz Age Adventures of Neysa McMein and Her Extravagant Circle of Friends* (New York: Times Books, 1987), 31–32. Gallagher's biography of McMein is one exception, although he spends little time exploring her work in the theatre.
12. Neysa McMein, "What's in My Name: Your Fate May Hinge upon Your Name," in *As I Look at Life: Intimate Stories of Love, Marriage, Divorce, Fortune, Adventure, Health by Fourteen Famous Men and Women Who Have Lived and Felt the Strange Experiences They Tell* (New York: International Magazine Company, 1925), 145–52. McMein changed her name after a consultation with a numerologist.
13. Norman I. Platnick, "The Lady Seldom Smiles: A Collector's Guide to Neysa McMein," p. 5, unpublished manuscript, September 2012.
14. McMein, "What's in My Name," 142.
15. Ibid., 143.
16. "Neysa McMein Might Have Been Actress but She Decided to Star as an Artist," *Milwaukee Journal*, January 27, 1931, 10.
17. Ibid.
18. Gallagher, *Anything Goes*, 31–32.
19. Ibid., 36.

20. "Neysa M'Mein Dies; Portrait Painter," *New York Times*, May 13, 1949.
21. Carolyn Kitch, *The Girl on the Magazine Cover: The Origins of Visual Stereotypes in American Mass Media* (Chapel Hill: University of North Carolina Press, 2001), 15.
22. Gallagher, *Anything Goes*, 37.
23. "Active in State Campaign Work," *Woman Citizen*, November 24, 1917, 222.
24. Nina Miller, *Making Love Modern: The Intimate Public Worlds of New York's Literary Women* (New York: Oxford University Press, 1999), 90. McMein maintained her name following her marriage to John C. Baragwanath.
25. Gallagher, *Anything Goes*, 3–4.
26. Andrew B. Harris, *Broadway Theatre* (London: Routledge, 1994), 12.
27. Stuart Y. Silverstein, introduction to *Not Much Fun: The Lost Poems of Dorothy Parker* (New York: Scribner, 2009), 29.
28. Marc Connelly, *Voices Offstage: A Book of Memoirs* (New York: Holt, Rinehart and Winston, 1968), 81.
29. Silverstein, introduction, 29; James R. Gaines, *Wit's End: Days and Nights of the Algonquin Round Table* (New York: Harcourt Brace Jovanovich, 1977), 58; Margot Peters, *Design for Living: Alfred Lunt and Lynn Fontanne, a Biography* (New York: Alfred A. Knopf, 2003), 77–78.
30. Noël Coward, *The Noël Coward Diaries*, ed. Graham Payn and Sheridan Morley (New York: Da Capo Press, 1982), 57.
31. Gaines, *Wit's End*, 62–66.
32. Marion, "Autobiography," 9.
33. Ibid., 12. Marion's first music hall engagement was at the "Star" Bermandsey, as part of a benefit performance for an older comedian. A theatrical agent whom she dubs "Mr. Dreck" informed her that he could not book her into other engagements until he had seen her "turn" on the stage. Although her performance was received well, Marion went back to the dressing room and cried following it. She writes, "Should any 'ancients' who knew the 'Star' some forty years ago read this, they will appreciate the situation of a quiet, shy, self-conscious, unsophisticated, sedate nineteen year old being thrown into that roughest of the rough, hard drinking, hard swearing crowd."
34. See Gardner, "Three Nobodies." See also Christine Woodworth, "The Company She Kept: The Radical Activism of Actress Kitty Marion from Piccadilly Circus to Times Square," *Theatre History Studies* 32, no. 1 (2012): 80–92.
35. Elizabeth Crawford, *The Women's Suffrage Movement: A Reference Guide, 1866–1928* (London: Routledge, 2001), 377. Crawford notes that Marion set five fires, including one that destroyed the Grand Stand at the Hurst Park Race Course in 1913.

36. Marion, "Autobiography," 22. She details the gruesome nature of these forcible feedings in her autobiography.
37. Richard Harding Davis, "How Courageous Kitty Marion Solved Her Hard Luck Problem," *Pittsburgh Press*, September 10, 1916, http://news.google.com/newspapers?nid=1144&dat=19160910&id=TuwbAAAAIBAJ&sjid=T0kEAAAAIBAJ&pg=5209,2817074 (accessed February 5, 2014).
38. Ibid. See also Marion, "Autobiography," 5: "The press soon 'found' me, and carried interviews, articles and pictures. A theatrical producer, with offices in the Haymarket London, called on me with the intention of 'rescuing' an 'English Actress and Suffragette from her menial position,' until I told him I was of German birth. Crash!"
39. Margaret Sanger, *An Autobiography* (New York: W. W. Norton, 1938), 257.
40. Kitty Marion, "Scrapbook," Kitty Marion Papers, Manuscripts and Archives Division, New York Public Library, Astor, Lenox, and Tilden Foundations. The cartoons were cut out and loosely placed in Marion's unfinished scrapbook. The provenance of the cartoons is unknown.
41. "Miss Kitty Marion of Suffrage Fame," *New York Times*, October 10, 1944, 23.

Part Two

Inscription, Erasure, and Recovery: Palimpsests of Labor

This section pushes beyond initial concerns about the worker and working conditions and into the ways that historically marginalized groups have used theatrical work to reclaim and resist limiting narratives. How is class worn on the bodies of workers? In what ways do the collision of work and the theatrical body constitute performative and historical palimpsests? How might these narratives be recovered? Dorothy Chansky, Max Shulman, Elizabeth A. Osborne, and Jerry Dickey delve into issues of class, race, and gender as they explore these underrepresented groups. Whether through Chansky's consideration of the kitchen as both trap and haven for women, Shulman's intriguing investigation of "class-based trauma," Osborne's careful reclamation of the Federal Theatre Project's traveling outdoor Caravan Theatre, or Dickey's intricate exploration of the cakewalk tradition, these pieces return a formerly neglected theatrical entertainment, worker, or audience to the forefront of the scholarly conversation. They also work in concert with the previous essays by engaging in an array of methodologies and by continuing to deepen the discourse on theatrical laborers and work.

5. Retooling the Kitchen Sink: Representing Domestic Labor in American Performance after 1963

Dorothy Chansky

> It will not do for women who are mostly housewives to say that Women's Liberation is fine for women who work, but has no relevance for them. Equal pay for equal work is only part of the argument—usually described as "the part I'll go along with." We are all housewives. We would prefer to be persons. That is the part they *don't* go along with.
>
> —Jane O'Reilly, *The Housewife's Moment of Truth*

> For most, housewifery will never have any utopian or dream-like quality but simply be a routine part of our lives.
>
> —Stéphanie Genz, "'I Am Not a Housewife, but . . .'"

In 1963 Betty Friedan and Julia Child shook the world of American domesticity in opposite ways. Friedan's *Feminine Mystique* urged women to leave the kitchen, while Child's *The French Chef* enticed them with its creative pleasures. This essay examines the effects of this Janus-faced battle cry in two particularly salient examples of pieces that depict and discuss domestic labor *as work*—Martha Rosler's performance piece *Semiotics of the Kitchen* (1975) and Sarah Ruhl's 2007 play, *The Clean House*. For Rosler, whose short piece features but a single performer in a claustrophobically small kitchen, that work is oppressive. In Ruhl's play, four women represent four different attitudes toward domestic labor, ranging from pleasure to loathing, indifference to the expectation of being exempt. Importantly, however, every position acknowledges housework as work that requires skill, takes time, and has value. The productions are separated by more than thirty years, during which time American women achieved professional parity in a number of white-collar realms and women's workplace presence in the United States more than doubled.[1] Despite these facts, however, women have remained both responsible for and sometimes obsessed with the housework that takes place in most American homes, making what Arlie Russell Hochschild calls the "second shift"—the domestic work regimen women begin at home after returning from their paid outside employment—an ongoing reality and housework qua work still a hot topic.[2]

Prior to the 1960s, myriad dramatic works—virtually all Aristotelian plays set in a recognizable present—addressed domestic labor as either a trap or a haven for middle-class, mostly white women.[3] These works basically fit the rubric of "kitchen sink realism," a term coined in the 1950s but since applied to plays written before and after that decade. Originally it referred to plays and other works of art depicting the gritty everyday of the working class and flying in the face of drawing room niceties.[4] It has also been used as shorthand for a genre whose mimetic naïveté is read by some as risible in the face of various avant-gardes or epic storytelling. Kitchen sink realism, however, always had a paradox at its heart. Namely, the materiality of its performative means that were concrete but idealized, glamorized, or truncated via conventionalized dramaturgy—primarily food, scenographic kitchens, and onstage domestic labor such as ironing or sewing—frequently belied their referents in order to sell tickets to audiences wanting escapism, easy legibility, and closure. In other words, the "real" in realism could be anything but real to those for whom its putative truths were patently false. And the supposed antirealism of nonlinear or non–character driven theatrical works can sometimes deliver far more truthfulness—by which I mean fidelity to a recognizable everyday—than the telescoped and idealized "realist" play. This is the case in the two works discussed here, works whose investigation of domestic labor as gendered work falls outside the realm of kitchen sink realism but solidly in the arena of truthfulness. Indeed, because so much feminist work about domestic labor resonates as truthful but uses nonlinear or collage techniques, putting pressure on the term that supposedly defines the way domestic labor can most honestly be represented remains important.

After 1963, credible means of staging questions surrounding domestic labor as work mushroomed with the advent of Off-Off-Broadway, performance art, feminist collective theatres, and the recognition that housework and cooking are both a trap *and* a haven. Material props, especially food, became more likely to be the real thing (rather than fakes or substitutes) in many performance contexts, and angry critiques of a domestic status quo were no longer necessarily tidy debates ending with marriage or career. Rosler's *Semiotics of the Kitchen* and Ruhl's *The Clean House* both expose the stifling nature of domestic labor but couple this, ironically and possibly oxymoronically, with demonstrations of the valuable expertise one can develop through repetition, even if it is boring.[5] Each piece also offers multiple ways in for audiences, making it easy to *identify* the actions, objects, and behaviors being depicted but forcing some thinking and choosing regarding how one will *identify with* these, if at all. Both identifying and identifying with something depend on real referents but need not dictate the nature of the reality perceived by the spectator or community of viewers. In the case of domestic labor, a kind of work to which most theatregoers will need little introduction, the probability of finding a "way in" is high.

Rather than treating these pieces as the beginning and end points of some kind of feminist teleological project, and at the risk of giving away the punch line, I state up front that I borrow from contemporary feminist art scholar and critic Helen Molesworth to make two points here that will recur throughout this essay. First, Molesworth argues that separating feminist work into essentialist versus theory camps prevents other interpretive strategies, settling for a kind of sealed-off stalemate. Molesworth shorthands these camps as, respectively, 1970s or second-wave feminism and 1980s or poststructuralist feminism, but she points out that these are camps that continue in the twenty-first century to offer generic homes to feminist works about domestic labor. Rosler's and Ruhl's work each individually lends itself to both essentialist and theoretical readings, not to mention to other possibilities, allowing for a way to take up what Molesworth sees as the really important question in feminist work that addresses domesticity, which is how to parse and address "the fault line between things considered private and things considered public," categories as defined by "the[ir] reciprocity and mutual dependence."[6] Domestic labor, in other words, may take place in the private realm, but it has been placed there by public policies. The most fundamental of these public policies are governmental unwillingness to recognize housework and child care as work worthy of pay and the industry assumption that paid male workers can devote themselves fully to their employers because their domestic needs are being taken care of for "free." Such conjectures pass muster only when paid workers are understood as men with dependent wives who provide their cooked food, clean clothes, and child care.

Second, Molesworth's invocation of feminist philosopher Moira Gatens to problematize equality gets to the heart of the standoff that Ruhl and Rosler expose in provocative, creative ways. Namely, unless capitalism and democracy are themselves denaturalized and identified as social constructions with a patriarchal agenda, the American system of capitalist labor, which "is founded on inequality [. . .] 'can involve only the abstract opportunity [for women] to become men.'"[7] Capitalism is a system wholly tethered to structures of work, meaning that anything considered in its light is one way or another linked to work as a source of money. Accordingly, while traditional capitalist theory cordons off domestic labor as *not work*, a recognition of this blind spot facilitates an examination of the housework versus waged work standoff as being, under capitalism, a battle of two kinds of work duking it out for shared respect.

Rosler's 1975 *Semiotics of the Kitchen* is a six-minute video performance featuring the artist herself and shot in her own compact kitchen. It mimics the form of the television cooking program in order to challenge the idea that women "belong" in the kitchen. In the piece, the "protagonist," a woman in her early thirties, displays and names in alphabetical order items found in ordinary kitchens. The entire spoken text of the piece is made up of her list of kitchen items. "Apron. Bowl. Chopper. Dish. Eggbeater. Fork. [. . .] Hamburger press. Ice pick. [. . .] Knife. Ladle. [. . .] Pan. Quart bottle. [. . .] Spoon. Tenderizer."[8] She performs a simple action with each, many of these either frivolously wasteful/empty or alarmingly violent. For instance, we see her stirring a bowl with nothing in it and tossing away the imaginary contents of a ladle. In another example, she slashes the air with a knife or pounds the table with the meat tenderizer. Beginning with the letter *u*, she abandons the connection of alphabet to items and shapes the letters with her arms like a kind of cheerleader. She concludes by tracing *z* in the air with a knife, putting her knife down, and shrugging. The piece is over.

Rosler describes the work as "[a] woman in a bare-bones kitchen demonstrating some hand tools and replacing their domesticated 'meaning' with a lexicon of rage and frustration [. . . an] antipodean Julia Child."[9] It is easy to see thinly suppressed rage in the slashing, the pounding, and the stabbing actions with the fork and ice pick. The monotone and expressionless face bespeak numbness, a recognizable response to a familiar setup of separate spheres. When *Semiotics of the Kitchen* was exhibited, three decades after its debut, as part of a 2006 show on food and memory at the Jewish Museum, a description on the museum's website called it "a critique of the commodification of food and traditional women's roles. The artist objected to those elements of her Orthodox upbringing which she saw as insisting that the only secure domain for a Jewish woman was the kitchen."[10] At the simplest level, plays and performance art presenting domestic labor as haven, trap, or both depend on someone—present or implied—suggesting precisely that housework ("the kitchen") is not the only secure domain for women.

Rosler is clear about wanting her feminist, antiwar performance work to be "accessible, to avoid sliding into recherché theorizing that general audiences won't get." She stated explicitly in a 1981 interview that her goal in *Semiotics of the Kitchen* was "to think about real, historically grounded social relations and the ways in which they inform the personal," noting that she "start[s] not with the self and its reflection in social interaction, but from the outside."[11] In the same interview, the artist noted that, regarding this piece, "everyone talks about anger, violence, and entrapment. Hip audiences also talk about semiotics and distantiation." She added that *Semiotics of the Kitchen* portrays "the transformation of the woman herself into a sign in a system of signs that represents a system of food production, a system of harnessed subjectivity. [. . .] This woman is implicated in a system of extreme reduction with respect to herself as a self." The shrug at the end, in Rosler's own interpretation, suggests stuckness, but not a permanent, hopeless condition, indicating that activism was a goal.[12] However constructed, imagined, reified, or symbolic the "real world" outside the kitchen may be, it has really and truly colonized the thinking of the culture that would relegate this woman, a representative "Everywoman," to her kitchen. Rosler's work protests this reification. "Everywoman" here knows the tools of her trade, but they drive her to anger and are empty of content and purpose in the context of isolation and expected confinement.

While Rosler invoked the "real" to name the social relations she sought to depict, however, she emphatically eschewed "naturalism," describing it as

> that which locks narrative into an almost inevitably uncritical relation to culture. Rather, I am aiming for the distancing effect that breaks the emotional identification with character and situation that naturalism implies, substituting for it, when it is effective, an emotional recognition coupled with a critical, intellectual understanding of the *systematic meaning* of the work, its meaning in relation to common issues.[13]

Little surprise, then, that Helen Molesworth's reading of Rosler's performance in *Semiotics of the Kitchen* is that it comprises what would logically occur "if the stage directions were written by Bertolt Brecht [. . .]. Should we giggle or shudder at the trapped quality of Rosler's slightly maniacal home cook?"[14]

Can a work be both realistic and Brechtian? If, as Brecht famously noted, petroleum resists the five-act form, surely so does the post-1963, first-world kitchen resist any Ibsenesque or Milleresque legacies. Likewise, if Brecht could insist contra Lukács that "realism" was the right term for his own work, it is possible to think about the multiplicities in Rosler's work as riffs on "kitchen sink realism." Brecht asserts that "realism is not a mere question of form" but the genre par excellence for representing the true "relations between appearance and essence without the need for any external commentary."[15]

> Realistic means: discovering the causal complexes of society / unmasking the prevailing view of things as the view of those who are in power / writing from the standpoint of the class which offers the broadest solutions for the pressing difficulties in which human society is caught up / emphasizing the element of development / making possible the concrete, and making possible abstraction from it.[16]

This work, then, draws on the recognizable but eschews naturalism or closure, achieving what Molesworth reads as having "combined an aesthetic of identification (traditionally associated with second-wave feminism) with one of distanciation [*sic*] (usually affiliated with poststructuralist feminism)" to show the imbrication of public and private under capitalism.[17] Along the way, *Semiotics* allows viewers to see whimsy, multiple and simultaneous responses to a single work situation, and perhaps even confidence. That is, we witness a shrug; an emotional spectrum spanning boredom, anger, and indifference; and the suggestion that the hands can function efficiently while the mind is somewhere else. Moreover, Rosler knows exactly what to do with all the kitchen implements and can get the job done in a very small, very clean place. The piece does not offer answers but it does stage questions and provocations. This is realism about kitchen work without being kitchen sink realism.

Accordingly, *Semiotics of the Kitchen* is a work that fits a feminist project that was its contemporary: the "wages for housework" movement. Kathi Weeks explains that this movement, which was articulated in a range of texts published between 1972 and 1976 in the United States, Italy, and Britain, sought to expose the financial worth of unwaged domestic labor in its capacity as necessary facilitator of keeping the paid workplace going. In other words, wages for housework wanted to show that the putatively non-productive—in Marxist terms "reproductive"—realm of the household is not separate from the putatively productive realm of the paid workplace but is "an economic unit with complex linkages to the waged-labor economy—a structural component of, rather than a haven from, the world of work." Weeks highlights the "cognitive dissonance" that results from an insistence that "a woman receive payment for what is supposed to be a spontaneous desire rooted in women's nature."[18] Of course, for those espousing the argument (or stabbing tables with ice picks in performance art videos), this was cognition without the dissonance, reality without the recuperative insistence of drama's generic "realism."

The problems with wages for housework included the fact that paying a housewife for her labor would not get her out of that labor, leaving a structure of gendered, separate spheres intact in the quest for "an expansion of the wage relation rather than a transformation of its terms."[19] Perhaps most troubling and challenging was the idea that, in focusing on housework as the thing all women supposedly had in common, the wages for housework leaders did not naively believe that all women were, in fact, housewives but rather that "the housewife could be imagined as a site of identification for women, on the basis of which they could be hailed into militancy as feminists."[20] At the time, the problem was that this again reified gender division. Weeks, writing in 2011, notes that a post-Fordist, post-Taylorist world of labor that increasingly blurs borders between work and home has resulted in production and reproduction coming to resemble each other. Fordism comes from Henry Ford's institutionalization of the assembly line, while "Taylorism" comes from the ideas of Frederick Winslow Taylor, whose theories of scientific management broke tasks into their small component parts in the quest for maximum worker efficiency. One might say that Taylorism is the theory and Fordism is the practice of streamlined, impersonal, worker-as-machine labor with humans functioning as interchangeable parts. In the post-post-world, one might think of gyms and day care centers at the office or of writing or seeing clients at home. Weeks notes particularly that "when the notion of reproduction is expanded to cover the reproduction of the socialities necessary for production, the distinction between production and reproduction becomes even more amorphous."[21] In Rosler's 1975 work, simply making the point that "woman equals domestic laborer" is wrong and unfair was an intervention. Thirty years later, American women had myriad work options beyond housewifedom. They had not, however, fully defeated a cultural imaginary in which domestic labor was to be their domain *even if they were also employed for wages or salaries.* The landscape was more varied, but the gendered connection between women and housework had not been severed.

What might theatre say about domestic labor and feminism in a post-Fordist world where globalization, cross-class alliances, a desire to work hard for goals that are not wages, personal income, and high stakes for domestic cleanliness are all on the table? Sarah Ruhl's *The Clean House* throws all these phenomena into relief and relationship, presenting both obvious and less obvious issues and tensions surrounding housework. The play features four women with radically differing relationships to housework and to waged work, thereby making it impossible to say that one or the other is better or more suitable to females, as none of the characters is fully happy with her lot nor a fully responsible role model. Lane, a doctor in her mid-fifties, is a workaholic who wears white and whose home—the main playing area—is all white. She hires Mathilde, a twenty-seven-year-old Brazilian, to clean her house. Mathilde hates cleaning, knowing that her calling is to follow in her parents' footsteps and write jokes. Lane's sister, Virginia, is a housewife for whom cleaning is a reason to get up in the morning; her marriage is boring, her husband is unable to father children, and she realized after majoring in Greek literature at Bryn Mawr that she could not be a critical writer because she has nothing to say. Virginia relishes domestic labor and covers for Mathilde by cleaning Lane's house every day after finishing with her own. The fourth woman, sixty-seven-year-old Ana, originally from Argentina, is a terminally ill, glowing free spirit who lives in a small house with a barebones amount of unmatched furniture and a balcony overlooking the sea. Her beloved husband died thirty-six years earlier, and while she wanted children, she refused to have them until he stopped drinking, which he did, but too late.

The distinct positions regarding domestic labor bear analysis in light of what Weeks calls "the problem with work"—the problem of Americans' worth and worthiness being defined by how they earn livings under capitalism and by the possibility that we unquestioningly link purposefulness with job titles. This problem has not to do with actions undertaken in order to accomplish tasks—that is, it is not an argument that we all quit our jobs to go fishing or read novels and eat bonbons, nor one pretending we can all go "back to the land." Rather the problem is with capitalist economic systems that dominate our entire social unconscious—our "taken for granted"s—and depend on the acceptance of waged labor as the *only* legitimate means of achieving human dignity, basic needs, moral worth, respect as a responsible citizen, and social standing. In this scheme, non-wage-earning housewives still depend on a wage earner for sustenance, health care, social status, and respect, whether they are married to that income producer or have inherited money from him or her. After the family, the workplace is the primary source of sociality for most Americans. "Raising children with attributes that will secure them forms of employment that can match if not surpass the class standing of their parents is the gold standard of parenting," notes Weeks. Paid work outside the home is sometimes the requirement for welfare, ironically wreaking havoc on the home in the name of some kind of moral fortitude and responsible citizenship. Meanwhile, despite "the fact that [social] wealth is collectively not individually produced," the normative expectations remain intact, thereby shoring up the imperative of "an individual responsibility [which] has more to do with the socially mediating role of work than its strictly productive function."[22] *The Clean House* offers a fascinating site to consider this nexus of values precisely in relation to domestic labor.

In the play, Lane is a clear-cut spokeswoman for paid labor as everyone's responsibility and for hierarchized paid labor at that. "I did not go to medical school to clean my own house," she declares.[23] Mathilde is caught between the rock and the hard place of needing income and, as an immigrant, most readily finding it as a domestic, even as she hates housework and knows her talent lies elsewhere. She agrees to work part-time for Ana, not only because Ana is also uninterested in housework but because Ana vigorously and affirmatively lives up to this stance by refusing to be "washerwoman" to her lover and doctor, Charles, who is also Lane's estranged husband.[24] Arguably, it is precisely Ana's lack of interest in housework that allows the anti-housework Mathilde to take a job as her part-time domestic. While we never see the interior of Ana's house, we know that it is not high-tech and all white; we also know that Ana treats Mathilde as a friend and equal, as they pick apples and laugh together. Conceivably it is not exactly housework that Mathilde refuses but housework that will be subject to clinical judgment by an employer for whom its sterile performance is by an ideally invisible servant. Mathilde, then, may be the healthy mean between the disinterested micromanager, Lane, and the immersed, hiding, obsessive Virginia.

The four women are thrown into direct contact in the second half of the play, when Charles leaves on a quest for an exotic plant that is supposed to have the power to arrest Ana's spreading cancer. Virginia goes into a rage at Lane's insults and completely trashes the white living room. Her willingness to destroy her own work in the interest of "talking back" to her unfeeling sister opens the channel of communication between them. Lane, the doctor, accepts the task of caring for Ana in her last days and takes the dying woman into her own home. Virginia provides home-cooked meals and even homemade ice cream, and Lane has learned to ask for and accept help that is offered rather than purchased. Mathilde finally assists Ana in dying, "killing" her with a joke, as Mathilde's father had her mother.

The Clean House does satisfy Molesworth's two putatively noncongruent forms of feminist arts work—essentialist and identificatory. There is female solidarity, as Virginia fantasizes about the days when women met together at public fountains to wash clothes and tell stories and observes that everyone living in separate, solitary houses is terrible. There is post-modernist distancing, as apples dropped from Ana's balcony fall into Lane's living room, and Mathilde's dead parents, performed by the same actors who play Charles and Ana, dance through Lane's "real" house. And there are easy readings: Lane needs to learn compassion; Virginia needs to stop hiding; Ana is exceptional and seems to have an independent income, making her less a mimetic character with whom to identify than a fantasy to relish. And there are no children in sight, which means that characters' taking and representing clear stances is perhaps easier than it would be in the face of multiple unknown and mutable factors.

But reading the domestic labor, or its refusal, here as a problematization of paid work itself offers rich possibilities. At the simplest level, neither Lane nor Virginia is either fulfilled or willing to take a good look in the mirror, and for both the problems are a combination of work *and* domestic life. That the two WASPs come to greater awareness via two Latinas might also suggest that an infusion of an "other" culture (this one traditionally read as machismo and gendered) is worth a second look. A post-work reading, however, offers more—and maybe more unsettling—ways of thinking about whether the Friedan/Child standoff is not better seen as a dance with two partners. What is the difference between Virginia's and Mathilde's cleaning of Lane's house? Lane asserts outright that she does not want to be cared for: she wants to pay a stranger. This has nothing to do with the labor or its use value but has everything to do with a wage system and a certain amount of consumerism for status. Mathilde first sustains and then kills Ana with her company and, specifically, with her jokes. While her jokes alleviate suffering, they also induce the laughter that ultimately kills Ana. Mathilde, then, is the one who offers work in the home that requires skills and would otherwise necessitate home care workers. Palliative care is presented as a very real form of domestic labor that may be invisible to those thinking only of cleaning. After Ana dies, Lane is momentarily at sea. She has seen many deaths in a hospital context but considers closing the deceased's eyes and washing the body to be nurses' tasks. When Lane undertakes these tasks, she is situating herself both lower on the capitalist wage scale and also conflating professional and domestic work. She is also, of course, recognizing the latter as real, and necessary, work.

Like *Semiotics of the Kitchen*, *The Clean House* does not offer answers, but it asks important questions. Domestic labor is the "Mrs." of professional or even blue-collar work. Women who imagine replacing one with the other still find themselves trafficking in the same currency—constrained by capitalism, with its disregard for the value of domestic labor unless one pays for it—albeit with the expectation that the coin will always land on the other side. People who do both kinds of work generally realize that neither is without some predictability and some comfort. Depictions of domestic labor in theatre have generally been recognized as facets of kitchen sink realism—a causality-driven, often recuperative genre. The two works discussed here aim to reference truthfulness without full reliance on realism in either the literary sense or as a defining feature of the mise-en-scène.

The Friedan/Child pas de deux is still with us. Most American women perform some domestic labor and find some parts of it fulfilling, other parts boring and demanding. Only the most privileged in our era of dual-income households can opt to "stay home," and those who claim to find satisfaction doing so often have household help for the least interesting and most physically taxing aspects of housework.[25] Creating complicated dishes for a party one is hosting or making Halloween costumes for children are simply more pleasurable if one is not also responsible for scrubbing out the bathtub, washing the windows, pretreating the laundry, and cleaning the kitty litter box. But the gourmet dinner, the inventive costume, and the immaculately kept decorated home can be very fulfilling, especially for the person who has skills and dedication, à la Julia Child. And participation in the paid workforce is often what gives the woman who performs domestic labor a place among an adult cohort involved in public concerns beyond at-home parties, sparkling bathrooms, and children's costumes. Performance is a place to play with these paradoxical pluralities, as Rosler and Ruhl so richly demonstrate.

Notes

1. Between 1967 and 2002 women's workplace presence increased by 177 percent. For men the increase was 37 percent.
2. Arlie Russell Hochschild, *The Second Shift* (New York: Avon Books, 1989). On women's numbers in the workforce, see U.S. Census Bureau, "Women in the Work Force" (2009), http://www.census.gov/newsroom/pdf/women_workforce_slides.pdf (accessed September 4, 2013). Regarding continued obsession with housework into the twenty-first century, see Laura Kipnis, *The Female Thing: Dirt, Sex, Envy, Vulnerability* (New York: Pantheon, 2006). The essay's epigraphs might be seen as bookends (1973 and 2009) of a continuous phenomenon and its attendant debates.
3. A short list might start with Jesse Lynch Williams's 1918 comedy, *Why Marry?*, the first play to win a Pulitzer Prize for drama. It addresses the questions central to many middlebrow dramas and comedies of the 1920s: what do intelligent, energetic women get out of marriages that tease with

the promise of romance but close with a guaranteed life of domesticity? Williams's play argues for careers, with the heroine a budding scientist. The heroines of *Desire under the Elms* (Eugene O'Neill, 1924) and the Pulitzer Prize–winning *They Knew What They Wanted* (Sidney Howard, 1925)—respectively a tragedy and a comedy—marry men almost old enough to be their grandfathers because housekeeping, they state explicitly, is the only profession that can guarantee them a home, autonomy, and (imagined?) freedom from service to others. The college-educated woman's trap is often dramatized as a haven for the less privileged. Social upheaval also inflects theatrical understandings of trap and haven. In Elmer Rice's 1933 *We, the People*, clearly set against the ravages of the Great Depression, domestic labor is presented as sufficiently satisfying for a farm woman in a good marriage but an overwhelming burden in the face of an abusive, indifferent husband and little outside social contact. Robert E. Sherwood's 1940 *There Shall Be No Night*—the Pulitzer Prize winner for 1941—codes patriotism in part via a decorative, charming, and domestically helpless wife who learns to cook and clean to keep her household intact when her husband and son become resistance fighters. Here domestic labor becomes a kind of political commitment. William Inge's 1953 *Picnic* features two teenage sisters: the brainy tomboy sees domestic labor as a trap; her beautiful sister cooks, sews, and snags the sexy drifter who arrives in their small town.

4. Amy Dempsey, in *Art in the Modern Era: A Guide to Styles, Schools and Movements* (New York: Harry N. Abrams, 2002), points out that Kitchen Sink School was the name given by critic David Sylvester in an article in 1954 to a group of British painters whose work depicted "drab, unheroic scenes of post-war austerity, the commonplace subject-matter of daily life: cluttered kitchens, bombed-out tenements and backyards" (199). In *Modern Drama in Theory and Practice*, vol. 1 (Cambridge: Cambridge University Press, 1981), J. L. Styan notes that kitchen sink drama, despite its originators' desire to dispense with tradition, never overcame an affinity for the structure of the well-made play with a conventional emotional climax (149).
5. *Semiotics* was released in 1975 but begun earlier. "Martha Rosler: The Art History Archive—Feminist Art" dates it 1974–75 (http://www.arthistoryarchive.com/arthistory/feminist/Martha-Rosler.html). *The Clean House* premiered at the Yale Repertory Theatre in 2004, opened in New York at Lincoln Center Theatre in 2006, and was published in 2007 by Samuel French.

6. Helen Molesworth, "House Work and Art Work," in *Art after Conceptual Art*, ed. Alexander Alberro and Sabeth Buchmann (Cambridge, Mass.: Generali Foundation and MIT Press, 2006), 79, 74.
7. Gatens quoted in ibid., 70.
8. *Semiotics of the Kitchen*, http://www.youtube.com/watch?v=3zSA9Rm2PZA (accessed October 7, 2013).
9. Martha Rosler, "For an Art against the Mythology of Everyday Life," in *Decoys and Disruptions: Selected Writings, 1975–2001* (Cambridge, Mass.: MIT Press, 2004), 7.
10. "Food for Thought: A Video Art Sampler," www.thejewishmuseum.org/site/pages/onlinex.php?id=152&PHPSESSID=69e501 (accessed October 5, 2013).
11. Martha Rosler and Jane Weinstock, "Interview with Martha Rosler," *October* 17 (Summer 1981): 90, 89, www.jstor.org/stable/778252 (accessed October 7, 2013).
12. Rosler explains her work as "didactic and expository; it makes an argument. [. . .] Yet oddly enough, my work isn't hortatory. It doesn't insist on an avenue of action, or say, 'Do this!' Ultimately it's more contemplative, in that it does not answer the questions it poses. [. . .] There are vacillations, changes of direction meant to point to a panoply of ways of thinking about a question." Ibid., 78, 85–86.
13. Rosler, "For an Art against the Mythology," 8.
14. Molesworth, "House Work and Art Work," *October* 92 (Spring 2000): 91.
15. Georg Lukács, "Realism in the Balance," in *Aesthetics and Politics* (London: NLB, 1977), 34.
16. Bertolt Brecht, "Against Georg Lukács," in *Aesthetics and Politics* (London: NLB, 1977), 81, 82.
17. Ibid., 91. For a broad view of second-wave feminist theatre that sought identification, see Charlotte Canning, *Feminist Theatres in the US: Staging Women's Experience* (New York: Routledge, 1995). Poststructuralist feminist theatre fits the rubric Jill Dolan calls "materialist" in *The Feminist Spectator as Critic* (Ann Arbor: University of Michigan Press, 1991). See chapters 1 and 6.
18. Kathi Weeks, *The Problem with Work: Feminism, Marxism, Antiwork Politics, and Postwork Imaginaries* (Durham, N.C.: Duke University Press, 2011), 130.
19. Ibid., 137.
20. Ibid., 148.
21. Ibid., 141.

22. Ibid., 6–8.
23. Sarah Ruhl, *The Clean House* (New York: Samuel French, 2007), 8.
24. Ibid., 52.
25. See Linda R. Hirshman, "Homeward Bound," *American Prospect* 16, no. 12 (December 2005): 20–26; Leslie Bennetts, *The Feminine Mistake: Are We Giving Up Too Much?* (New York: Hyperion, 2007); and Anne Kingston, *The Meaning of Wife: A Provocative Look at Women and Marriage in the Twenty-first Century* (New York: Farrar, Straus and Giroux, 2004).

6. Beaten, Battered, and Brawny: American Variety Entertainers and the Working-Class Body

Max Shulman

Highlighting the dangers faced by North American railroad workers, a history of the industry from 1923 notes that any nineteenth-century "freight man who did not carry one or more marks of injury must have borne a charmed life."[1] In 1906 the first-ever survey of workplace deaths in the mining region of Pennsylvania's Allegheny County reported 526 worker fatalities in that year alone.[2] This figure can only hint at the rates in earlier years. Accident rates for American workers did not begin to fall nationwide until 1910 when pressure from activists and new compensation laws began to take effect. Still, in 1911 New York City saw the deadly Triangle Shirtwaist Factory fire, and in 1912 an estimated 18,000 to 21,000 work-related deaths occurred nationwide.[3] As these statistics attest, injury was rightly considered an inevitable part of a life of labor at the turn of the century. This dangerous state of affairs was the result of the explosion of mechanized industry that redefined the North American landscape. The jobs created by these developments gave rise to a new labor class in the country. However, the instruments and conditions of modern industry also brought with them a number of hardships. The troubling interaction between the fragile human body and the overwhelming agents of modernity created particular anxieties among the new working class.

This essay examines the ways in which the bodies of entertainers registered these anxieties in an attempt to diffuse them. Analysis considers three performers whose careers spanned from the latter half of the nineteenth century to the first decades of the twentieth. These performers provide extreme examples of the human body's response to the conditions of working-class life as part of what can be interpreted as a larger societal exploration of class identity.

The first two entertainers considered here exhibited the destructive capabilities of the industrial landscape and the limits of bodily suffering in an attempt to engender pathos or humor. Leonard Trask was a freak show and dime museum attraction from the 1860s. Nat Wills was a well-recognized vaudevillian tramp comedian who performed from the 1890s to the 1910s. As analysis of their performances shows, Trask and Wills demonstrate the way that physical trauma could function as a signifier of working-class identity. I designate the visible evidence of this kind of damage on performing bodies as "class-based trauma," a term that I use to connote disfiguration, deformation, and the prominent wear and tear that the laboring body could experience. Though featured at different times and in different venues, both Trask and Wills portrayed the individual's capacity to subvert the degradations of class-based trauma through adherence to working-class ideals, such as an intensified work ethic and the centrality of the family unit.

At the same time, the popular strongmen of the period offered a contrasting image of the body on stage. Devoid of visible trauma, such performers could be found in diverse venues, from county sideshows to the polished spectacles of the Ziegfeld Follies. Eugen Sandow, arguably the most famous performing strongman, is considered here. Sandow's feats of strength negated the threat of industrial life as he portrayed the superiority of man's might over his environment. The muscles that the laboring populace had developed as they built the nation brick by brick and steel beam by steel beam gained cultural cachet through Sandow's fame. His performances explored the capacity to transcend, if not escape, class hierarchies through this celebration of the working body. A comparison of the degraded physiques of Trask and Wills with the brawny musculature of Sandow reveals the range of ways that popular entertainers portrayed the relationship between the body and the perils of working-class life.

The audience of late nineteenth-century popular entertainment was a mix of newly arrived immigrants, assimilated foreigners, and those who considered themselves natives. However, Susan Kattwinkel asserts that these diverse types were unified through their shared experience of class struggle and the reflection of that struggle on stage.[4] It was the working class with concerns over financial status, the family unit, and respectability that funded variety entertainments and thus determined the content. Janet Davis maintains that the range of entertainment forms visited by this audience was also unified. Vaudeville, burlesque, circuses, and freak shows functioned jointly to provide a response to the national shift from agrarian communities to industrialized urbanity. To Davis, popular entertainments all took part in testing the "body's capacity for pain, pleasure, and fear and [. . .] the boundary between the real and the fake, the animal and the human, the self and other, and the local and the global."[5] Considering both Kattwinkel and Davis, we can see that the interconnected performance forms and their amalgamated audiences were functioning in a participatory venture of national self-definition. This process included a preoccupation with how the body might manifest class. The working-class body became a text on which ideals of resilience, self-determination, and the mutability of class status could be inscribed through performance. For audiences across the country, these performances helped to define and unify a working-class identity.

The freak show performer Leonard Trask offers an example of how this identity could be defined through a relationship to pain. Trask was a farmer and lumberjack who began exhibiting himself in the late 1850s at sideshows and dime museums once he was no longer able to work. Today, Trask is identified as the first documented case of ankylosing spondylitis in America. This rare disease caused the vertebrae in Trask's neck to slowly fuse together, bending his head so severely forward that he had to lean backwards to see in front of him.[6] In performance, Trask would do little more than present himself to his audience; the sight of his disfigurement was the source of viewer fascination. Raised in Maine, Trask limited his performances to one of the northeastern exhibition circuits, where his audience would have been predominantly made up of laborers and working-class townspeople.[7] Trask lived during a period of increased national production and thus of danger to the working body. Mechanization and large-scale industry would continue to mount in subsequent decades, creating increasingly hazardous conditions. Trask serves as an early example of what I contend is a pattern in which degraded bodies on stage were linked to the American worker.

Evidence of Trask comes primarily from an 1858 pitch book that was sold for fifteen cents wherever he exhibited himself (figure 6.1). The booklet of some fifty pages offered a biography of its subject. Such memorabilia are highly specious; while the pitch book lists Trask himself as author, it was just as likely written by a manager who knew how to shape a compelling tale. However, much can be discerned through the attempt to fashion Trask's disability into a marketable attraction.

The booklet claims that Trask's spine began to bend after he fell headlong from his horse while working on his farm, reassigning a hereditary deformity as a form of work-related, and thus class-based, trauma. The book also maintains a preoccupation with Trask's ability to perform labor, the severity of his condition measured by the extent to which it hampered his capacity to work. Further toil only compounded his hardships as nights

Fig. 6.1. Cover of pitch book for *The Life and Suffering of Leonard Trask: The Wonderful Invalid*. Printed by David Tucker in Portland, Maine, 1858. General Research Division, The New York Public Library, Astor, Lenox, and Tilden Foundations.

without shelter in the logging woods, his second fall from a hay wagon, and continued attempts at farm duties worsened his bent spine. How much of this is true and to what extent Trask understood his disability is unknown; medical science had not yet identified the disease, and the potentially skewed history offered by the booklet leaves it suspect. Even so, it is clear that the writer of the pitch book chose to publicize Trask's misfortunes as stemming from occupational hazards, ones intimately familiar to a local working-class audience.

In homiletic prose the book urges its readers to recognize that they could potentially experience a similar fate, noting "how soon may be the transit from joy to sorrow, from hope to despair; and from the height of worldly pleasure to the depth of human wo [*sic*]." What truly set Trask apart as "the Wonderful Invalid," the book asserts, was his ability to transcend his suffering through spirit. The book claims that by "being of a hardy and almost iron constitution [Trask] performed labor and endured hardships that would have shattered and broken down the constitution and health of most men."[8] By glorifying his body's ability to tolerate suffering and reminding audiences that they avoided a similar fate by the "grace of God," Trask presented himself as a kind of idealized working man.

Popular science of the era also reflected this connection between those who performed labor and their capacity to withstand pain. In their widely circulated 1896 encyclopedia, *Anomalies and Curiosities of Medicine*, George M. Gould and Walter L. Pyle claimed, "The question of the endurance of pain is, necessarily, one of comparison. There is little doubt that in the lower classes the sensation of pain is felt in a much less degree than in those of a highly intellectual and nervous temperament."[9] In accordance with such essentialism, class was not simply a measure of material wealth but a result of an inherited predisposition that enhanced the worker's threshold for suffering. Trask was the manifestation of this phenomenon, as his working-class body had been put to a tremendous test and found to exhibit a steel determination. The pitch book claimed that Trask worked until his disability rendered it impossible and exhibited himself only to keep his family from indigence, even going so far as to portray Trask as a rustic version of the Bible's Job who had remained stalwart in his working-class values of industriousness and family. Audiences might have felt sympathy for Trask, but the pitch book assured them that such degradation could not rob an honest worker of his pride. As a victim of his class and environment, Trask both embodied and dispelled the anxieties of a populace that faced the unforgiving and unpredictable life of the laborer in America. Trask did so by demonstrating the extent of potential suffering in the form of class-based trauma and, at the same time, the resilience of an individual who, according to contemporaneous science, was inherently fit to withstand it. Trask offers an early example of how popular entertainment could craft working-class identity, promoting an ethos of inner strength as a means of enduring the strain of prolonged toil.[10]

By the 1880s, twenty years after Trask made his rounds, expansion of industry had created the working conditions that could produce death tolls like those experienced in Allegheny County in 1906. This involved a shift from the agrarian world in which Trask suffered his "accident" to the widespread mechanization of factories, the stretching of the national railroad, and the growth of cityscapes that were home to sweatshops, overpopulation, and unhygienic living situations. It was at this time that the fast-paced format of vaudeville became the most popular performance style for working-class people. Trask's very real disfigurement stands in stark contrast to the traumas featured on vaudeville stages, which were more often simulated and typically less crippling. Performers presented versions of class-based trauma aimed at engendering laughter rather than pathos. This comic treatment is exemplified by the tramp comedians of the day whom Douglas Gilbert identifies as so popular at the turn of the twentieth century as to qualify as a national symbol.[11]

The stage-tramp convention developed in response to a contemporary phenomenon. America had long had transients or vagrants, but with the end of the Civil War and an economic depression beginning in 1873, the number of homeless men roaming the countryside swelled to alarming numbers. In 1877 there were over one million vagrancy arrests in New York City alone.[12] The resultant "hobo army" was made up partially of menial laborers looking for work, but there was also a subset of wanderers who took to tramping as a preferred lifestyle. Public response to the tramp was twofold. On the one hand, the perception of these men as lawless and aggressive provoked fear; regular reports in newspapers of violence involving drifters reinforced this impression. On the other hand, there was a fascination with these men who had abandoned all that was supposedly fundamentally American. Tramps rejected the hard work, diligence, and family stability that were the presumed backbone of the American ideal. Instead, the tramp willfully subjected himself to the wear and tear of a life of poverty within both rural and urban environments. Symbolic of his willingness to battle the hazards of modern life, the tramp spent his time perilously hitching rides on the railroad, which was the very emblem of industrial modernity's unrelenting character. It was this broad rejection of social norms that the tramp comedians represented.

Nat Wills—a famous vaudevillian tramp for more than twenty-five years—played a character with a darkly lined face, wild eyes, rough beard, and a gaping mouth of blacked-out teeth. His bedraggled hair shot out in all directions, leaving his face unframed and giving the impression that his giant grin might eventually expand to encompass his whole head. His ragged costume included a chest full of indeterminate military medals, according him a kind of "king-tramp" status or signifying a celebrated rank in the hobo army, usurping and parodying a ruling-class identity (figure 6.2).

Fig. 6.2. Nat Wills as "the Happy Tramp" in *Luck Dog* (1907). Billy Rose Theatre Division, The New York Public Library for the Performing Arts, Astor, Lenox, and Tilden Foundations.

Wills's appearance corresponds to Mikhail Bakhtin's concept of the grotesque body as unfinished and continually in the "act of becoming."[13] Unlike the classical body that was solid, smooth, and finished, Wills seemed to repudiate the limits of his own anatomy, expanding outlandishly in a comic renunciation of reason, rationale, and proportion.[14] Bakhtin identified such characters as providing lower-class "folk" a means of victory over systems of "power, of earthly kings, of the earthly upper classes, of all that oppresses and restricts."[15] Accordingly, Wills's act, which resembled the stand-up comedians of today, lampooned the official power structures in an attempt to subvert their authority. As World War I reached its height in 1917, toward the end of Wills's career, he featured war-related jokes like, "John D. Rockefeller wants to go the front, but I don't think he'll do much for the country. When the officer says advance he'll raise the price of gasoline."[16]

Other targets of his act were Henry Ford and Teddy Roosevelt; the working class had a particular interest in seeing these titans of industry ridiculed as a way of deflating their status.[17]

In a song recorded in 1908 called "B.P.O.E.," Wills waggishly accuses the members of the honorable Elk Society of assaulting him and stealing his wife.[18] At the core of his humor was the incompetence and hypocrisy of the ruling class and respected society. For Wills, the shortcomings of the established elites always resulted in the suffering of the little man. In his tramp getup, Wills appeared insignificant to the moneyed world of industry and politics, a trait he shared with his audience. However, he was empowered by the fact that his low social status could not dampen his jollity.

Moreover, tramp performers alleviated deep-seated fears regarding the loss of one's home and the threat of poverty. Wills's degraded body was the result of his abandonment of conventional values and safeguards. His mangy appearance, missing teeth, and creased face were evidence of how the trying environs of the urban and rural landscapes could batter those without hearth and home. In this way, the trauma to his body was class-specific. For working-class audience members who existed in an economically precarious position or whose well-being was threatened by their daily employment, Wills demonstrated a triumph of spirit over bodily concerns; he treated his destitution with gleeful insouciance. Like Trask's resilience in the face of his debilitating condition, Wills assured audiences that the working-class body possessed an inherent vivacity in spite of the worst possible situations.

At the same time, Wills's act affirmed allegiances to the very ideals he rejected. Unlike Trask, Wills's physical deterioration was decidedly artificial, expertly created with makeup and costume. Audiences could enjoy Wills's character while recognizing that he was providing a safe version of something that should be avoided in reality. Trask could not escape his physicality and was thus to be pitied. Wills was providing a facsimile against which audience members could measure themselves without any necessary sense of compassion. Audiences, unified by class struggle but whose bodies were unmarked by class-based trauma, might be reassured that they were superior to the degraded figure that Wills presented. As Wills's outward decay was supposedly the result of his renunciation of certain values, the popular audience could recognize the importance of maintaining those very ideals. In this way, bodies of the tramp comedians reinforced ethics of productivity, hard work, and perseverance. It was the adherence to these values that elevated the working class above the dire straits of the tramp. Wills's act provided a foil against which the working class could define and declare the integrity of its identity.

In almost perfect opposition to Wills's tramp were the popular strongmen of the period. If Wills and, before him, Trask portrayed how the body could be degraded by the violent industrial landscape even as the working-class spirit triumphed, the strongmen demonstrated the body's superhuman capacity to survive and even thrive within that landscape. A number of strength performers could claim celebrity status at the turn of the century. However, none was as famous or as important to the redefinition of American manhood as Eugen Sandow, known as "The Perfect Man."[19] Sandow's fame signaled the interest in his ability to exceed the designated limits of the human body, which were more and more defined by the confrontation between man and mechanized industry.

Sandow first appeared in New York City in 1893 and soon became the centerpiece of Florenz Ziegfeld's first financial success in a show designed to compete with the Chicago World's Fair. Along with his regular tours of the country between 1893 and 1906, Sandow's image was widely circulated in newspapers, magazines, and some of the very first moving pictures. Whereas the worn and ragged body of the tramp was evidence of modernity's toll on the nation's labor force, Sandow's body was a defiant example of man's potential to defend himself against the hostile tide of industry. John F. Kasson notes that, "starkly exposed and thoroughly publicized as [Sandow] was, he became an icon of the hypermasculine who with his extraordinary muscular development literally embodied characteristics that many men and women believed were threatened by modern life."[20] Sandow's remarkable strength represented a kind of autonomy in an environment that had reduced the individual to his or her material utility. He stood for the salvaging of a uniquely American identity, one that was originally connected to the taming of the nation's frontier and the formation of the country. It is no surprise that the American folklore figures of John Henry and Paul Bunyan flourished at the turn of the century.[21] At a time when machines seemed to surpass humans in every respect, the popular imagination celebrated any proof that people were still superior, particularly when it came to industriousness. Physical strength was reborn as an American ideal, and Sandow helped to identify the working class as representative of this newly valued physicality.

The connection between the strongman and the working class becomes clearer when we consider that, in performance, strongmen often confronted the implements of industry directly. Standard feats of strength included bending iron bars, breaking chains, or snapping wires by expanding the chest (figure 6.3). Sandow completed these tasks and also lifted large dumbbells, audience members, and even horses.[22] Louis Cyr, another famous strongman, lifted barrels of cement, pushed an empty train car up an incline, and resisted the pull of four horses.[23] The tools of their trade were iron and steel—the materials that formed the great cities and railroads of the nation—just as they were for those spectators who labored in factories and mines, on the docks, and in construction. The effect of the demonstrations was to show the body's ability to destroy the unbreakable and overpower the relentless.

The strength of the strongman was tied to a proletarian base. It did not come from money or privilege; rather, it reflected power that was earned through struggle and hard work, and it was potentially accessible to all. Coming out of a Victorian era that had rejected the body, the American populace came to idolize the development of physical prowess and the masculine virility it came to represent. This is a fact that Sandow did not fail to

Fig. 6.3. Cabinet card of Eugen Sandow breaking a chain. Photograph by Napoleon Sarony. Courtesy of the Laurence Senelick Collection (private), Medford, Mass.

capitalize on. He regularly invoked his own past as a "scrawny whelp" who had built his stupendous strength through work and perseverance.[24] Ever industrious, he marketed his own training equipment, including "Sandow's Patent Spring Grip Dumb Bells" and manuals such as *Sandow on Physical Training*.[25] Theoretically, anyone with the proper motivation (and the right equipment) could become a Sandow. Thus, while Trask and Wills triumphed over their bodily degradation via internal spirit, Sandow's inner strength resulted in a robust and virile outer appearance; his hard work negated any possibility of bodily suffering.

Other performance conventions that were typical of strongman acts accentuated the beauty of the sculpted physique. Scantily clad in costumes inspired by both Greek and Roman imagery, strength performers took on the characters of Hercules, Ajax, and Achilles, posing as living statues or in *tableaux vivants*. The performers would portray famous scenes from the lives of the mythic heroes by moving through a cycle of poses, holding each for a period. Though many incorporated the practice of mimicking statuary, it was Sandow's chiseled definition and his control of every muscle that gained him the title of "The Perfect Man" and brought him widespread notoriety.[26] None could compete with his capacity to emanate beauty and polish through his carefully rippling physique and celebrated classical beauty.

Through such performances, Sandow deliberately strove to portray his body as a work of art, bringing prestige to his act and making it appropriate for a more sophisticated audience. Kasson notes in his excellent study of Sandow that the performer purposely "cultivated an air of bourgeois respectability."[27] To enhance this perception, he often appeared in public in a well-tailored tuxedo. However, Sandow performed primarily on vaudeville stages that catered to middle-class and working-class audiences. By embodying both animal strength and classical beauty, Sandow represented a connection between the development of physical potency and that of civility. He helped to redefine the modern body as one that was both brawny and refined. In the tradition of American social mobility, Sandow represented a new kind of self-made man. As his carefully cultivated public image demonstrates, developed muscles, so often a result of hard labor, could also coincide with polished gentility. By celebrating this new respectability, his audience participated in the resituating of the working class from victim to victor. Sandow's celebrity helped to disseminate this new vision of the American worker on a national scale.

The fact that superhuman strongmen and withered tramps were popular at the same time is intriguing. It is highly probable that an audience could have experienced both extremes in one sitting, thus seeing opposing limits of the physical response to the conditions of industrialized society.

Between the complete abandonment to the elements by the tramp and the iron-willed revolt of the strongman, a middle stance may have seemed the appropriate path for the working-class individuals taking a moment out of their daily struggle for a little entertainment. This range of popular entertainment conventions created a broad discourse on the working-class body that functioned to celebrate and affirm working-class ideals.

By the turn of the century, dime museums and freak shows, like the ones that featured Leonard Trask, could not compete with the ever-growing vaudeville and variety circuits. Managers like Tony Pastor, B. F. Keith, and Edward Albee opened theatres nationwide, and the smaller, makeshift venues were subsumed.[28] These same managers endeavored to clean up the vaudeville stages, ridding them of anything potentially offensive or troubling so as to create a family-friendly entertainment that adhered to the glossy sheen of twentieth-century American showbiz. Tramps like W. C. Fields and Charlie Chaplin no longer portrayed the kind of physical wear and tear that made Wills such a sight, and no other strongman ever reached Sandow's level of fame.[29] By the end of World War I, humanity's physical confrontation with the industrial landscape was no longer such a troubling issue. More families found economic stability and were safer from the strain of manual labor. Additionally, labor laws and regulations reduced the dangers that people faced in the workplace, while cities began to remedy the unhygienic living situations that contributed to mass debilitation. Finally, with the conclusion of the First World War and the return of the walking wounded, the depiction of the mangled or degraded body lost much of its comic potential.[30]

This research has proposed a way of reading the bodies of popular entertainers as they relate to the nation's developing working class between the mid-nineteenth and early twentieth centuries.[31] For working-class audiences, performers like Trask, Wills, and Sandow helped to validate confidence in the capacity of the American worker to both endure and transcend the hardships that defined American labor. Working-class values developed in response to these hardships and were reified by such performances. Working-class identity became an amalgamation of the belief in an inherent durability of spirit, of the celebration of strength developed through toil, and of the maintenance of particular priorities regarding family. Certainly, there are other examples in which this complex process of identity production can be further examined, and it is my hope that the concept of class-based trauma can serve as a tool to recognize them. The valorizing of working-class identity, which these performances enabled, was more than simply the unification of a less-privileged sect of society. It was, in fact, a search for and celebration of humanity's supremacy in the modern world that they had created.

Notes

1. Railroad and Locomotive Historical Society, *Railroad History, No. 6* (Cambridge: Harvard University Press, 1923), 55.
2. Crystal Eastman, *Work-accidents and the Law* (New York: Russell Sage Foundation, Charities Publications Committee, 1910), http://www.cdc.gov/mmwr/preview/mmwrhtml/mm4822a1.htm (accessed May 10, 2012).
3. National Safety Council, *Accident Facts, 1998 Edition* (Itasca, Ill.: National Safety Council, 1998), http://www.cdc.gov/mmwr/preview/mmwrhtml/mm4822a1.htm (accessed May 10, 2012).
4. Susan Kattwinkel, "The Tradition of the Eccentric Body in Vaudeville: Subversion and Power in Performance," *Journal of American Drama and Theatre* 24, no. 3 (2012): 8.
5. Janet M. Davis, "Freakishly, Fraudulently Modern," *American Quarterly* 55, no. 3 (September 2003): 526.
6. Malcolm I. V. Jayson, "Leonard Trask: The Wonderful Invalid: The First American Description of Ankylosing Spondylitis," *Arthritis and Rheumatism* 48, no. 3 (March 2003): 612–13.
7. Trask was likely on the circuit for at least three years before his death in 1861.
8. *The Life and Suffering of Leonard Trask: The Wonderful Invalid* (Portland: Tucker, 1858), 33, 12.
9. George M. Gould and Walter L. Pyle, *Anomalies and Curiosities of Medicine* (New York: Bell Publishing, 1896), 475.
10. There are examples of later freak show exhibits similar to Trask. Barney Baldwin, "the Broken Neck Wonder," would remove his neck brace and demonstrate for audiences how his head could fall well below his shoulders. Barney's pitch book from the 1890s relates how he broke his neck in an accident while at work on the railroad, causing him to topple from the roof of a train car.
11. Douglas Gilbert, *American Vaudeville: Its Life and Times* (New York: Dover Publications, 1940), 269. Nat Wills was joined by countless other stage tramps like Lew Bloom, Walter Jones, Joe Jackson, Bozo Snyder, Bobby Barry, and later Emmett Kelly.
12. Paul T. Ringenbach, *Tramps and Reformers, 1873–1916: The Discovery of Unemployment in New York* (Westport, Conn.: Greenwood Press, 1973), 5.
13. Mikhail Bakhtin, *Rabelais and His World* (Cambridge, Mass.: MIT Press, 1968), 315.
14. Todd Despastino, *Citizen Hobo: How a Century of Homelessness Shaped America* (Chicago: University of Chicago Press, 2003), 154.
15. Bakhtin, *Rabelais*, 92.

16. "Vaudeville Wit," *Chicago Tribune*, June 10, 1917.
17. Segments of Wills's act may be in found in newspaper clippings in the Locke Collection, Billy Rose Theatre Division, New York Public Library.
18. Nat M. Wills, "B.P.O.E. (Elks' Song)" (New Jersey: Victor Record, 1908), Library of Congress, http://www.loc.gov/jukebox/recordings/detail/id/1542 (accessed March 13, 2013).
19. John F. Kasson, *Houdini, Tarzan, and the Perfect Man: The White Male Body and the Challenge of Modernity in America* (New York: Macmillan, 2001), 38.
20. Ibid., 30.
21. Michael S. Kimmel, *Manhood in America: A Cultural History*, 2nd ed. (New York: Oxford University Press, 2006), 96.
22. Kasson, *Houdini*, 28. Kasson reports that what were advertised as "horses" were more like small ponies.
23. David Norwood, "The Sport Hero Concept and Louis Cyr" (thesis, University of Windsor, 1971), 21–22, 38; David Waller, *The Perfect Man: The Muscular Life and Times of Eugen Sandow* (Brighton: Victorian Secrets Limited, 2011), 52.
24. Kasson, *Houdini*, 30.
25. Ibid.
26. The title was officially bestowed by Dudley A. Sargent in 1893.
27. Kasson, *Houdini*, 30.
28. Kattwinkel, "Tradition of the Eccentric Body," 18–19.
29. That being said, Chaplin's *Modern Times* (1936) was a direct commentary on the mechanization of the individual by the forces of industry.
30. Jenna Kubly's recent dissertation finds little evidence that popular performance touched on the physical or mental trauma inflicted during the war. Jenna Kubly, "Vaudeville and the American Experience of the First World War as Seen by Variety" (PhD diss., Tufts University, 2010), 82.
31. Admittedly, this examination has focused exclusively on white male performers and the male physique. Pain as it registers on the female body or on the body of the ethnic and racial "other" is itself a complex issue, and study should be extended to investigate how these performers manifested the struggle with the modern industrial landscape.

7. Hidden in Plain Sight: Recovering the Federal Theatre Project's Caravan Theatre

Elizabeth A. Osborne

The enormous reach of the Federal Theatre Project (FTP) spread throughout the United States between 1935 and 1939, taking live theatre and performance to poor and working-class audiences in diverse cities and rural areas. While much is known about the FTP's particularly celebrated activities—the politically aware living newspapers, simultaneous nationwide openings of *It Can't Happen Here* (1936), and the infamous Orson Welles production of *The Cradle Will Rock* (1937), for example—many of the vast organization's less well known activities have fallen into history's blind spots. Though frequently challenging to research, these community-based projects speak to the possibilities of a national theatre that was tied to serving the people rather than to the box office. The following are just a few examples of the many ways the FTP met the working-class Americans who served as its target audience on their own terms.

* * *

In 1936 the FTP established a small company in Muskogee, Oklahoma—the Federal Theatre for the Blind. Highlighted in a 1937 issue of *Federal Theatre* magazine, this tiny company consisted of only two individuals on the federal payroll: director Floyd Qualls, one of the only completely blind and trained directors in the country, and supervisor Gladys Fearnside. The Oklahoma School for the Blind supplied other personnel, including actors, designers, and technicians, and the public library donated rehearsal and performance space. The project cost only the salaries of Qualls and Fearnside, both of whom were eligible for government relief, and the only accommodations made for the actors' lack of sight was a slightly longer rehearsal period that enabled the translation of plays into braille and the use of a "long narrow strip of carpet stretched across the front edge of the stage [. . . which] serve[d] as a warning to prevent a blind actor from walking too near the edge." By mid-1937, the company had produced three plays for both seeing and non-seeing audiences.[1]

* * *

For a five-month period in 1936–37, the New York City FTP's Community Drama Unit participated in a program unofficially called the Psychiatric Theatre, which experimented with the use of different dramatic techniques to diagnose and treat patients at Bellevue Hospital. Initially incited by the results that Dr. Karl Bowman, director of Bellevue's psychiatry division, observed in mental patients following performances of FTP marionette shows, Bellevue and the FTP worked in concert to design theatrical experiences that would help mental patients work through various issues, ranging from social maladjustment to their deepest fears. Donald McHenry, a dramatic coach trained on the FTP's Community Drama Unit, supervised the theatrical components of the work while Bellevue's Dr. Nathaniel Ross sought ways to use these experiences as one aspect of treatment. Patients wrote plays, designed sets and costumes, and acted in both original and classical pieces. Similar to Oklahoma's Theatre for the Blind, this activity relied on the expertise of a single FTP worker and cost only his salary. According to Bowman, it helped many of his mental patients "make unconscious revelations of the underlying causes of their ills that no other technique had brought forth."[2]

* * *

In January and February 1937, the United States experienced one of the most devastating floods in its history. Killing hundreds and leaving well over a million people homeless, the Great Flood of 1937 wreaked havoc through the Ohio and lower Mississippi River valleys, leaving evacuees from thirteen states trapped in refugee camps often several hundred miles from home.[3] The FTP reached out to the American Red Cross that February, and by midmonth a traveling company of vaudeville players—comprised entirely of volunteers—joined FTP recreational drama expert Herbert Stratton Price in a morale-boosting tour throughout the flood zone. Since the Red Cross had established its own Recreational Refuge Program in the largest refugee camps, the FTP Flood Tour focused on midsized refugee camps. As with the Federal Theatre for the Blind in Oklahoma and the experimental forays into drama therapy at Bellevue in New York, the flood tour's financial cost was minimal; the company traveled in a single truck with a portable stage, slept and ate with the refugees after their performances, and performed original variety shows that could be easily adapted to the needs of the actor, audience, or the physical space.[4]

* * *

Far from the more prominent FTP productions, these units all focused on quietly serving their communities, whether those communities consisted of students, faculty, and families connected to the Oklahoma School for the Blind, the mentally ill patients in the psychiatric wing of Bellevue Hospital, or flood refugees displaced by one of the worst natural disasters of the era. These FTP activities all serve as examples of the ways in which this vast national undertaking—which employed more than thirteen thousand theatre practitioners, drew an audience of more than thirty million Americans, and operated under a constant barrage of media attention—was, in many ways, hidden in plain sight; these little-known activities simply did not attract the same media attention as the high-profile, politically leftist works that dominated media attention.

Like many of the government programs put into place during the Great Depression, the FTP's primary mission was to put the unemployed to work, preferably in their own fields. Yet national director Hallie Flanagan had a more complex agenda as well. She imagined a "federation of theatres" scattered throughout the country, each with the ability to call on the resources of the larger organization but focused on creating theatre that addressed the needs of local communities, developing new audiences for live theatre, and preserving the cultural value of theatre and the skills of those who produced it. Flanagan's decentralized organization introduced a wide range of performance and viewing opportunities for audiences nationwide, but much of the public attention—both in the 1930s and today—focused instead on a small percentage of contentious, politicized, big-city shows. Famously memorialized productions such as the aforementioned *The Cradle Will Rock*[5] and *It Can't Happen Here*, while certainly important components of the FTP's work as a whole, reveal only a fraction of the phenomenal range of theatrical activities engaged in, encouraged by, or created by the FTP.

As numerous scholars have noted, the FTP became the lightning rod for critics of President Franklin Delano Roosevelt's wide-ranging and expensive New Deal.[6] When the U.S. Congress ultimately terminated the FTP, it did so by approving a spending bill that continued funding for all WPA programs except for those projects that included theatre, thereby simultaneously forcing the closure of the FTP and ensuring that no other federally funded project could absorb those workers and continue the work of the FTP. As Flanagan wrote in her memoir:

> Just as it sometimes happens that a drop of water in a certain light mirrors a landscape, so the Federal Theatre was a microcosm reflecting changes in American attitudes. [. . .] The Federal Theatre cost money; it represented labor unions, old and new; it did not bar aliens or members of minority parties. In other words Federal Theatre presented a small but graphic example of the [Roosevelt] administration's characteristics, which were regarded, of course, as defects by all enemies of that administration.[7]

My intention here is not to argue one way or the other that the FTP was defunded arbitrarily or capriciously, or that it was unjustly made the WPA poster child by those who intended to destroy Roosevelt or his New Deal. Some FTP productions did indeed have communist overtones or overt political agendas, and some FTP productions appeared in particularly inopportune social and historical moments. However, the productions that made political waves—whether due to subject matter, timing, or general public brouhaha—became emblematic of the FTP at the expense of many of the other activities that the organization funded, encouraged, and instigated in communities across the nation. And so, popular and community-based work frequently fell into the shadow of the contentious public debates that surrounded the national FTP, leading to widespread misconceptions about the organization, its workers, its audience, and its role as a cultural stronghold in the nation. In other words, much of the work of the FTP effectively disappeared from the views of both the contemporaneous public and the contemporary scholar. As the examples at the beginning of this essay begin to suggest, such instances of invisibility occurred in every region of the country, in big cities and small rural communities, regarding award-winning shows and activities intended to rebuild communities in some way. This essay explores one case study as a way to decenter modes of thinking about FTP activities in the city that is most widely studied: the monumentally popular summer Caravan Theatre in New York City.

The Caravan Theatre, also known as the "Portable Theatre" or "WPA Outdoor Shows," opened June 16, 1936, with a four-show program.[8] Designed to take live theatre to poor and working-class audiences, four distinct companies traveled a nineteen-park circuit through the five boroughs of New York, playing a variety of shows ranging from classics to vaudeville. In fact, all local FTP productions that were rehearsed and "not scheduled to play in the regular theatres during the summer months [were] at the disposal of the portable theater management."[9] Overseen by former Theatre Guild actor Julius Evans, each company traveled with its own portable stage, dressing rooms for up to sixty actors, costumes, and lighting and sound equipment, all tucked inside one intricately designed and collapsible trailer. Tractor units towed the trailers to the performance location—city park, baseball field, blocked-off street, and the like—where a crew of stagehands and technicians "transform[ed] the prosaic box into a magic house of dreams" (figure 7.1).[10]

The performances—all free—attracted more than thirty thousand people in a single opening night. Having come out to Staten Island for a production of *A Midsummer Night's Dream*, *New York Times* critic Brooks Atkinson compared his evening with the Caravan Theatre to the festivals of ancient Greece and described his own surprise by the audience at the production:

> A writhing mass of children is crowded as close to the [stage] as the law will permit; young legs protrude from under the spotlight platform and dangle out of the trees. When the warning lights go up, they are the ones that cheer, clap, and whistle; and when the play finally begins in the twilight, they all move forward as though someone had pushed them.[11]

Much of Atkinson's review focuses on the ways in which the Caravan Theatre attracted an audience of children—he later describes himself as "engulfed in children" who were enthralled by the production of *A Midsummer Night's Dream* and who made up nearly half of the audience.[12] Caravan Theatre director Julius Evans similarly noted that the "most delightful portion of [the Caravan Theatre's] audience was always to be found in the first fifteen rows of solidly packed children ranging in ages from 3 to 12."[13]

While no recordings of these productions are extant, Atkinson describes a "rough-and-ready performance at a lively physical pace" in his review. Productions like *A Midsummer Night's Dream*, *The Comedy of Errors*, *Melodies on Parade*, and *The Emperor's New Clothes* made use of physical comedy, tumbling, music, loudspeakers, and colorful costumes, and the vaudeville unit was always one of the most well attended. Though the Caravan Theatre companies each performed only four or five shows per week, they averaged weekly audiences of 120,000 during their sixteen-week season. FTP publicity teams compared the numbers to those of Broadway's four most popular shows during the same period in 1936—*Boy Meets Girl*, *Dead End*, *Three Men on a Horse*, and *Tobacco Road*—and found that the FTP Caravan Theatre companies attracted nearly seven times more audience members than did the top Broadway shows, and they did so with just over half the number of performances.[14] Crotona Park (in the Bronx) was one of the Caravan Theatre's most popular and well-attended sites. There, audiences averaged between fifteen thousand and eighteen thousand people per performance. Crotona Park's largest audience during the summer of 1936 reached nearly twenty-five thousand people (figure 7.2).[15]

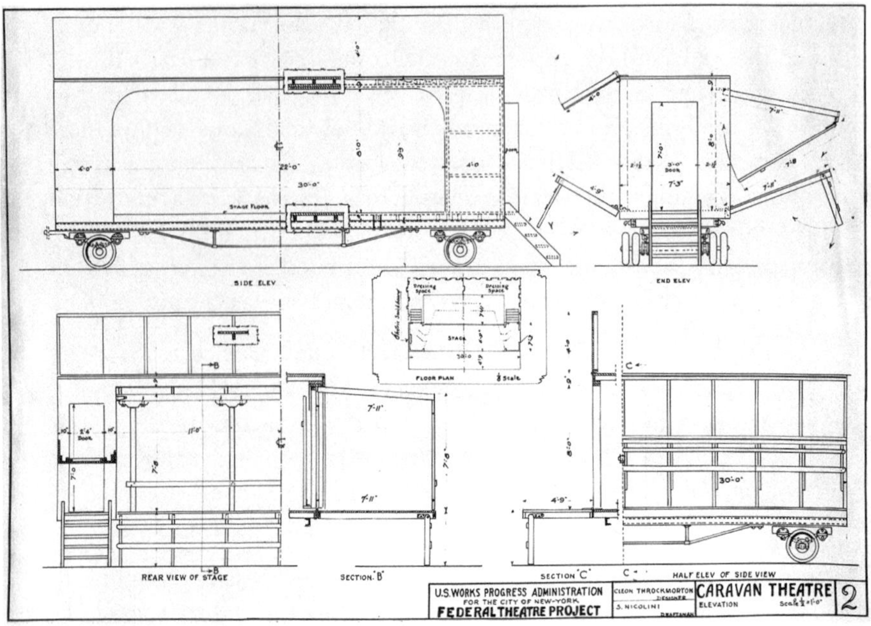

Fig. 7.1. Schematics of the Caravan Theatre trailer, showing floor plans, side and end elevations, and dimensions. Federal Theatre Project collection C0002, Special Collections and Archives, George Mason University, Fairfax, Va.

The following summer—despite massive budget and personnel cuts and the very public controversy surrounding *The Cradle Will Rock*—the FTP added a fifth company and additional locations to the Caravan Theatre. In *Arena*, Flanagan writes of the Caravan Theatre as a bright spot in a period of otherwise deep despair.[16] Again, audiences turned out by the tens of thousands when given the opportunity to spend their summer nights experiencing free theatre in the park. Between June 1 and September 18, 1937, Caravan Theatre companies played a repertoire of sixteen productions in twenty-two different sites throughout the parks and public areas of New York City. In this, the second summer of Caravan Theatre productions, each performance averaged an audience of 6,500 people. To again compare the popularity of the Caravan Theatre productions to Broadway: during the week of August 2, 1937, the five top-grossing shows on Broadway had a combined audience of 32,500.[17] That week the Caravan Theatre's five shows—*Just Ten Days*, *Riddle Me This*, *The Pirates of Penzance*, *Jack and the Beanstalk*, and a series of vaudeville sketches—played to an audience of 168,000, more than five times that of the Broadway shows.[18] Testimonials praised the Caravan Theatre and viewers begged the FTP to expand, asking for additional spaces, performances, and productions and explaining that summer theatre in the park had become fundamental to their families.[19]

Yet the end of the Caravan Theatre was already in sight. Following the deep cutbacks ordained by Congress in the summer of 1937, the FTP was forced to end the Caravan Theatre season three weeks earlier than planned. Evans's account of the summer hinted at the possibility of charging five or ten cents for admission to upcoming Caravan Theatre performances. By the summer of 1938, one of the Caravan Theatre's five touring companies had been completely disbanded, the repertory had been cut to twelve plays, and longtime director Julius Evans was reassigned. While it still employed more than three hundred theatre workers and the 201 performances attracted an audience of more than 1.1 million—more than 38 percent of the New York City FTP's annual attendance—the Caravan Theatre appeared less frequently in the newspapers, and the season emphasized one-act plays, children's shows, and vaudeville.[20] It soon became clear that the FTP simply did not have the funding to continue in future summers.

In his published report on FTP activities in the 1938–39 season, New York City project director George Kondolf provided a series of figures to demonstrate "all the activities [that] show how much more the Project achieves than

Fig. 7.2. Caravan Theatre performance and audience at Crotona Park in the Bronx, 1936 or 1937. Federal Theatre Project Photographs, collection C0205, Special Collections and Archives, George Mason University, Fairfax, Va.

the general theatergoing public knows about." Indeed, between the circus, marionette shows, vaudeville, companies presenting at local schools, out-of-town tours, community drama, and the Caravan Theatre, the "permanent" theatre productions taking place in theatre buildings and intended to attract a more traditional audience accounted for only 12 percent of the attendance and about 22 percent of the performances in New York City. Kondolf went on to discuss the Caravan Theatre specifically:

> Such presentations, while they may get the least attention in the metropolitan press and probably are not comparable to the very best Broadway presentations, are highly prized by the Project for their unquestioned contribution to the community's cultural life. [. . .] Such an enterprise represents some of the most socially useful work the Project can accomplish; but work of this sort, because it is not revenue-producing, has had to be severely curtailed for lack of funds.[21]

True to Kondolf's prediction, the Caravan Theatre did not return in the summer of 1939. In another sign of diminished resources, while the FTP created detailed scrapbooks and clippings files following the 1936 and 1937 seasons, the 1938 season is all but unremarked in the primary collections of FTP materials at the Library of Congress and in the National Archives.

As the above figures demonstrate, the Caravan Theatre was extraordinarily popular, attracting approximately 5.1 million audience members during its three brief summer seasons and appearing in numerous city newspapers. To put this into perspective, in these three summers the four or five Caravan Theatre companies played to approximately 41 percent of the total audiences that attended all FTP shows in New York City—and 17 percent of the total audience nationwide—during the entire four years of the program.[22] Articles on the Caravan Theatre appeared in numerous newspapers as well, including the *New York Times*, the *New York Telegraph*, the *New York Post*, the *New York Herald-Tribune*, the *Bronx Home News*, the *Brooklyn Eagle*, the *New York American*, the *New York News*, the *Staten Island Advance*, the *Long Island Star*, the *Brooklyn and Coney Island Times*, and *Women's Wear*. A *New York Enquirer* article succinctly explained the value of the Caravan Theatre, saying that the loss of the FTP would strike a severe blow to Broadway and popular entertainments alike: "At least 200,000 will see the WPA's two-bit circus this summer. More than 2,000,000 will see the Caravan shows. That's no longer an audience. It's a social obligation."[23] Yet the success of the Caravan Theatre faded into the shadows of the national battle over censorship and funding that the FTP would face in the summer of 1937 and became nearly invisible publicly by 1938. And so, instead of celebrating a program that served as a model of popular, family-oriented entertainment, was endorsed by Mayor Fiorello La Guardia and various commissioners on the New York Board of Transportation, and drew the joint efforts of the federal government and local businesses that donated advertising space, goods, and labor to the cause, the FTP struggled to remind the public that many of its programs served the social and cultural needs of the nation.

As newspaper critics, Flanagan, and New York City project director George Kondolf all noted, the Caravan Theatre satisfied the multiple and varied goals of both the FTP and the federal government. First and foremost, it employed several hundred relief workers during the summer season and during the rehearsal and preparation period while operating on a minimal other-than-labor budget.[24] It also encouraged the invention of a variety of portable stages addressing different traveling company needs; the blueprints for them, designed, built, and refined by the FTP's technical department, were eventually compiled by manager Irwin A. Rubinstein into a booklet titled *Caravan Theatre and Portable Frames* and distributed to unit directors across the country. Just as important, the Caravan Theatre established a system through which the FTP could physically transport theatre to the poor and working-class audiences that Flanagan targeted. An evening of quality, live theatrical entertainment was free for anyone who cared to see it and required no time-consuming, expensive trip into the theatre district. Moreover, based on plans discussed in letters and memos exchanged by Flanagan, Evans, and FTP publicity-man Charles Plotkin, the traveling Caravan Theatre was simultaneously a goal in and of itself and a stepping stone toward long-term plans. The FTP intended to establish a "Five-Boro Theatre circuit" that would include thirty-six permanent playhouses in various neighborhoods throughout the city. As Plotkin explained, "Great effort has gone into making this plan bring to a culmination the Federal Theatre's ultimate goal—of bringing the flesh-and-blood theatre to the people—, and we are receiving the cooperation of organizations, societies, lodges, institutions and labor unions throughout the city."[25] These plans for permanent theatres outside of the primary theatre district would have meant year-round, sustained, high-quality theatre for millions of poor and working-class audience members who lived outside of Manhattan and long-term employment for the workers employed by the Caravan Theatre units.

While the sheer volume of audience numbers, the list of enthusiastic supporters, and the praise the Caravan Theatre units garnered in New York newspapers are impressive, the distinction that the general public seemed to make between the high-profile performances in permanent theatres and popular entertainments like the circus or Caravan Theatre and the fact that the Caravan Theatre closed after its 1938 season signal the need for further study. In this way, the Caravan Theatre served as one of the proverbial canaries in a coal mine for the FTP; just as the canaries first passed out and then died from poisonous gases, so too did the Caravan Theatre falter in the rapidly changing political environment of 1937 and eventually expire in 1938. One of several signals that the FTP had reached dangerous ground by mid-1937 was that the Caravan Theatre had joined the ranks of the battle over censorship that surrounded *The Cradle Will Rock* and the premature closing of the nationally appreciated *Federal Theatre* magazine that publicized the people, stories, and achievements of the FTP. Flanagan's discussion of the debate over *Federal Theatre* magazine during the pivotal summer of 1937 seems eerily prescient when considering the fall of the Caravan Theatre:

> Gradually the real reasons began to come out, not all in one conversation, a little at a time. Was it true that the magazine was on sale at workers' bookshops? [. . .] Wasn't Pierre de Rohan, the editor, a Communist? [. . .] Wasn't there too much emphasis on poor audiences, too many pictures of squatters in Oklahoma and shirt-sleeved crowds in city parks—was this the kind of audience we wanted? We wanted our plays to be good enough for any kind of an audience, but our chief obligation was to people who weren't able to afford other theatre-going. Wasn't that still the idea? Or was it?[26]

With this description, Flanagan points to a sort of identity crisis that reverberated through Congress, the nation, and the FTP. Years of bloody strikes, hunger, and the ever-enduring economic depression took their toll as fears of a proletariat revolt percolated through political circles, and rising tensions abroad would soon lead to World War II. As Flanagan so astutely notes, priorities were changing; the "shirt-sleeved crowds in city parks" that were the hallmark of the Caravan Theatre had become a force to be feared in the aftermath of the worker strikes that plagued the era. Indeed, the work—and public perception—of the FTP would need to adapt to survive.

This crisis of identity occurred in a pivotal moment for the FTP. Having finally identified its audience, determined various best practices to connect with that audience, and trained its personnel to do so in the midst of managing the bureaucracy that accompanies institutions attempting to operate within the federal and state governments, the FTP was poised to explode onto the national scene as the decentralized but unified "federation of theatres" Flanagan imagined. However, the FTP failed to find ways to consistently highlight these less "traditional" approaches to theatre for critics, politicians, and potential audiences who prioritized those more commercial—and often controversial—productions that were scripted, rehearsed, and performed in permanent theatre buildings. As Kondolf demonstrated in his article regarding activities in New York City during the 1938–39 season, the FTP's community-oriented, socially aware programming constituted 80–90 percent of the organization's activities—and that rate in a city famous for the range and breadth of its professional theatre. Whether through efforts to create a theatre for the blind in Oklahoma, to assist in the treatment of the mentally ill in the psychiatric ward of Bellevue Hospital, or to join forces with the American Red Cross to boost morale among flood refugees, the work of the FTP was to create a theatre that gave a voice to poor and working-class Americans. Through this "democratic" or "people's theatre," the FTP invited the disenfranchised into the theatre, built morale, trained and supported creative artists who would have otherwise been left to digging ditches, and created a "federation of theatres" that spoke to the concerns of the nation. As the aforementioned statistics regarding the popularity of the Caravan Theatre suggest, any FTP unit that accounted for 17 percent of the FTP's total nationwide audience and averaged at least 40 percent of the annual New York City audience is worthy of scholarly examination. These figures speak to the overall character and measure of the FTP as a whole; they are the rule rather than the exception.

Though Flanagan—and many others writing publicly on the FTP—repeatedly drew attention to these acts, they remained largely invisible to the FTP's critics in the years that led to its untimely demise. As I have worked my way through the archives, it has become abundantly clear that many individuals enjoyed their local FTP branches immensely but thought of them as entirely different entities from the controversial, outspoken, and—to their minds—problematic New York City units. Even those who would otherwise be considered critical of the organization as a whole sometimes found much to enjoy in their local units. Flanagan recounts one famous example in which a congressman called to inquire about the glacial speed with which the FTP was handling an actor friend's application:

> "I've always been very much interested in the Federal Theatre and its work in our State, and a few weeks ago I suggested that a certain fine professional actor of my acquaintance be considered for your rolls. I've heard nothing, and my friend, who is very much in need of work, is getting impatient."
>
> I told the Congressman that I would look up the particular case and inform him, and then I added, "Of course, you know, however, that the

> Federal Theatre is no longer in existence. [. . .] [T]he Federal Theatre was abolished on June 30 by Act of Congress?"
>
> Again a loud silence. Then a shocked and heavy voice said, "Was that the Federal Theatre?"[27]

This congressman was not alone in his dissociation—his misperception—that the New York City FTP was an entirely different animal from the typically less controversial and more community-based programs that took place in his state. In his remarks on the FTP in Portland, Oregon, for example, Burns Mantle commented that it appeared to be "completely detached" from the national organization.[28] Nick Chaivoe, a socially conscious worker on the Portland FTP, likewise noted this apparent disconnect between his local unit and the provocative New York City units: "We were in the hinterlands, after all. [. . .] We were completely insulated from what was going on in any other state."[29]

In my research, I have noted similar disconnects in the accounts of both working-class and wealthy individuals from Washington, Massachusetts, West Virginia, Illinois, Alabama, Georgia, and numerous other locations. Over and over, individuals were surprised to learn that the new community theatre director or the small company of actors traveling through the countryside to perform for tens of thousands of Civilian Conservation Corps boys each week were part of the same FTP that was accused of pushing communist propaganda on children, attacking federal government policies and attitudes, and boondoggling with federal dollars. While the work of the FTP was not exactly invisible in these cases, examples such as the Caravan Theatre foreground the widespread misperceptions that surrounded the organization and remind scholars of the importance of considering the range of roles the FTP played in sustaining the nation.

Notes

1. Dunn quotes from Qualls's report on the company's activities in his article. Qualls notes that he chose plays based on the preferences of the company members rather than on any particular outside agenda. Qualls also explained that plays sometimes required adaptation for his actors, as when a completely blind actor played a character that relied on visually identifying or noticing a person or object. The three shows the company had presented by mid-1937 were *The Florist Shop* (Winifred Harkridge), *Heaven Will Help the Working Girl* (anonymous), and *The Moonshiner* (Arthur Hopkins). John W. Dunn, "Oklahoma's Federal Theatre for the Blind," *Federal Theatre* 2, no. 1 (1937): 10, 28.

2. Directed by Madelyn O'Shea, the Community Drama Unit operated out of the Provincetown Playhouse on MacDougal Street in New York with the goal of training qualified individuals who could be sent out into cities and towns in need of a locally relevant community theatre. Training consisted of both theory and practice in directing, designing, building, lighting, construction, speech, and "theory of community drama" courses. Combined, these offered students the means to lead their respective communities in nearly every aspect of theatre as well as an awareness of their own potential role as "positive community forces" creating "plays of value to the life of the people." Anthony Buttitta, "Teaching Teachers: Complete Technique of Production," *Federal Theatre* 2, no. 1 (1937): 19–21; "Mental Patients Find Aid in Drama: Bellevue Uses Plays as Help in Diagnosing and Treating Maladjusted Girls," *New York Times*, April 7, 1937, 9. This article is also featured in *Federal Theatre* 2, no. 5 (1937): 18.
3. While Kentucky and Ohio saw the worst flooding overall (sometimes in excess of thirty feet above flood stage), the other eleven states (Illinois, Wisconsin, Iowa, Missouri, Pennsylvania, Indiana, West Virginia, Tennessee, Arkansas, Louisiana, and Mississippi) also experienced some of the worst flooding in their history. For further information on the flood and weather patterns, see Bennett Swenson, "Rivers and Floods," *Monthly Weather Review* 65, no. 2 (February 1937): 71–77, http://docs.lib.noaa.gov/rescue/mwr/065/mwr-065-02-0071.pdf; additional local reports are also available in this issue of *Monthly Weather Review*.
4. For further information on the FTP's flood tour, see my article "A Nation in Need: Revelations and Disaster Relief in the Federal Theatre Project," *Journal of American Drama and Theatre* 20, no. 2 (Spring 2008): 49–64, or my book, *Staging the People: Community and Identity in the Federal Theatre Project* (New York: Palgrave Macmillan Press, 2011).
5. While often linked to the FTP, it must be noted that *The Cradle Will Rock* did not, in fact, open as an FTP production. Due to a series of convoluted events, Orson Welles and John Houseman broke with the FTP on the eve of *Cradle*'s opening performance. Instead, *Cradle* became the first offering of their newly created Mercury Theatre. For an intriguing discussion, see Barry Witham, "Backstage at *The Cradle Will Rock*," *Theatre History Studies* 12 (1992): 213–19.
6. See, for example, John O'Connor and Lorraine Brown, *Free Adult, Uncensored: The Living History of the Federal Theatre Project* (New York: Simon and Schuster, 1978); Paul Sporn, *Against Itself: The Federal Theatre and Writers' Projects in the Midwest* (Detroit: Wayne State University Press, 1995); Jane De Hart Mathews, *The Federal Theatre, 1935–1939: Plays, Relief,*

and Politics (Princeton, N.J.: Princeton University Press, 1967); and Barry Witham, *The Federal Theatre Project: A Case Study* (New York: Cambridge University Press, 2003).

7. Hallie Flanagan, *Arena* (New York: Duell, Sloan and Pearce, 1940), 347.
8. The FTP modeled the idea for the Caravan Theatre after the summer theatre done under the Temporary Emergency Relief Administration (TERA), which was the New York State version of the Federal Emergency Relief Administration (FERA) and an early New Deal program. In 1935 the Works Progress Administration replaced FERA. Newspaper accounts suggest that the TERA summer theatre was also quite popular with audiences. June 16, 1936, was the first day that all of the Caravan Theatre productions ran simultaneously. "2 Million Witness Free WPA Shows," unnamed/undated newspaper clipping, National Archives and Records Administration, College Park, Md. (hereafter NARA), Records of the Work Projects Administration, 1922–1944, Record Group 69 (RG69), Records of the Federal Theatre Project, entry 877, box 145, "Caravan Theatre, NYC—Photographs."
9. "Bronx Premiere of WPA Portable Theater Will Be Staged in Crotona Park on Tuesday," *(Bronx) Home News*, June 14, 1936, Library of Congress (hereafter LOC), Federal Theatre Project Collection, box 963, "Portable Theatre," 17.
10. The portable stages had one important design flaw: when mounted on the trailer bed, they were precariously weighted and tall. On June 19, 1936, just after the first summer season opened, one of the portable stages got stuck under an elevated structure at First Avenue and Eighth Street. Police assisted the driver in removing the truck's tires and rims in order to free the vehicle and stage without further damage. "WPA Portable Theatre Stuck under Elevated," *New York Post*, June 19, 1936, LOC, Federal Theatre Project Collection, box 963, "Newspaper Clippings on FTP Activities"; "New York City Caravan Theatre, 1936," NARA, RG 69, E986, "Scrapbooks Relating to the New York Caravan Theatre, 1936–1937" (hereafter "Scrapbooks"), 12; "Caravan Theatres and Portable Frames," NARA, RG 69, E938, box 483, 9.
11. Brooks Atkinson, "Caravan Theatre of the WPA Opens on Staten Island with 'A Midsummer Night's Dream,'" *New York Times*, June 2, 1937, 21.
12. Ibid., 21.
13. Julius Evans, "From the Drama Mailbag: The Caravan Season Ends," *New York Times*, October 3, 1937, J2.
14. The four Portable or Caravan Theatre units combined gave nineteen performances per week to a total audience of approximately 120,000, while the four most popular Broadway shows gave thirty-two performances per

week to a total audience of approximately 18,000. "New York City Caravan Theatre, 1936," NARA, RG 69, E986, "Scrapbooks," 5–8.

15. Other sites included Forest Park, Kings Park, Smith Field, Leavitt Field, and Astoria Park on Long Island; St. Mary's Park and Franz-Siegal Park in the Bronx; Owls Head Park, Gravesend Park, Randstand, and Thomas Jefferson High School in Brooklyn; Silver Lake Park, Robin Hood Field, Semlers Field, and Fitzgerald Field on Staten Island; and Yeshiva Ball Field, Washington Square Park, and Roosevelt Park in Manhattan. Ibid., 3, 9.
16. Flanagan, *Arena*, 205.
17. The five Broadway shows used for comparison included *You Can't Take It with You*, *Room Service*, *The Women*, *Babes in Arms*, and *Having a Wonderful Time.*
18. "Caravan Theatre Schedule," *New York Times*, August 19, 1937, 22.
19. "New York City Caravan Theatre, 1936," NARA, RG 69, E986, "Scrapbooks"; "New York City Caravan Theatre, 1937," ibid.
20. Figures are based on those given by Kondolf in his published report of the 1938–39 season. Kondolf noted that 1,131,600 people attended 201 Caravan Theatre performances, while 2,960,427 people attended 4,522 total FTP performances (including the Caravan Theatre) for the year. George Kondolf, "The Federal Theatre Season: In Which the Local Director Summarizes the WPA Theatre Activities during the Past Year," *New York Times*, June 18, 1939, 113–14.
21. Ibid., 113.
22. Flanagan catalogs the employment, expenditures, performances, attendance, and receipts by state in *Arena* as of March 31, 1939 (three months before the FTP closed). At that time, New York City's attendance was 12,558,738 and national attendance was 30,398,726. "New York City Caravan Theatre, 1937," NARA, RG 69, E986, "Scrapbooks"; Flanagan, *Arena*, 435.
23. "Caravan Shows Worth While Summer Fare," undated, *New York Enquirer*, NARA, RG 69, E877, box 145, "Caravan Theatre, NYC—Photographs."
24. As a relief organization, 90 percent of the FTP's funding was designated as wages for theatre professionals eligible for government-funded relief, leaving only 10 percent of the budget for any worker not eligible for relief, costumes, lighting, sets, theatre rental, utilities, play royalties (called "play rental" because the federal government could not pay royalties), and other equipment, space, or technology costs. After extensive negotiation, the government approved the use of admission fees for these other-than-labor costs as well.
25. Charles Plotkin to E. A. Belding, September 2, 1937, LOC, Federal Theatre Project Collection, box 964, "Caravan Theatre—Posters/Correspondence: Publicity."

26. Flanagan, *Arena*, 204.
27. Hallie Flanagan, "Congress Takes the Stage," *New York Times*, August 20, 1939, sec. 9, p. 1.
28. "Noted Critic Pays Brief Visit While on Lecture Tour," *Oregon Journal*, March 16, 1939, 21.
29. Nick Chaivoe, interview by Shirley Tanzer, January 18, 1978, Portland, Ore., transcript, WPA Oral Histories Collection, Special Collections and Archives, George Mason University, Fairfax, Va., 61.

8. African American Waiters and Cakewalk Contests in Florida East Coast Resorts of the Gilded Age

Jerry Dickey

In the late 1880s and the 1890s, the African American cakewalk served as the most popular event in the weekly social calendars of exclusive East Coast resort hotels. Many surviving documents of the cakewalk—notably, grotesquely stereotypical cover art for sheet music and advertising, as well as frequent association with elements of minstrelsy—reflect more the persistent attitudes of white racial superiority than the actual innovations of the black dancers. While well-known professional entertainers such as George Walker and Bert Williams helped popularize cakewalk dancing, little scholarly attention has been given to the numerous contests and amateur dancers who brought the cakewalk into national prominence and established it as the first social dance in American history that was shared by both the black and white communities.[1]

Especially as performed by black waiters and bellmen in Henry M. Flagler's Florida East Coast hotels in St. Augustine and Palm Beach, the cakewalk ultimately proved the most prominent form of African American cultural expression appropriated by the Gilded Age social elite, paving the way for jazz-era dance crazes like the Charleston and black bottom. Flagler's waiters developed two distinctly different styles for the cakewalk, one that satisfied white expectations for black demeanor within narrowly defined, racially restricted stereotypes, and another that attempted to expand these caricatured limitations with a fuller, more refined exhibition of dignity and creativity. This essay focuses primarily upon these waiters/dancers and on their background, training, and occupational challenges as hotel staff; on their innovation and perseverance for self-advancement in society and in emerging forms of musical theatre; and on the relationship of manners and behavior to the white clientele's demands for servitude (both in the dining room and on the dance floor).

The cakewalk may be described more as a stylized manner of walking than what one would normally think of as a nineteenth-century social dance. Elegantly dressed couples would assemble around the edges of a ballroom or dance floor. To the music of a march or polka or, more frequently, to the syncopation or "ragging" of ragtime music, each couple would interlock arms or hold hands, then promenade around the dance floor. James Clouser, in *Looking at Dance*, describes the cakewalk as "a dance in which you lean, or rear way back and kick your feet alternately in front of you while moving forward from foot to foot. The lifted leg is long but the knee remains bent until the foot achieves its ultimate highpoint with a quickly extended flick."[2] During the dance, couples struck exaggerated poses and improvised gestures and steps in attempts to gain favor and audience response. Not all cakewalkers exhibited flamboyant athleticism, however, and the relative ease with which the basic movement of the dance could be executed led to the equation of the cakewalk with anything simple, as in the phrase "It's a cakewalk." The variety and coexistence of different cakewalk styles may be seen in three short films produced in 1903 by the American Mutoscope and Biograph Company. One film shows the lively tempo of the cakewalk, as well as the dignified and graceful manner of the black dancers. In a second film, dancers display comic gyrations and high-stepping antics more typical of the comic cakewalk that held special sway for whites attending the contests. The third film shows members of white high society on a beach mimicking elements of the comic cakewalk as a means for frolics and buffoonery.[3]

Historians attribute multiple origins to the cakewalk. Many look back to its precursors in African dances like the ring shouts and walk-about, perhaps coming to the United States by way of Caribbean plantations. In southern plantations, the dance, sometimes referred to as the chalk line walk, seems to have been performed as part of slaves' parody of white mannered dances such as the promenade and grand march. Plantation owners often encouraged performances of the dance as contests for their own amusement, not recognizing the satirical elements in the encoded movements. Cakes or hoecakes were awarded to the winning couple. The cakewalk's movement into mainstream white society came initially at a showcase at the Centennial Exhibition in Philadelphia in 1876, but more significantly as a result of the newly erected, lavish resort hotels, where black waiters performed the cakewalk in widely attended formal contests for the resorts' guests and surrounding communities. The dance's popularity sparked a national competition in 1892 in Madison Square Garden before becoming a European sensation shortly after the turn of the century.[4]

The Florida East Coast resort contests originated with the bellmen at Flagler's famed Hotel Ponce de Leon in St. Augustine in 1888, the year of the hotel's opening.[5] The contest became institutionalized the following year with the first annual cakewalk contest at Flagler's second St. Augustine hotel, the Hotel Alcazar, a slightly less formal resort with a fifteen-thousand-square-foot ballroom in its casino that played host to a range of theatrical entertainments. The Hotel Ponce de Leon waiters and bellmen performed in this first and subsequent annual contest, but as its popularity grew the waitstaff from the Alcazar and a third Flagler resort, the Cordova, joined the mix, sometimes competing among themselves and sometimes against each other.[6] During the height of the winter resort season, from mid-February to early April, the Alcazar Casino typically presented a cakewalk contest each week, embedded within a more formal program of entertainment that featured the hotel staff and waiters. A jubilee concert by black quartets and sextets preceded the cakewalk and included spirituals as well as popular songs from both black and white composers. Buck-and-wing dancing, a precursor to tap dancing, also featured prominently on the bill, often interspersed between musical selections.[7]

The cakewalk followed the jubilee concert, typically beginning between nine and ten o'clock, after the final evening shifts for waiters assigned to morning and day crews.[8] Competing couples ranged in number from half a dozen to as many as fifty and consisted of waiters and their female partners from domestic staff at the hotels or from the segregated black communities near the resorts.[9] Their carefully choreographed pivots around the corners of the dancing area received close scrutiny by three or four judges selected from notable dignitaries staying at the resort—politicians, entrepreneurs, visiting royalty, or popular personalities like the actor Joseph Jefferson or Admiral George Dewey.[10] The judges gradually eliminated dance teams until only three or four couples remained. The competitive nature of the contest intensified the audience's response, with crowds often ranging between five hundred to more than a thousand viewers shouting encouragement for their favored couple.[11] The judges' mock seriousness, most evident in their speech announcing the winners, contributed to the overall merriment of the occasion. In addition to prizes such as gold watches and cash, the winning couple would receive the lavishly decorated cake that had frequently been on display in the hotel throughout the day.[12] Thus, the dance coined another popular phrase, "It takes the cake," signifying something that wins out over competition (figure 8.1).

Fig. 8.1. Cakewalk couple with prize cake, St. Augustine, Florida. Courtesy of the St. Augustine Historical Society Research Library.

The waiters who performed the cakewalk contests held a precarious position within the exclusively white resort social scene. The history of African American waiters serving in restaurants dates back to the early 1800s, as black workers assumed service positions that many white workers deemed inferior. Ironically, the years after the Civil War saw a decrease in skilled black tradesmen, and the U.S. Census records of 1890 and 1900 show that

87 percent of all black workers maintained employment in agricultural or domestic service fields.[13] Positions at resort hotels offered more regular hours and greater prospects for advancement than farming or domestic servitude. In the turn-of-the-century *Commanders of the Dining Room*, E. A. Maccannon further explained why black individuals gravitated to hotel service for employment: "For some time to come," he wrote, "it is better for educated black men to enter this and similar callings" where he may have more influence and receive more compensation than in "those channels in which the resistance is much greater and the pay inadequate."[14]

Although inexpensive labor undoubtedly served as a major factor in the hiring of black waiters at resorts, their acceptance in the exclusive dining rooms, where knowledge of formal dining etiquette and precise table settings was a prerequisite, might also reflect contemporaneous social progressives' attitudes toward race relations. While many Gilded Age elite supported emancipation, few believed that the black race was the equal of the white race. For example, in April 1900, the *St. Augustine Record* reported on a bill before Congress that dismissed both segregation and deportation as "practically impossible" solutions to the "negro problem" of population expansion. Instead, the bill proposed the "rapid multiplication of [. . .] industrial, not academic," training schools for black youth throughout the South.[15] Theories of social Darwinism gave rise to the notion that it was the responsibility of the superior race to educate and elevate inferior groups, and the movement of black workers into the dining room served as one step in this direction.[16] The fact that waiters had demonstrated their mastery over what black headwaiter John B. Goins referred to in 1902 as the "fine art" of the formal dining room may have helped pave the way for their acceptance by white resort guests as fellow social dancers in the grand ballrooms.[17] Nowhere can the recognition by white individuals of black organizational and managerial prowess be seen better than in the position of the headwaiter.

With the emergence of the leisure resorts, the role of the headwaiter took on increasing prominence. Black headwaiters at late nineteenth-century resorts typically had received varying levels of formal schooling, most having been born in the years during or shortly after the Civil War. Many began some form of hotel service—as bellmen, busboys, and the like—in their early teens. Some rapidly advanced to the role of headwaiter in their early to mid-twenties, finding initial employment with steamships and Pullman cars before moving to resort hotels for better salaries and working conditions. These individuals possessed immense organizational skills and talents, often commanding a small army of male waitstaff. The title of Maccannon's book—*Commanders of the Dining Room*—applied the military title of commander to the headwaiter for his ability to marshal up to four hundred men trained in a variety of specializations within clearly defined ranks, such as second waiter or side waiter.[18] This comparison of the headwaiter with a military commander was not uncommon. The *Tatler of Society in Florida*, the weekly social paper aimed at St. Augustine resort guests of the time, records that as headwaiter of the Hotel Ponce de Leon, "Frank Thompson marshals his corps of waiters as a general would his army, with subordinate officers as well known to the regular guests as he is."[19] With limited employment options for black workers in business or government, the position of headwaiter proved one of the most prestigious available.

While headwaiters organized many aspects of their staffs' life and work, they seem not to have taken a direct hand in organizing the cakewalk contests, a task often assumed by the hotel's or casino's general manager. When the cakewalk contests began at the Hotel Alcazar Casino, journalistic accounts suggest that these managers preferred the largely comic and grotesque elements of the dance over those of a more dignified character. The *Tatler* called the cakewalk "as inane a performance as can be imagined," where "guests laugh immoderately at the contest for a cake."[20] By the end of the first decade of the contests, however, Anna Marcotte, the popular editor of the *Tatler*, perhaps spoke on behalf of her resort peers in noting a shift to a new, more subdued and elegant style of cakewalk: "The only trouble with the cake-walks [is that] those walking are much too serious, '*just like white folks*' [emphasis mine]. This is unfortunate; they should do 'jes like de old-time darkie;' that is what the public wants."[21] Four years later, Marcotte still longed for the waiters' old style of dancing: "But why can we not have an old-fashioned cake walk? They were worth seeing; boys take a hint."[22] In that same season of 1901, articles in the local newspaper, the *St. Augustine Record*, provide further evidence of a changing sensibility regarding the cakewalk, referring to black walkers carrying "themselves with an air of pride and grace" and noting that "the best and most graceful couples in the city" would be entering an upcoming contest at the casino.[23] Both styles coexisted for several years, for in 1902, the year before the American Mutoscope and Biograph Company recorded its films, the *Tatler* announced the final dance of the season in which "the old and new styles of cakewalking will be contested."[24]

As Marcotte demonstrates, the new style of a more subdued, graceful cakewalk did not receive an immediate welcome by the white community in St. Augustine. Her statements suggest a discomfort with the clear level of achievement in the black dancers and their ability to engage in a form of social dancing that was at least on a par with, if not superior to, the social dances seen in the formal balls of the resorts. Yet the changing style paved the way for the cakewalk's acceptance as a social dance for the white community as well, and those of the social elite quickly began performing the cakewalk themselves.[25] In Palm Beach, the young socialite Juliana Cutting gained a rapid reputation as an excellent interpreter of the cakewalk. *Town and Country* magazine noted that Cutting "was a leader in the gaiety at the Florida resort last winter. She is an unusually graceful dancer. Her ability in this direction extends to fancy dances, and last winter just after the cakewalk in the Cocoanut Grove, at which Mr. James Henry Smith and Mr. John Jacob Astor were judges, she and the latter essayed at a little impromptu dance in a private ballroom."[26] Palm Beach notables such as Henry Flagler's third wife, Mary Lily Kenan, also performed the cakewalk, as did Frederick Townsend Martin, writer and critic of the extravagant social elite within whose circle he traveled.[27] In New York, William K. Vanderbilt hired a noted black cakewalk dancer, Tom Fletcher, to teach him the dance. In fact, Fletcher's hiring sparked a well-publicized, semicomic rebuke by the musical-comedy duo George Walker and Bert Williams, who accused Vanderbilt of distracting "the attention of the public" from black dancers and their own position as "world-renowned cake-walkers."[28]

The social implication of black and white people dancing together did not go without notice. Marcotte editorialized in the *Tatler*, "They are murdering [that is, lynching] colored men who hold Federal positions up in Georgia and Carolina, while in the old Southern city of St. Augustine [. . .] we are attending cake-walks with our colored brethren dancing in the same room and to the same music with them. Why not establish cake-walks in our sister States?"[29] Marcotte's statement reveals the unique character of St. Augustine as a resort destination. Although a southern town in many respects, and part of the Confederacy in the Civil War, turn-of-the-century St. Augustine found itself during the winter season infused with white vacationers primarily from the Northeast and Midwest. The popularity of the *Tatler* suggests that Marcotte's statement reflected the prevailing attitude of St. Augustine resort guests as remaining apart from—and more progressive than—the attitudes found in the cities and resort towns in neighboring southern states. While resort guests in St. Augustine may have resisted the black dancers' refined style of cakewalk, they at least viewed their cohabitation of the dance floor as a sign of progressivism. The evolving style of performance in the cakewalk contests may well have precipitated this small step toward racial integration. But what led to this change in performance style in the first place?

While the cakewalk contests were approaching the heyday of their popularity, African American waiters experienced a severe challenge to their profession. At the turn of the twentieth century, resort hotels across the

United States increasingly began replacing black waiters with white waiters and sometimes white waitresses. This shift in the labor force coincided with hotels' widespread adoption of the European dining plan, in which guests ordered dinner items separately off a menu, as opposed to the previously commonplace American plan, in which a fixed plate was offered at a set price. Many hotel managers presumed that black waiters lacked the ability to adapt to the European plan and turned their favor to available white labor from the masses of newly immigrated Europeans.

Leading headwaiters responded to this occupational challenge by forming an all-black labor association to facilitate communication, education, and advanced training for waiters. The Head, Second, and Side Waiters Association was formed in 1899, holding annual meetings to facilitate black labor organization, even as it remained vehemently opposed to the concept of labor strikes.[30] The association aimed to better prepare black waiters for the new dining experiences. W. Forrest Cozart and John B. Goins authored two instructional manuals for black waiters, respectively titled *The Waiter's Manual* (c. 1898) and *The American Colored Waiter* (c. 1902). These manuals, as well as the weekly column "The Waiter" that appeared in the *Freeman*, the black newspaper of Indianapolis, placed emphasis not only on proper dining service techniques but also on continuing education for waiters in the areas of "spelling, letter writing and grammar."[31] By the turn of the century, Cozart and others wrote of "two classes" of waiters: "the grand old comrades of the old School," also less affectionately referred to as "chair pullers," and a "new school" of "aspiring, progressive" individuals.[32] Not surprisingly, then, Cozart occasionally took issue with black waiters who "still denigrate their race" by performing in the comic cakewalks that remained popular in Palm Beach and many other resort locales. The "better element" of waiter, Cozart noted, "has relegated these follies to the rear."[33]

While white society appropriated the genteel version of the cakewalk, the comic version of the dance grew increasingly commodified, often inspiring the composition of commercial musical scores and serving as an entertainment vehicle for both professional and amateur blackface minstrel companies. In their 1992 study of African American popular music, *From Cakewalks to Concert Halls*, Thomas L. Morgan and William Barlow discuss what they call "pseudonegro" popular music devised by white composers such as Kerry Mills and Abe Holzmann. The cover art selected by Tin Pan Alley music publishers of these tunes did much to relegate the cakewalk to the realm of racial stereotype and comic exaggeration.[34] In her insightful critical examination of the cakewalk, Brooke Baldwin theorizes on the rationale behind white society's takeover of the dance: "The cakewalk can be identified as [. . .] a genuinely black cultural product, which is exactly why whites, from the beginning, attempted to coopt and stereotype it."[35]

Especially through blackface minstrelsy, which was staged throughout the country but most popularly in southern states, white performers attempted to use the comic cakewalk to seize power from black entertainers by reducing their dance and personas to buffoonery. As Baldwin notes, "By 1898 white popular culture had so denigrated the image of the black cakewalker [. . .] that white society was convinced that the dance was now its rightful province."[36] In St. Augustine, for example, the local military unit, the St. Augustine Rifles, regularly performed cakewalk contests at the Alcazar Casino for the amusement of the community. The *St. Augustine Record* offered an opinion that undoubtedly would have been shared by many white resort guests and that reveals the unresolved contradictions within their social Darwinian and socially progressive beliefs: "Visitors who have watched the darkeys in their graceful evolutions, probably have never had the opportunity of seeing the darkey outdone by his white imitator. The Rifles can imitate the darkeys and give a truer to nature walk than the most graceful and accomplished coons."[37] Sixty-two years later, Imamu Amiri Baraka could not help but comment on the idea of blackface cakewalks in a manner that offers a rebuttal to the *Record*'s remarks: "If it is a Negro dance caricaturing white customs, what is that dance when a white theatre company tries to satirize it as a Negro dance? I find the idea of white minstrels in blackface satirizing a dance satirizing themselves a remarkable kind of irony."[38]

While black hotel workers formed a labor association, they and other black organizations featured the cakewalk at their own formal balls and fund-raising events. For example, the United States Hotel Waiters Club in Newport staged annual cakewalk contests in the 1890s.[39] In 1891 the NePlus Ultra Club of Pine Bluff, Arkansas, offered a cakewalk as part of a benefit for the community's new African Methodist Episcopal church. More than twenty-five couples "got their Sunday's graceful step," while the winning couple was selected for "being the most graceful walking couple in the march."[40] And in St. Augustine in 1892, the black community staged a "colored ball" fund-raiser at the Alcazar Casino, which featured "ladies handsomely dressed, the men in full dress," and some curious and supportive white attendees who purchased tickets for charity and watched the dancers.[41] Although descriptive details of these events are scant, there is enough evidence to suggest that the refined cakewalk was performed as a black entertainment for black participation and viewing, not simply as a performance on demand for white amusement.

In terms of race relations at the turn of the twentieth century, the history of the cakewalk is a mixed bag. In some respects, it served as a vehicle for the perpetuation of racial stereotypes, depicting black people as gaudily dressed, lacking in sophistication, and happily strutting for the white boss's pleasure. In other respects, it paved the way for widespread popularity of later forms of black dance, including the shimmy, Charleston, and black bottom. As Jayna Brown notes in *Babylon Girls*, "The meaning of the [cakewalk] dance—class parody, serious self-fashioning, intra-racial satire—depended to some degree on where and when and by whom the dance was performed."[42]

The same ambivalence could apply to the waiters who performed in cakewalk contests. Some accounts suggest that as the cakewalk reverted back to its stereotypical associations, waiters in the Florida resorts began pulling away from performing the dance. By 1903 the *Tatler* reported that "it is very unfortunate that the waiters and bellmen do not do their own cakewalking, as they formerly did."[43] In 1905 a troupe of "professional dancers from Atlantic City" was hired to perform in Palm Beach cakewalks, although this practice was not consistently employed at that time.[44] The Palm Beach resorts, especially the Hotel Royal Poinciana, heavily preferred the "old-fashioned" style emphasizing comic antics, and there the cakewalk contests retained their popularity before large outdoor crowds throughout the 1920s.[45]

In his 1912 *Autobiography of an Ex-Coloured Man*, James Weldon Johnson's unidentified narrator describes his first encounter with a cakewalk contest in Jacksonville, Florida, before going on to provide an assessment of the dance form: "There are a great many coloured people who are ashamed of the cake-walk, but I think they ought to be proud of it." Johnson's narrator discusses the cakewalk alongside ragtime music in terms of black artistic achievements of international appeal. "These are lower forms of art," the narrator states, "but they give evidence of a power that will some day be applied to the higher forms. In this measure, at least, [. . .] the race has been a world influence."[46] At Florida East Coast hotels between 1889 and approximately 1905, the cakewalk provided black waiters with a venue to express their attitudes toward their employment, self-identity, and ability to produce an art form of original creation. For the Gilded Age as a whole, the cakewalk served as a transitional step toward more widespread recognition by white society of African American culture, innovation, and elegance.

Notes

1. Ralph G. Giordano provides a brief overview of the cakewalk contests in resort hotels in *Social Dancing in America* (Westport, Conn.: Greenwood, 2007), while discussions of dancers transitioning from amateur to

professional status may be found in Marshall Stearns and Jean Stearns, *Jazz Dance: The Story of American Vernacular Dance* (New York: Macmillan, 1968); and Jayna Brown, *Babylon Girls: Black Women Performers and the Shaping of the Modern* (Durham, N.C.: Duke University Press, 2008).

2. James Clouser, *Looking at Dance: One Dancer's Guide to His World* (Dubuque, Iowa: Kendall/Hunt, 2005), 80.
3. These short films are included in the DVD *America Dances! 1897–1948* (Dallas: Dancetime Publications, 2003). The originals are housed at the Library of Congress.
4. For an account of the cakewalk in France, see Davinia Caddy, "Parisian Cake Walks," *19th-Century Music* 30, no. 3 (2007): 288–317.
5. Thomas Graham, "Opening Season for the Hotel Ponce de Leon, January through May 1888," *El Escribano: The St. Augustine Journal of History* 49 (2012): 23–24.
6. The Cordova was originally built by Franklin W. Smith as the Casa Monica Hotel but was purchased by Flagler after its first season in 1888 and immediately renamed. All three Flagler hotels remain today, although only the Cordova is a functioning hotel, having returned to its original name, the Casa Monica. The Hotel Ponce de Leon is the home of Flagler College, and the Alcazar has been transformed into the Lightner Museum.
7. Waiters may have been hired not only for their abilities in the dining room but also for the possibility of contributing to a variety of leisure entertainments for resort guests. For example, headwaiter Frank P. Thompson is credited with forming the first professional black baseball team, the Cuban Giants, to which black waiters contributed. For a discussion of Thompson and the Giants, see Greg Schneider, "Baseball: The Legacy of the Negro Leagues," *Helium*, 2012, www.helium.com/items/964192-baseball-the-legacy-of-the-negro-leagues/print (accessed January 6, 2012).
8. The shifts for working the dining room were arranged with gaps of between one and three hours, which allowed for rest or contribution to these extra leisure entertainments. For more information on waiters' shifts, see John B. Goins, *The American Colored Waiter* (Chicago: Hotel Monthly, c. 1902), 4. The *St. Augustine Record*, March 13, 1901, mentions that Ponce de Leon waiters rehearsed in the afternoon for a cakewalk contest the next evening.
9. *St. Augustine Record*, March 13, 1901; *St. Augustine News*, March 1, 1891. For information on these and similar black communities near white resort hotels, see Myra B. Young Armstead, *"Lord, Please Don't Take Me in August": African Americans in Newport and Saratoga Springs, 1870–1930* (Urbana: University of Illinois Press, 1999), 19–34, 56–58; and David R. Colburn, *Racial Change and Community Crisis: St. Augustine, Florida,*

1877–1980 (New York: Columbia University Press, 1985), 19. The *Palm Beach Daily News*, March 7, 1903 identifies a "parlor maid" as one of the cakewalk dancers.

10. Admiral Dewey's triumph over the Spanish fleet in the Battle of Manila in 1898 signaled for many the emergence of the United States as an international power. Dewey staged an unsuccessful candidacy for the U.S. presidency in 1900.
11. *St. Augustine Record*, March 15, 1901.
12. *Tatler of Society in Florida* (St. Augustine), March 23, 1895; *Palm Beach Daily News*, March 7, 1903.
13. Nelson Jordan, *The Northside: African Americans and the Creation of Atlantic City* (Medford, N.J.: Plexus, 2010), 38. Comparative census data from earlier in the nineteenth century is not available.
14. E. A. Maccannon, *Commanders of the Dining Room: Biographic Sketches and Portraits of Successful Head Waiters* (New York: Gwendolyn Publishing Co., 1904), 12.
15. *St. Augustine Record*, April 12, 1900.
16. For relevant discussions of social Darwinism and race relations, see Tiffany Jones Miller, "Progressivism, Race, and the Training Wheels of Freedom," *National Review*, November 14, 2011, www.nationalreview.com/articles/283075/progressivism-race-and-training-wheels-freedom-tiffany-jones-miller?pg+1 (accessed November 14, 2011); Armstead, *"Lord, Please Don't Take Me in August,"* 102–3; and Mary Cable, *Top Drawer: American High Society from the Gilded Age to the Roaring Twenties* (New York: Atheneum, 1984), 166–67.
17. Goins, *American Colored Waiter*, 15.
18. Maccannon, *Commanders of the Dining Room*, 10.
19. *Tatler of Society in Florida*, January 19, 1901.
20. Ibid., March 21, 1896.
21. Ibid., March 6, 1897.
22. Ibid., March 2, 1901.
23. *St. Augustine Record*, February 27 and 28, 1901.
24. *Tatler of Society in Florida*, March 25, 1902.
25. Ibid., February 23, 1901.
26. Quoted in Jerry E. Patterson, *The Best Families: The Town and Country Social Directory, 1846–1996*, ed. Anthony T. Mazzola and Frank Zachary (New York: Harry N. Abrams in association with Hearst Magazines, 1996), 52.
27. *Tatler of Society in Florida*, March 22, 1901; *Palm Beach News*, March 21, 1902.

28. Quoted in Stearns and Stearns, *Jazz Dance*, 122–23. By 1896, Walker and Williams garnished widespread acclaim as cakewalkers during their forty-week engagement at Koster and Bial's variety theatre in New York City. Their performance in the 1903 London run of the musical *In Dahomey* initiated an international dance craze for the cakewalk.
29. *Tatler of Society in Florida*, March 5, 1898.
30. This association appears to have been relatively short-lived, most likely dissolving as other unions and organizations arose for hospitality workers.
31. "The Waiter," *Freeman*, April 13, 1901. "The Waiter" column was typically written or compiled by W. Forrest Cozart.
32. "The Leading Headwaiters," *Freeman*, December 27, 1902; "The Waiter," ibid., January 24, 1903.
33. "The Waiter," ibid., April 7, 1900.
34. Thomas L. Morgan and William Barlow, *From Cakewalks to Concert Halls: An Illustrated History of African American Popular Music from 1895 to 1930* (Washington, D.C.: Elliott and Clark, 1992), 49–56.
35. Brooke Baldwin, "The Cakewalk: A Study in Stereotype and Reality," *Journal of Social History* 15 (Winter 1981): 211.
36. Ibid., 215.
37. *St. Augustine Record*, March 13, 1901.
38. LeRoi Jones, *Blues People: Negro Music in White America* (New York: William Morrow, 1963), 86.
39. Armstead, *"Lord, Please Don't Take Me in August,"* 135.
40. "Great Cakewalk, Church Work—Suicide by a Woman for Unrequited Love," *Freeman*, May 30, 1891.
41. *Tatler of Society in Florida*, March 5, 1892.
42. Brown, *Babylon Girls*, 138.
43. *Tatler of Society in Florida*, March 14, 1903.
44. Ibid., February 4 and 11, 1905.
45. *Palm Beach Life*, February 8, 1929, 8. These outdoor cakewalks in Cocoanut Grove began during the 1903 winter season (*Palm Beach Daily News*, February 11, 1903).
46. James Weldon Johnson, *The Autobiography of an Ex-Coloured Man*, introduction by Henry Louis Gates Jr. (New York: Vintage Books, 1989), 87–88.

Part Three

Myth, Memory, and Manifestation: The Work of the Public Mind

The essays in this section add further complexity to the consideration of work and theatre, situating theatre itself as the "work of the public mind." These essays seek connections between the work of art and larger ideological narratives of cultural, political, and historical identity. How might works of art and the process of imagining those works factor into the public imagining of identity and history? How might history itself become a work of art? What role does theatre play in the outside world? Elizabeth Reitz Mullenix, AnnMarie T. Saunders, and Rosemarie K. Bank trouble these complex negotiations of personal, communal, and national identity. Whether exploring the intricate ramifications of Dion Boucicault's *The Octoroon* in its contemporaneous political moment, detailing the sometimes ridiculously complex process of attempting to bring a national theatre to life in an emerging nation, or investigating performances of cultural workers in Chicago's Columbian Exposition of 1893, their work bridges the gaps between politics, dramatic literature, performance, geography, and culture. By probing the ways that people of the past have used theatre and performance to make myth manifest, Mullenix, Saunders, and Bank unite theatre, work, and the process of imagining a new nation. Their readings expand the ways scholars can write about theatre and work.

9. Dion Boucicault's *The Octoroon* and the Work of Republicanism

Elizabeth Reitz Mullenix

Nineteenth-century playwright Dion Boucicault's melodrama *The Octoroon; or Life in Louisiana* invited a great deal of press when it was written in 1859 and still garners perhaps more critical interest than other antebellum dramatic texts. While most nineteenth-century American melodrama resides in obscurity within dusty reels of microfilm, Boucicault's play is anthologized and frequently makes its way into twenty-first-century college syllabi.[1] Students and scholars of *The Octoroon*—both past and present—seem to think they understand how this play works and acknowledge Boucicault's clever way of dodging the critical issue of abolition just days after John Brown's execution and months before Abraham Lincoln's election as the first Republican president of the United States. Much ink has been spilled by historians who describe the playwright's Barnumesque strategies, including his way of introducing a controversial topic in order to lure patrons to the theatre without rendering a discernible political opinion and his careful attempt to refrain from disparaging southern institutions even as he laments the difficulties associated with slavery.

Indeed, it appears that we have figured out Boucicault's strategy. Despite the difficulty in determining whether or not this play was working for northern antislavery factions or for the southern-sympathizing Copperheads of New York—which included the city's new mayor Fernando Wood, elected to office on the same day the play opened, December 6, 1859[2]—it is easy to see that Boucicault *worked* to construct an ambivalent dramatic and performance text for his audience at the Winter Garden in New York. His attempt to flummox critics and theatregoers alike was simply an example of a successful playwright at work, his job being—qua the ancient Horace—to instruct (on a significant topical issue, slavery) and to entertain (through popular melodrama and controversial subject matter) and to make money in the meantime by writing a politically charged play on the eve of the Civil War.

Prior to the opening of *The Octoroon* that winter in 1859, Sidney Kaplan reports that Boucicault supposedly urged the theatre's manager William Stuart to "work up the anti-slavery feeling of the community for the purpose of benefitting the run of the piece."[3] Though I have discovered no evidence of this in my own research, if such a plan was designed, it was successful. As soon as the play opened, the proslavery press was incensed: the Democratic *New York Herald* found the play criminal—"calumnious"—and the *Spirit of the Times* categorized the drama as a sensation piece, "disgusting" and "poisonous." Indeed James Gordon Bennett, editor of the *Herald*, asked that it be immediately removed from the boards, for the result of introducing texts like *The Octoroon* "will inevitably be disunion and civil war."[4] Boucicault took offense at Bennett's fighting words and, in a letter to the editor published in the *Herald* the morning after the melodrama's premiere, declared, "I believe the drama to be a proper and very effective instrument to use in the dissection of all social matters. The Greeks thought so, who founded it; Molière thought so when he wrote *Tartuffe*; and a very humble follower of theirs thinks so too."[5] Even the *New York Times*, a moderate sheet relative to the proslavery *Herald* and the abolitionist *Tribune*, called the play a "formidable political engine" and commended "the matter to those 'geese of the Capitol,' the Presidential organs here and at Washington. It demands their prompt attention."[6]

Six days after *The Octoroon* opened, Boucicault, seemingly rattled by southern vitriol, filed a complaint with the U.S. circuit court against Stuart, who proceeded to produce the play even after Boucicault secured a copyright and requested termination of the piece. The playwright argued that his wife, Agnes Robertson, who played the titular octoroon, Zoe, was receiving death threats. In his biography of Boucicault, Richard Fawkes claims that Boucicault "knew exactly what he was doing when he wrote the play" and purposefully balanced northern and southern positions on slavery. "The day before the play opened (four days after John Brown had been hanged, and not the same day as Boucicault later claimed), Agnes [. . .] received an anonymous letter saying that if she went ahead with the performance she would be shot. In all probability the letter was written by her husband, but its mere existence enabled Boucicault to gain column inches of free publicity."[7] In his claim, Boucicault professed neutrality, stating that *The Octoroon* presented the social conditions of slavery "as fact," rendering the subject for dramatic effect and topical interest rather than for targeted political debate. It was the public and the press, he insisted, "to the chagrin and disappointment of the plaintiff," who were bent on assigning the play partisan significance. According to the playwright, the controversy was unwelcome and inspired him to ask for the revocation of the production at the Winter Garden.[8] Despite Boucicault's published statement, New York audiences continued to read the play as political. The *Times* critic wrote,

> Everybody talks about the "Octoroon," wonders about the "Octoroon," goes to see the "Octoroon"; and thus the "Octoroon" becomes, in point of fact, the work of the public mind [. . .]. Still, the public having insisted in rewriting the piece according to its own notions [. . .] the "Octoroon" may prove after all to be a political treatise of great emphasis and significance, very much to the author's amazement.[9]

Considering the charged political climate of 1859, it is no surprise that the public became so fixed upon this melodrama in this historical moment, working out the play's meaning in light of intensifying political convictions. Though we might think the playwright protested too much (thus likely scripting the controversy that followed), Boucicault introduced this hot-button issue, either deliberately or naively, then stood back and let the people and the pundits do the rest.

When I began my research on this play, I was interested in the way that Boucicault intentionally worked this sectional line at a time of unprecedented national crisis.[10] I saw the play's calculated ambivalence as not just a shrewd equivocation but as a symptom of national crisis, as I have examined in previous work the idea that performance texts become permeable and seemingly open during historical moments that are marked by radical ideological shifts.[11] However, the more I studied the play, the more I became convinced that the text was working toward another purpose, that it was indeed a "formidable political engine" and that a select public was "rewriting" the piece in order to serve an emerging and urgent Republican Party prior to the election of Lincoln in 1860.

As noted by American studies scholar Bluford Adams, "What made Boucicault's play controversial was not so much the content as the timing."[12] Because the play premiered just days after John Brown's hanging, contemporary audiences and critics read the performance text within the context of insurrection, and, argues Adams, Boucicault benefited from such a reading. Indeed, the events of October 16, 1859, were well known by New York audiences: John Brown (also known as Osawatomie Brown for his bloody escapades fighting slavery near Osawatomie, Kansas, in the mid-1850s) and a small band of diverse "soldiers" seized the federal arsenal in Harpers Ferry, Virginia, in the hopes of arming uprising slaves, who would join Brown and his men in hiding along the two-thousand-mile mountain range that stretched from the North to the Deep South; from this highland base, Brown's men would enact hit-and-run liberation raids, creating a widespread southern panic that would somehow imperil the future of slavery.

Adams argues that John Brown—heralded as both martyr and madman in the wake of his infamous raid, well-publicized trial, and subsequent hanging—was recognized by audiences in Boucicault's character of the stage Yankee, Salem Scudder. Despite the fact that Scudder "devotes himself to saving the fortunes of his slaveholding employers, rather than to freeing their slaves," explains Adams, throughout the play the Yankee "echoes the combination of moral vigilantism, racial paternalism, and insurrection with which Brown was synonymous."[13] The *Herald*, bent on vilifying Boucicault for introducing a subject that would fan the flame of sectionalism, compared the playwright to James Redpath, Brown's sycophantic abolitionist biographer, and Scudder to Captain Brown: "an exaggerated delineation intended to pander to those fanatical passions which brought John Brown and his unhappy associates to the gallows."[14] Both the *New York Evening Post* and the *Spirit of the Times* carried a story in mid-December titled "John Brown on the Stage," a slanderous review of *The Octoroon* that noted the play's dangerous "revolutionary sentiment"; questioned the critic, "Of what use to pass resolutions against John Brown and servile insurrection, when audiences nightly applaud a slaver-girl for exclaiming, 'I go to a land where there is *no* law, only *justice*?' Is there not 'mutiny and rage' here?"[15] Adams argues that Boucicault's interest in drawing similarities between Scudder and Brown was a marketing strategy and that the playwright wove together fictional accounts and front-page news stories to help him construct his character.[16]

While the comparison between Brown and Scudder is apt, no critic, past or present, explores the implications of this association. In his book *The Haunted Stage: The Theatre as Memory Machine*, Marvin Carlson discusses the intertextuality of the actor's body on stage, a body that audiences "read" as text, bringing to their reception the memory of previous theatrical "ghosts." Carlson argues, "Ghosting presents the identical thing they have encountered before, although now in a somewhat different context." For Carlson, the haunted body of an actor might include the recognition of a particular type of role in a performer's characterization, including the popular stage Yankee type; the "Yankee, like the *commedia* mask, was particularly associated with certain actors [. . . and] possessed certain general qualities."[17] Significantly, the actor who played Salem Scudder in the 1859 Winter Garden production was Joseph Jefferson III, a performer well known for his Yankee delineations in the nineteenth century. Jefferson, who would go on to be most famous for a stage adaptation of Washington Irving's Rip Van Winkle—arguably a prototypic Yankee—was celebrated for his representations of several Yankees (including an early Rip) prior to 1859. In a review of *The Octoroon* on December 8, the *New York Times* critic wrote:

> Mr. Jefferson's new parts will always bear commendation; no artist, comic or serious, has such a range of individuality, or such a varied style of interpreting it. [. . .] The Yankee being nevertheless his specialty, Mr. Boucicault has of course measured him for it, and the fit was pronounced perfect. In all the broader phases of the character Mr. Jefferson brought down the house with abundant laughter, and in the sadder ones achieved the greater triumph of true and earnest pathos. He has undoubtedly added a new part to his already extensive catalogue.[18]

Because the stage Yankee was Jefferson's "specialty," as the critic notes above, it is likely that his performances of Scudder were ghosted by other stage Yankees. It is also possible that Jefferson's Scudder was haunted by real-life Yankee John Brown, as Adams and contemporary critics suggest. According to Carlson, media images of an actor's other roles (or other important stage representations) can also affect his or her work, creating a body that is haunted by an amalgam of roles that were not necessarily "identical" to the role the actor portrays at any given moment.[19] While Carlson does not entertain the possibility of other types of media images contributing to a haunted body, I would argue that the construction of a cultural icon in the popular consciousness that was as profoundly influential as John Brown—arguably an important catalyst for the Civil War—was a specter indeed. And while theatrical Yankees were not insurrectionists, they were often outlaws in a sense, using their folksy good nature and common sense to challenge mainstream viewpoints or to question dominant ideology.

The thought of Salem Scudder *as* John Brown is a compelling idea, and one not simply borne out of the anxiety of a proslavery press looking for excuses to pan Boucicault's play. Certainly these unlikely heroes shared many qualities: both lived in Massachusetts (which in December 1859 was code for abolitionist); both were tall, rugged, and willowy; both were comfortable expressing open affection for their friends of color; and both were advocates of higher law theory. A concept popularized by New York senator and future secretary of state William Seward, higher law theory maintained that American law was no longer just, because it sanctioned slavery. Rather, advocates like Seward and Brown urged the conscientious citizen to look instead to God's law or a "higher" morality. Thus physically and ideologically Brown and Scudder were similar in many ways, but as workers they had even more in common. Brown, successful only as a warrior against slavery, failed in all lines of work he embraced; after years of laboring as a tanner, wool merchant, cattle tradesman, land surveyor, and businessman, Brown barely made enough money to feed his family and even in jail was writing letters to patrons asking for funds to support his starving flock. Similarly, Boucicault describes Scudder as "a Yankee from Massachusetts, now Overseer of Terrebonne, great on improvements and inventions, once a Photographic Operator, and been a little of everything generally."[20] Scudder himself laments that all his various efforts and failed inventions have only contributed to Terrebonne's financial ruin.

If John Brown were indeed being ghosted in the character of Salem Scudder, this might simply be another example of how the stage Yankee often becomes a barometer of public sentiment in abolitionist drama: Gumption Cute in George Aiken's 1852 stage adaptation of *Uncle Tom's Cabin* is a filibusterer and a racist, introduced in this compromise text, along with minstrel tunes, as an ameliorating balance to Harriet Beecher Stowe's antislavery message;[21] Penetrate Partyside, the Yankee in H. J. Conway's 1853 version of *Uncle Tom's Cabin*, who always "sees both sides of the question," speaks openly about compromise politics (the idea that northern and southern interests should be balanced by legislators); Cipher Cute in Conway's 1856 revision of Stowe's second antislavery novel, *Dred*, "studies law but practices justice" like Seward, arguably his own ghost; and finally Jeptha, a female Yankee and a Republican in Kate Edwards Swayze's 1859 *Ossawattomie Brown; or, the Insurrection at Harpers' Ferry*, a play that ran concurrently with *The Octoroon*, who serves as the playwright's mouthpiece.[22] Scudder, of course, is next in this lineup—a representation of John Brown. Yet if Salem Scudder is John Brown, John Brown is an overseer. An overseer? Significantly, scholars and critics who hint at this ghosting do not unpack this extraordinary paradox, perhaps assuming that Scudder's identity as a worker mitigated any connections to abolitionism an audience might glean and thus contributed to the play's ambivalence.

Exploring the profession of overseeing, however, is informative indeed. Even northern audiences in 1859 might have thought themselves quite knowledgeable about this line of work, as Frederick Douglass's autobiography, *Narrative of the Life of Frederick Douglass*, was published in 1845 and sold almost thirty thousand copies by 1860. The former slave describes this occupation:

> I speak of overseers as a class, for they were such. They were as distinct from the slaveholding gentry of the south as are the fish-women of Paris, and the coal-heavers of London, distinct from other grades of society. They constituted a separate fraternity at the south. They were arranged and classified by that great law of attraction which determines the sphere and affinities of men; which ordains that men whose malign and brutal propensities preponderate over their moral and intellectual endowments shall naturally fall into those employments which promise the largest gratification to those predominating instincts or propensities. The office of overseer took this raw material of vulgarity and brutality, and stamped it as a distinct class in southern life.[23]

Not only does Scudder not fit this description, but the audience never once sees the character engaged in the work of overseeing. He has no whip, no brand; he does not leer or lust; he expresses only tenderness and sympathy toward slave characters and toward the Choctaw, Wah-notee.[24] Rather, the work done by Salem Scudder is the work of a politician: he talks and charms, campaigns for causes that he sees as just, and inspires others to follow his lead through passionate and eloquent public speeches. If New Yorkers glimpsed John Brown in Salem Scudder, they saw a Republican Yankee who functioned more as a lawyer/politician (in a kangaroo court) than as a plantation overseer.

In December 1859, in addition to the execution of Brown and the simultaneous productions of *The Octoroon* and Swayze's *Ossawattomie Brown*, William Lloyd Garrison's abolitionist newspaper the *National Era* printed the new platform of the Republican Party in its entirety, and big-city dailies in New York regularly reported on party politics. The Republicans, hoping to gain votes from various constituencies prior to the election in 1860—including Boucicault's Irish immigrant population of New York[25]—cast a wide net, fishing for former southern Whigs and northern Democrats, Free Soilers and Know-Nothings.[26] They were opposed to the expansion of slavery into the territories but were not advocates of abolition, which they, like the Democratic opposition, regarded as an extreme doctrine. Republicans such as Lincoln and Seward also condemned the Kansas-Nebraska Act of 1854, which allowed residents of those western territories to decide the slavery question through popular sovereignty rather than to follow the Missouri Compromise of 1820. Thus, the Republicans were moderates and non-expansionists—proponents of a compromise ideology for the late 1850s. They believed in an idealistic higher law philosophy that read slavery out of the Constitution but were adamantly against all forms of violence that would be needed to bring it to an abrupt end. The Republican stance on John Brown was, as historian David Reynolds notes, "to admire the man but not the deed."[27]

Both higher law and violence are evident in the final acts of *The Octoroon*. As a lynch mob assembles to kill Wah-notee for supposedly murdering the slave boy Paul, Scudder appeals to the better angels of their nature:

> This lynch law is a wild and lawless proceeding. Here's a pictur' for a civilized community to afford; yonder, a poor ignorant savage, and round him a circle of hearts, white with revenge and hate, thirsting for his blood: you call yourselves judges—you ain't—you're a jury of executioners. It is such scenes as these that bring disgrace on our Western life. [. . .] Fellow-citizens, you are convened and assembled here under a higher power than the law. What's the law? When the ship's abroad on the ocean—when the army is before the enemy—where in thunder's the law? It is in the hearts of brave men who can tell right from wrong, and from whom justice can't be bought. So it is here, in the wilds of the West, where our hatred of crime is measured by the speed of our executions—where necessity is law![28]

Immediately after this speech, Wah-notee is exonerated as a photograph is discovered convicting McClosky of murder. The *law* prevails and the villain is not lynched but taken off to the steamboat, which will take him to jail. McClosky sets fire to the boat and escapes but is hunted by Wah-notee, who enacts *justice* by killing him. Prior to McClosky's death, however, there is a final scene in which he appeals to the lawyer/politician Scudder, as Wah-notee tracks him through the night. In response to the villain's appeal, "You are a white man; you'll not leave one of your own blood to be butchered by the red-skin," Scudder replies,

> Here we are on the selvage of civilization. It ain't our side, I believe, rightly; but Nature has said that where man sets his foot, the red man and the black man shall up sticks and stand around. But what do we pay for that possession? In cash? No—in kind—that is, in protection, forbearance, gentleness, in all them goods that show the critters the difference between the Christian and the savage. [. . .] You have been tried—honestly tried and convicted. Providence has chosen your executioner. I shan't interfere.[29]

Several ideas in these scenes are striking relative to thinking about theatre as the "work of the public mind."

Scudder makes reference to life in Louisiana as "our Western life," "the wilds of the West," and "the selvage of civilization." As Joseph Roach points out, "In the mouth of Salem Scudder, a homespun character in the Anglo-American tradition of Yankee Jonathan, the word *selvage* does a lot of work in Boucicault's play. It literally means the edge of a fabric woven thickly so that it will not ravel. It more figuratively suggests a margin, a boundary, or a perimeter that by opposition defines the center—in short, the frontier."[30] For Roach, this frontier is plural and one that invites multiple encounters, the "paradigm of creolized interculture on the Caribbean model." But what if this frontier were also—or instead, or simultaneously—Kansas: the bleeding edge of a country locked in mortal combat over popular sovereignty, the borderland of a nation on the brink of war, the territory where John Brown lived and fought between 1855 and 1856, and where he and his sons hacked five proslavery men to death with broadswords? What if the reference to the "wilds of the West" evoked for audiences an association with the vigilante Osawatomie Brown, a household name and front-page story in the late 1850s?[31]

Furthermore, Scudder, like Brown and Seward, is a proponent of the higher law. Both Adams and Gary A. Richardson, in his essay "Boucicault's *The Octoroon* and American Law," support this idea. Richardson argues that Boucicault was indicting American law as unjust by depicting Zoe, the heroine, being sold to the villain; she must kill herself so as not to suffer rape and oppression at the hands of the sexual predator McClosky. Stowe makes a similar point in her first two antislavery novels, *Uncle Tom's Cabin* and *Dred*, noting that slaves are mistreated because the law is unjust, not because they have a "good" master or a "bad" master. In short, the law sanctions unjust practices, as Zoe's fate makes clear. The higher law seems to render "justice" in McClosky's case but not in Zoe's, for with her death, the law can no longer produce justice: "Indeed, justice, and its attempted practical application, law, have become by the end of the play the center of attention. The deaths of Zoe and M'Closky, which close the drama, are not only the consequences of conflicting definitions of justice, but also representations of the inadequacy of law to deal with fundamental human impulses which are not based on reason."[32] For while Scudder/Brown advocates an American heart "bustin' up with freedom, truth, and right," he does not engage in the violence necessary to engender justice but leaves that to the noble savage. Perhaps this separation of law from justice allows Scudder to be Brown in a way that is politic, that allows audiences to "admire the man but not the deed," effectively mirroring contemporaneous Republican doctrine. And yet we are happy for Wah-notee's deed. Audiences of melodrama want to see justice rendered, just as Brown's more extreme fans (Henry David Thoreau and Ralph Waldo Emerson among them) lionized him as a martyr for his savage deeds, and his prophetic note from the gallows made clear that "the crimes of this guilty land will never be purged away but with Blood."[33] By engaging in the work of law and justice rather than in the brutal business of overseeing, Scudder performs a role that allows the audience to see him as Brown and yet not as Brown—a John Brown whose politics were just, even if his work was outside the law.

Is it plausible that Dion Boucicault, an "out" nonpartisan, was a closet Republican? That he, like Kate Edwards Swayze, was attempting to recoup John Brown to help an embryonic Republican Party bent on spinning Brown's life and works so as to avoid associations with fanaticism? According to his biographer Richard Fawkes, Boucicault was against slavery. A letter in the London *Times* in 1861—written by the playwright to respond to British requests for an alternative ending for *The Octoroon*—proves, in fact, that he saw the play as an indictment of American law, which failed to produce justice.[34] Boucicault notes that "there are features in slavery far more objectionable than any of those hitherto held up to human execration, by the side of which physical suffering appears as a vulgar detail. Some of these features are, for the first time, boldly exhibited in *The Octoroon*."[35] As Richardson explains, "The aspect of slavery which Boucicault found most 'objectionable' was that it was an institution, an injustice that American society sanctioned by law."[36] This was, again, Stowe's point exactly and a central tenet of the Republican platform, thus providing the rationale to prohibit slavery's further expansion into the territories.

Furthermore, Boucicault socialized regularly with important Republicans—Emerson, Oliver Wendell Holmes, William Cullen Bryant—all members of the New York City Sketch Club, which met biweekly throughout the 1850s. *The Octoroon* was also compared on several occasions to Hinton Rowan Helper's *The Impending Crisis of the South*, a popular and controversial book that condemned slavery from a southerner's perspective. A correspondent for the *New York Herald* wrote,

> The stage is an institution of great influence for good or evil. It is a school of instruction in which susceptible youth are liable to be deeply impressed with the most erroneous views of men and things. "The Octoroon" is more pernicious than "Uncle Tom's Cabin," and would do more mischief than "Helper's Impending Crisis" were its representation capable of being multiplied like copies of the book.

Helper, a white supremacist, opposed slavery despite his own personal bigotry because he felt that the slavery system had a detrimental economic effect on the South and inhibited the progress of industry. His book was appropriated by the Republican Party, which decided to use it as campaign literature in December 1859, the very month that Brown was hanged and *The Octoroon*'s run began.[37]

Perhaps it was Boucicault's evasive *performance*, his calculated ambivalence, and not the play's content that attracted audiences to the theatre. Certainly *The Octoroon* became a hit while Swayze's play about Brown survived only four performances and other abolitionist dramas of the late 1850s such as *Dred* and the New York production of John Townsend Trowbridge's *Neighbor Jackwood* also experienced short runs. By seeming to support "both sides of the question," a tactic used by earlier adaptors like Aiken and Conway, Boucicault provided fuel for his "formidable political engine." Indeed, because everyone was talking about, wondering about, and going to see *The Octoroon*, the emerging Republican Party had an opportunity to do some important recovery work regarding the catalytic actions of John Brown. And shortly after the opening of *The Octoroon* in New York, yet another tall, rugged, willowy Yankee employed similar recuperative strategies; on February 27, 1860, Abraham Lincoln gave an important speech about John Brown at the Cooper Institute, an impassioned performance that historians believe secured his presidency.

Notes

1. *The Octoroon* is included in the twentieth anniversary edition of *The Wadsworth Anthology of Drama*, ed. W. B. Worthen (Boston: Wadsworth Cengage Learning, 2011), 1141–63. See also *The Broadview Anthology of British Literature*, ed. Joseph Black et al. (Buffalo, N.Y.: Broadview Press, 2012), 443–51; *The Longman Anthology of American Drama*, ed. Lee A. Jacobus (New York: Longman, 1982); *The Meridian Anthology of 18th- and 19th-Century British Drama*, ed. Katharine M. Rogers (New York: Meridian/Penguin, 1979); and *Early American Drama*, ed. Jeffrey H. Richards (New York: Penguin Books, 1997), 444–94.
2. *New York Herald*, December 7, 1859, 4. Wood, a Democrat and Unionist, sympathized with the South, knowing that the cotton industry was critically important to the city's economic health, and even proposed New York's secession in 1861 after Lincoln's election threatened relations with the South.
3. Sidney Kaplan quotes this in his essay "*The Octoroon*: Early History of the Drama of Miscegenation" (*Journal of Negro Education* 20, no. 4 [Autumn 1951]: 548) but provides no reference. I have not discovered this quote in any contemporary newspapers or in biographies of Boucicault. It is indeed

evident that the audience was "worked up," but whether or not this was deliberately done by Stuart is difficult to ascertain.

4. "Anti-Slavery Theatres and Literatures," *New York Herald*, December 9, 1859, 6; "'The Octoroon': A Disgrace to the North, a Libel on the South," *Spirit of the Times* 29, no. 45 (December 17, 1859): 529; *New York Herald*, December 5, 1859, 6.
5. *New York Herald*, December 7, 1859, 5.
6. "The Octoroon," *New York Times*, December 15, 1859, 4.
7. *New York Times*, December 16, 1859, 8; Richard Fawkes, *Dion Boucicault: A Biography* (New York: Quartet Books, 1979), 107.
8. "'The Octoroon' Copyright," *New York Times*, December 20, 1859, 2. The *Herald* also republished the complaint.
9. "The Octoroon," *New York Times*, December 15, 1859, 4.
10. Sectionalism, the condition of having an allegiance to one's own part of the country, was a common term in the 1850s because former political parties like the Whigs and the Democrats were breaking down or redefining themselves based on the politics of region, specifically concerning issues surrounding slavery. Sectional fealties began to trump former ties to a political party, so, for example, northern Democrats would have more in common with members of the Free Soil Party than they would with members of the southern Democratic Party.
11. I use Mikhail Bakhtin's theory of the grotesque and carnival ambivalence—the symbolic emergence in culture of one thing and its opposite—as a way of exploring textual instability during times of crisis. See my essays "From Carnival to Myth: Performing Nationhood in Pre–Civil War New York," *Journal of Dramatic Theory and Criticism* 18, no. 1 (Fall 2003): 29–43, and "Yankee Doodle Dixie: Performing Nationhood on the Eve of War," *Journal of American Drama and Theatre* 18, no. 3 (Fall 2006): 33–54.
12. Bluford Adams, *E Pluribus Barnum: The Great Showman and the Making of U.S. Popular Culture* (Minneapolis: University of Minnesota Press, 1997), 148.
13. Ibid., 151.
14. "Anti-Slavery Theatres and Literatures," *New York Herald*, December 9, 1859, 6. James Redpath's *The Public Life of Captain John Brown* was published in 1860 and thus too late to influence audiences watching the play in December 1859. As Redpath traveled with Brown in 1856, however, he had sent dispatches back from Kansas that were published in the *New York Tribune*, the *Chicago Tribune*, and the *St. Louis Democrat*. He also started his own Kansas newspaper, *Crusader of Freedom*, to ensure that his stories would be accessible to Kansans. Because of this regular reporting from

what was at that time the front line of an imminent civil war, audiences would have been familiar with Redpath's "fanatical" politics as a radical abolitionist and supporter of John Brown.

15. "John Brown on Stage," *New York Evening Post*, reprinted in the *Spirit of the Times* 29, no. 45 (December 17, 1859): 529. The critic quotes Shakespeare's *Julius Caesar*, act 3, scene 2.
16. Adams, *E Pluribus Barnum*, 150.
17. Marvin Carlson, *The Haunted Stage: The Theatre as Memory Machine* (Ann Arbor: University of Michigan Press, 2005), 5–7, 63.
18. "The Octoroon," *New York Times*, December 8, 1859, 1. The critic refers to other Yankee roles: Caleb Plummer from an adaptation of Dickens's *The Cricket on the Hearth* and Newman Noggs from Dickens's *Nicholas Nickleby*.
19. Carlson, *Haunted Stage*, 67–68.
20. Dion Boucicault, *The Octoroon; or Life in Louisiana*, in *Nineteenth-Century American Plays*, ed. Myron Matlaw (New York: Applause, 1985), 100.
21. The Compromise of 1850 was a political measure introduced by Congress to stave off civil war because of the increased debate about slavery. This legislation contained elements that appealed to both the North and the South (California entered the Union as a free state, but a stricter Fugitive Slave Law was imposed) and thus allowed lawmakers to compromise. Striking this balance, attempting to give each side something that it wanted with regard to the slavery debate, was referred to as compromise politics in the 1850s.
22. I argue in my upcoming book that Jeptha is a deliberately constructed Republican *raisonneur* and that her rhetoric attempts to recoup the controversial actions of John Brown for a burgeoning Republican Party as Kate Edwards Swayze and her husband, Jason Clarke Swayze, were both politically aligned with the new Republican Party. Swayze's play—which ran simultaneously with *The Octoroon*—was only on the boards for a handful of performances. For texts of these stage adaptations of *Uncle Tom's Cabin*, see the University of Virginia's excellent online archive at http://utc.iath.virginia.edu/. H. J. Conway's stage adaptation of *Dred: or the Tale of the Dismal Swamp* was published in New York in 1856 by Amerman Press. Swayze's play is anthologized in Walter Meserve and Mollie Meserve's *Fateful Lightning: America's Civil War Plays* (New York: Feedback Theatre Books, 2000). Please note that Swayze spells the Kansas town of Osawatomie as "Ossawattomie" in her play. I have chosen to use the correct spelling when referring to the place and her spelling when referring to the play's title.

23. Frederick Douglass, *Life and Times of Frederick Douglass*, 1881, electronic ed., http://docsouth.unc.edu/neh/douglasslife/douglass.html (University of North Carolina at Chapel Hill, 1999), 55–56. While Douglass writes of the overseer years after the audience viewing of *The Octoroon*, he describes a time in his life that would have been concurrent with the "work" of Salem Scudder.
24. In *Midnight Rising: John Brown and the Raid That Sparked the Civil War* (New York: Henry Holt, 2011), Tony Horowitz talks of Brown's friendship with Native Americans in Ohio during his youth. He writes that Brown had "a lifelong sympathy for natives that stood in stark contrast to the prevailing hostility of white Americans" (16).
25. For more information on Boucicault's relationship to the Irish immigrant population in New York City, see Deirdre McFeely's *Dion Boucicault: Irish Identity on Stage* (New York: Cambridge University Press, 2012), 14–21.
26. Political parties broke down in the 1850s and reemerged along regional lines—North and South—inspired by the slavery issue. Whigs were traditionally anti-slave as opposed to Democrats, who were typically proslave. The Free Soil Party was a single-issue party created in the late 1840s to campaign against the spread of slavery into the western territories. The Know-Nothing Movement was another political party that was born in the 1840s but declined in 1855. Like other parties, it was bitterly divided over slavery.
27. David Reynolds, *John Brown, Abolitionist: The Man Who Killed Slavery, Sparked the Civil War, and Seeded Civil Rights* (New York: Vintage Books, 2005), 425.
28. Boucicault, *Octoroon*, 141.
29. Ibid., 147.
30. Joseph Roach, "Mardi Gras Indians and Others: Genealogies of American Performance," *Theatre Journal* 44, no. 4 (December 1992): 461.
31. Bluford Adams supports this idea, stating, "In the wake of Harper's Ferry [. . .] Boucicault's audience may also have heard an allusion to John Brown's Western exploits." Adams, *E Pluribus Barnum*, 151.
32. Gary A. Richardson, "Boucicault's *The Octoroon* and American Law," *Theatre Journal* 34, no. 2 (May 1982): 159.
33. Boucicault, *Octoroon*, 141; Horowitz, *Midnight Rising*, 256.
34. In England the play was produced with an alternative ending in which Zoe lives and she and George are married. If Boucicault, through his original tragic ending, was indicting American law, as Richardson argues, changing the ending for a British audience was unproblematic for slavery as the institution did not exist in Britain; the English audience did not require schooling about the horrors of slavery.

35. *Times*, November 20, 1861, 5.
36. Richardson, "Boucicault's *The Octoroon*," 158.
37. "Anti-Slavery Theatres and Literatures," *New York Herald*, December 9, 1859, 6. See also http://www.northcarolinahistory.org/commentary/345/entry.

10. Myth Made Manifest: Labor, Landscape, and the First Washington Theatre

AnnMarie T. Saunders

On a June day in 1803, "a number of respectable gentlemen, citizens of Washington," gathered at Morin's Tavern on the south side of Pennsylvania Avenue in the new capital of the United States of America.[1] At that time, the view across the broad avenue that stretched from the President's House to the Capitol (both unfinished) included only a handful of buildings. Most of the would-be metropolis remained a tree-filled countryside, exhibiting more the pastoral beauty that had so captivated the city's namesake than the majestic urban plan designed by Peter Charles L'Enfant.[2] When the time arrived, a band led the group in a procession over the short distance down the avenue to the site of the soon-to-be Washington Theatre. Major John P. Van Ness, as chair of the theatre committee, spoke briefly to the crowd before ceremoniously laying the cornerstone for what would be Washington's first purpose-built playhouse.

Laying a cornerstone is a symbolic act but one that reflects the actual physical labor of the building process; the ceremony is both a celebration and a promise of work to come. Poised on the border between the ideal and the reality, the theatre founders presented their future playhouse to the citizens of Washington as "an object which may conduce materially to the advantage of the city," as one newspaper advertisement declaimed.[3] The formality of the ceremony in Washington, at least as it was described in print, stood in sharp contrast to the rural surroundings. Congress's arrival in the new American capital at the end of 1800 had done little to hasten the city's progress to becoming the manifestation of freedom and democracy intended by the capital's planners. The theatre founders saw building a playhouse as a way to improve the city, to put Washington (and thus America) on par with the capitals of Europe, and to participate in manifesting the myth of America.

Constructing a playhouse on the unstable foundations of the newly created American capital was arduous labor to say the least. Funds and interest had to be raised, plans drawn, land procured, walls framed, and bricks laid. Carpenters, plasterers, financiers, and organizers worked together to create a space for performance and to give a home to the institution of theatre. Often in theatre histories, this fundamental labor is overlooked in favor of focus on the plays and the players. Many scholars have turned to dramatic literature for evidence of an emerging American national identity. However, perhaps a more illuminating approach is to look at the act of constructing a playhouse and the placement of that playhouse within the urban landscape as suggestive of regional and, especially in the case of Washington, D.C., national identity creation. The era's conception of American identity was implicated in a complex project that simultaneously invoked and rejected European precedents. This ambivalence is evident in the creation of the Washington playhouse. On the one hand, theatre proponents in Washington desired to establish a European lineage in which American cultural institutions could be seen as operating on par with their Old World counterparts. Yet the founders also worked to create a theatre community that rejected elitist models in favor of institutional processes inspired by democratic idealism. The labor done by moneyed men and manual laborers alike turned the potential playhouse into an actuality—myth made manifest.

Expectations for the capital's first playhouse were high. Even in the earliest phases of the city's planning, theatre had been given a place of importance. City designer L'Enfant wrote to George Washington of his dreams for the grand avenues of the capital, describing "play houses, rooms of assembly, academies and all such sort of places" that would be "convenient to the whole city."[4] Such lofty expectations for the city and the institutions within its borders are important considerations in assessing and interpreting the construction of the Washington Theatre. The plans for the new capital were closely tied to a utopic vision for the future of the United States, a vision that influenced the debates in the 1780s over the site and function of the American capital as well as about the layout and design of the city. As that utopian ideal grew tangible in the form of a capital that the nation's leaders could create from the ground up, the proponents of the Washington playhouse imagined that theatre could be a part of that vision and instill audiences with Republican virtue and values.

Early in 1803, fewer than three years after the city officially became the nation's capital, Washington residents and nascent civic leaders Thomas

Law, Samuel Harrison Smith, John P. Van Ness, and brothers Robert and William Brent led a campaign to integrate theatre into the plan for the city by building a permanent playhouse. The proposal seemed to be enthusiastically received by other residents of the District; an Alexandria newspaper claimed that "one of the proposers actually obtained in less than 20 days subscriptions in shares of 50 dollars each, amounting to 7,500 dollars." One month later, a notice in the *National Intelligencer* announced that $10,000 had been raised for the project, almost the full cost of construction.[5]

Remarkably, shareholding in the playhouse was extended beyond the purses of the wealthy; early in the fund-raising process, the Washington Theatre Committee, made up of Law, Smith, Van Ness, the Brent brothers, and the other committed stockholders, encouraged subscriptions paid in trade, not just in cash. A newspaper announcement in July 1803 requested that "those subscribers to the Theatre who propose contributing work or materials" attend a meeting with the committee at a local hotel and tavern.[6] Painters, plasterers, bricklayers, men employed in hauling and carting, and tradesmen who supplied lumber, lime, and brick contributed to the construction of the Washington Theatre, trading their labor for shares in the playhouse.

This offer was quite unusual. Although other early American playhouses provided space for working people to attend performances—lower priced tickets for seats in the pit and later in the upper galleries—they were rarely offered ownership of the building. Playhouses were most often owned by theatre managers or by a group of wealthy investors, sometimes by a combination of the two.[7] The Washington Theatre created a different model of shareholding, one in which the public space of the playhouse could be possessed by a broader public. In creating a new model, the founders magnified the role that theatre could play in presenting American ideals. They wove democracy into their playhouse's foundation, expanding the ways in which theatre could manifest American identity beyond plays and playgoing to the building itself.

In reality, the founders of the first Washington theatre did not include *everyone* in their imagining of the public, no matter how high-minded their rhetoric. Although they claimed to represent "the citizens" of Washington, all the members of the theatre committee were white men, all owned property, and all held significant personal wealth.[8] They had extended ownership to other men, the tradesmen whose labor built the playhouse; however, their definition of citizenry likely did not include women, and it definitely did not include African Americans. Ownership of the space, even in the metaphorical sense, was limited by the societal conventions of the day.[9] Nevertheless, a theatre belonging to "the citizens" was an important part of the rhetoric of planning and promoting the playhouse; and in much the same way, it was part of the construction of the nation itself. The extension of ownership to laborers and tradesmen was a popular proposition. In the final tally, work and materials subscriptions were nearly equal to cash subscriptions.[10]

Once the initial assets were secured, the supporters directed their attention to the playhouse's location. The theatre committee first wrote to President Thomas Jefferson to request the use of public land for the playhouse.[11] Although they were privately financing the project, the playhouse founders viewed the theatre as a public institution. The theatre was for Washington—its citizens and visitors. Their request attests to their understanding of the government's role in managing key aspects of the city plan, including land use; and while they recognized Congress's authority over implementation of the plan, these men appreciated that development of projects that would serve the community would fall to their own purview and purses.[12] Although he seemed to support the playhouse project, Jefferson, who was still at Monticello, hesitated to alter the established city plan without conferring with the city commissioners in person.[13] Eager to begin the work, the founders sought additional prospects.

The committee then received two offers of property for the site of the future playhouse. Van Ness offered to donate a plot along Pennsylvania Avenue between the President's House and the Capitol, and prominent local landowner Daniel Carroll volunteered ground on the opposite side of Tiber Creek. Both among the early advocates of the theatre project, Van Ness and Carroll each owned substantial property in the District but offered particular plots for the theatre. According to the city plan, Carroll's lot would eventually be part of the core of the city once the Tiber was rerouted through a series of canals that would be filled in to form the long green space of the National Mall; however, in 1803, the canal system was barely begun and the wide creek remained with no convenient bridge across it.[14] The committee voted, not surprisingly, in favor of the Pennsylvania Avenue site.[15]

The location of theatres and other institutions within an urban plan can provide clues as to the values of the society that constructs and places them. In *Places of Performance: The Semiotics of Theatre Architecture*, Marvin Carlson argues that playhouses, when placed prominently within the city landscape, serve as "highly visible signs of civic dedication to the arts."[16] I would go one step further and assert that in the capital city, a prominently situated playhouse represents a national interest—or at least seeks to give the impression of such an interest. By building their theatre in the center of the city, the Washington Theatre proponents worked to place America's capital on par with cities such as London and Paris that enjoyed established theatre traditions and grand playhouses.

The site for the Washington Theatre was certainly conspicuous, situated almost directly between the city's two major landmarks, the Capitol and the President's House. At that time, apart from Pennsylvania Avenue, only a handful of roads had been completed of the dozens laid out in the urban plan. Rather than the intricate pattern of avenues and property squares devised by L'Enfant, the land remained covered with trees, rolling hills, and only the occasional building (figure 10.1). The sparseness of the landscape emphasized the structures that were placed upon it, even if such emphasis was unintentional. The significant placement of the playhouse primed the institution of theatre to play a significant role in the identity of the city.

With the site confirmed, the committee set to work hiring an architect and various craftsmen and soliciting additional subscriptions of money, labor, and materials. The initial announcement in March 1803 estimated that the playhouse would be ready by the end of the year, which was quite an ambitious goal. The foundation was poured at the end of May, and the cornerstone was laid June 24.[17] Throughout the summer, laborers cleared the lot and delivered construction supplies such as lime and brick. Records kept by Van Ness suggest that the first story was near completion in mid-August.[18]

Although no plans of the theatre have been recovered, by all accounts it was much smaller than those being built in established American cities such as Philadelphia, New York, and Charleston, accommodating fewer than seven hundred people.[19] The exterior of the theatre was likely made of brick, judging by the amount delivered to the building site. The interior walls were covered in plaster and painted and were described as drab and devoid of decoration. There were two to three tiers of box seating surrounding the pit. One review in the *National Intelligencer* described bare benches, awkwardly sized boxes, and poor ventilation, although the author did concede that the smallness of the space permitted better acoustics.[20] Tickets were priced at one dollar for box seats and seventy-five cents for the pit, indicating that the wealthier patrons inhabited the boxes.[21] This audience arrangement was common in American theatres in the late eighteenth and early nineteenth centuries; by midcentury the "parquet" had replaced the pit and galleries accommodated the working class and African Americans, reversing the social hierarchy within playhouses across the country.[22]

After a summer of productive work in 1803, the fall arrived bearing a number of problems that threatened to derail the project. Doubts of the building's structural integrity, loss of promised support, and threats to the city's status as capital challenged the theatre committee members' resolve

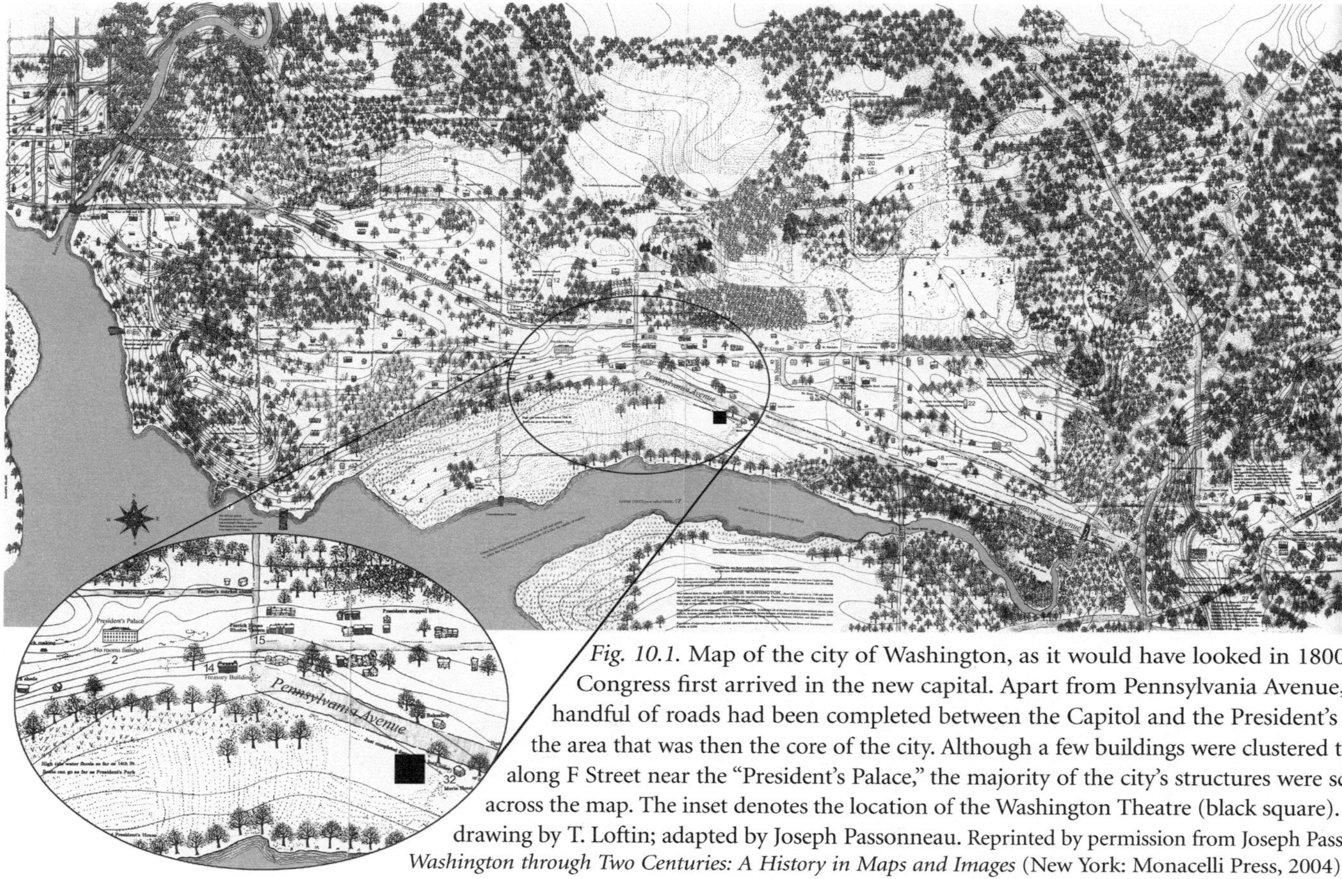

Fig. 10.1. Map of the city of Washington, as it would have looked in 1800, when Congress first arrived in the new capital. Apart from Pennsylvania Avenue, only a handful of roads had been completed between the Capitol and the President's House, the area that was then the core of the city. Although a few buildings were clustered together along F Street near the "President's Palace," the majority of the city's structures were scattered across the map. The inset denotes the location of the Washington Theatre (black square). From a drawing by T. Loftin; adapted by Joseph Passonneau. Reprinted by permission from Joseph Passonneau, *Washington through Two Centuries: A History in Maps and Images* (New York: Monacelli Press, 2004), 34–35.

and their ability to complete the theatre. Rather than debuting its first season of shows that winter as planned, the playhouse sat empty and unfinished.

Carpenters working on the building expressed doubts that the mode of framing proposed by the theatre's architect was structurally sound, prompting a meeting of the theatre committee in September 1803.[23] Washington engineer and surveyor Nicholas King recommended a review of the plans to address potential flaws in the architectural design. It is unclear whether new plans were implemented; however, as King's letter to the committee emphasized, "the execution of the Roof [original underlining] depends on it," it seems unlikely that the committee would disregard his advice.[24] As the roof had already been raised at the end of July, this certainly would have caused a considerable delay.[25]

In addition to architectural concerns, the project faced fiscal losses. While at the start, the theatre committee believed it had the funds to finance the project, when the subscription installments came due many of those who had promised support were either unwilling or unable to give it. Repeated calls for delinquent payments appeared in the newspapers. Even after the playhouse began holding performances, the committee directors warned those subscribers "who have not made full payments on their shares, or contributed the materials or work promised," that forfeiture of their shares was imminent.[26] Not only were the financial backers falling short of their obligations, the workers were defaulting as well. Indeed, as committee members struggled to collect pledged labor, materials, and funding, their groundbreaking attempt at democratic shareholding—and with it, the possibilities of the Washington Theatre—seemed doomed to fail.

The committee's troubles collecting payments from the subscribers resulted in slow (or no) payments to contractors and in construction delays. William Coombs, who supplied lumber for the playhouse, was not paid until 1808—four years after the playhouse finally opened—a fact he bemoaned in his letter settling with the committee, stating, "It is not my wish to have any further costs or trouble in this business of yours."[27] The committee was forced to take out a bank loan in the amount of $3,000 to cover expenses. It is unclear when the loan was obtained, but it is evident from numerous reports in the press that the founders had not originally planned to borrow any of the money but rather had relied on the previously pledged donations and subscriptions to cover the full amount anticipated. Even with the bank's infusion of cash, the committee listed an additional $2,000 in outstanding debts (roughly 17 percent of the total cost of the building) when the theatre opened.[28]

In early 1804, federal politics placed another obstacle in the path of the theatre committee when Senator Robert Wright of Maryland put forth a motion to Congress suggesting the federal seat of government be moved to

Baltimore. This was not the first time someone had proposed abandoning Washington as a failed experiment. In fact, the U.S. capital had moved so frequently in the past that there was plenty of speculation that Washington would not be Congress's final resting place. As historian Kenneth Bowling points out, the threat of removal of the capital from the Potomac site loomed large over the city until after the Civil War.[29] The residents who supported the theatre had invested not only their money but their families and futures in the belief that Washington would become a flourishing metropolis grounded by its ties to the federal government and had much to lose should the site be abandoned.

The founders' promotion of the playhouse to this point had emphasized its benefits for the *city*, with only passing reference to a *national* purpose. Early in the construction process, an editorial by "Dramaticus," likely one of the playhouse subscribers, had promoted the power of theatre "to be productive of the best effects," writing, "It fixes the principles yet fluctuating in the inexperienced mind, confirms the man of honor, arouses the valour of the soldier, and inspires the patriotic breast with that sacred love of his country, which he parts but with life."[30] Apart from Dramaticus's words, proponents of the playhouse had framed the theatre project as a city improvement benefiting full-time residents in particular. After Wright's motion, even brief public notices had decidedly more national emphasis, suggesting that supporters specifically reframed the function of the theatre for the nation. Following Congress's debate on Wright's motion, theatre committee member Smith, editor of the *National Intelligencer*, published a preview of the performer who was to open the theatre later that year, highlighting in enlarged capital letters that the evening's entertainments would now "commence with a PATRIOTIC ADDRESS."[31] The timing of this notice is conspicuous as the theatre's opening was many months away. A press release celebrating the raising of the playhouse roof heralded, "[The theatre] will be ready for performance by the next Session of Congress."[32] No previous announcements had indicated that the playhouse schedule would coincide with that of the federal government. Although committee members and potential patrons may have assumed the theatre would be open for the seasonal influx of government workers, the connection was given clearer articulation. Even a year later, Smith found it necessary to emphasize this aspect of the project, writing that the Washington Theatre's "great and primary object unquestionably is to strew the path of legislation with a few flowers in addition to those already in it," a statement that suggests that the new playhouse was to be placed in service to the nation by easing the burden of the democratic process through these "moral and entertaining" diversions.[33] Especially in the capital, employment of national rhetoric allowed supporters and subscribers to tie the playhouse to America.

Unfortunately for the committee, its rebranding came too late to remedy its troubles collecting money and materials that spring. Committee member John Tayloe blamed "the late motion of Mr. Wright in the Senate" for his inability to obtain new subscribers, even though the motion had been dropped.[34] In August 1804, a year and a half after the original subscriptions were taken, the directors were still pleading for the cash, labor, and resources that had been promised: "The Directors have thought proper to give this public notice, that every subscriber may come forward in the manner promised at the time of subscribing."[35] In October, the committee endeavored to entice new contributors by offering twelve free tickets with a subscription of $200.[36] Perhaps these entreaties were finally successful in motivating subscribers. Perhaps because shareholders were getting anxious, or because the committee feared the public's decreasing interest in the playhouse, the committee chose simply to get the playhouse open. In any case, even as the committee continued to solicit money and materials, the playhouse held its first performances in November 1804. The grand idea was officially a reality.

Unfortunately for the theatre proponents, the manifestation of their ideal did not fulfill its promise. On November 16, 1804, Mr. Maginnis's "Grand Medley of Entertainments" christened the stage of the Washington Theatre. Advertised as "Moral and Entertaining," Maginnis's performances consisted primarily of spectacle and magic, including automatons, lighted transparencies, feats of paper folding, numerously detailed card tricks, and fire eating, "with a number of other experiments composed of cards, eggs, and money."[37] Maginnis's one-man show was likely not what Dramaticus had imagined as "inspir[ing] the patriotic breast with that sacred love of [. . .] country." The *Washington Federalist* reported that the shows were thinly attended and that the first performances did not impress many in the audience.[38]

In addition to the first performances, the physical building itself was also a disappointment, an example of the difficulty of translating expectations to reality. It is unclear exactly when the little playhouse was considered "finished," if it ever was. Reports of renovations and improvements undertaken by theatre company managers appear as early as 1805, and near the close of the 1809 season, "a benefit for the improvement of the theatre" was held, reportedly agreed upon by William Warren, the company manager in residence at the time, and the directors of the theatre.[39] Even as late as 1811, actor James Fennell observed, "On my first visit to the Washington theatre, I was surprised in contemplating its unfinished state."[40] Fennell reported that when he attempted an entrance he found "a column of water, descending from the clouds and extending its base so far and wide, that the door-way I had to pass through, was completely secured against any direct entrance."[41]

In the years that followed the opening season, critiques of the playhouse were numerous, falling in line with the poor opinions of the city as a whole. A significant number of contemporaneous diarists included the theatre in their descriptions of their visits to the capital; they frequently disparaged its humble form, and their impressions of the city seemed to be heavily influenced by their experiences at the theatre. Even writers who did not attend performances at the playhouse often included the building in their narrative sketches of the city, which certainly did not enhance the reputation of the nation's capital with Americans or with the foreign visitors they hoped to impress. Reality for both the city and the theatre was a compromise of the myth the founders had conjured for themselves and for the Washington public.

And yet, despite the clear problems the committee had in completing the physical structure, the requests for materials and money that seem to have gone unanswered years after they had been pledged, and a dearth of quality talent, the theatre founders continued to be committed to providing the city of Washington with a playhouse befitting its enlightened citizenry. The myth remained alive. The day the theatre opened for its second season in 1805, the *National Intelligencer* carried three different announcements about the theatre; one listed the evening's bill, a second requested yet again that delinquent subscribers remit payment on their shares, while a third urged the public's patronage of the playhouse:

> The encouragement which we can give to this amusement is not to be tried. If it be liberal, we shall hereafter be able to command the ablest performers on the continent, some of which will this night appear on the boards. If they are this season welcomed by overflowing houses, and if among the spectators are seen the most respectable of our citizens, the reputation of Washington will be fixed, and the dramatic art will look to the metropolis for its most flattering reward, that reward which consists in a liberal pecuniary support, and the approbation (at least during the winter) of the most enlightened audience of America.[42]

The theatre founders mythologized their little playhouse, reimagining the disappointing manifestation of their plan as a grand playhouse befitting an equally grand vision of the capital landscape destined to showcase America's most celebrated talents. Though it would be many more years before the institution of theatre would find a foothold in the national capital, the Washington Theatre eventually found its stride and began to fulfill at least some of the founders' expectations. In the fall of 1808, William Warren and William B. Wood brought the reputable Chestnut Street Theatre Company from Philadelphia to the Washington Theatre and provided the playhouse with a consistent performing troupe and regular entertainment for the next decade.[43]

The idealism that informed and propelled the creation of the Washington Theatre mirrors the idealism with which Americans conceived of and pursued their own identities as citizens of a new nation. The planning and placement of the Washington Theatre illuminates the post-Revolutionary era's vision of American identity. The rhetoric of citizenship, as employed by the Washington Theatre stockholders, was a way in which patrons could reimagine their inherited theatrical tradition as "American" theatre. Even as they imported plays and performers, the ways in which they went about the work of constructing the playhouse redefined the model.

In 1771 French architect Jacques-François Blondel wrote that "nothing contributes so much to the magnificence of cities as public theatres, and these edifices should indicate by their grandeur and exterior disposition the importance of the cities in which they are situated."[44] Washington's first public playhouse, much like the city it represented, was certainly much grander in the planning than in the execution. However, the statements in the press issued from the theatre committee suggest that the founders' goals were in line with the ideas expressed by Blondel and Carlson. They imagined the Washington Theatre as more than just an entertainment venue; it was a physical manifestation of the nation itself and of the idealism of that nation.

Notes

1. *National Intelligencer*, June 24, 1803.
2. Pierre Charles L'Enfant anglicized his name to "Peter" shortly after immigrating to America, a sign of his love for his adopted country. Scott W. Berg, *Grand Avenues: The Story of the French Visionary Who Designed Washington, D.C.* (New York: Pantheon Books, 2007), xi.
3. *National Intelligencer*, June 24, 1803, and August 6, 1804. Information on the city's landscape at the time of the cornerstone ceremony was drawn from multiple sources, most substantially from Wilhelmus Bogart Bryan, *A History of the National Capital from Its Foundation Through the Period of the Adoption of the Organic Act*, vol. 1 (New York: Macmillan, 1914), and Joseph Passonneau, *Washington through Two Centuries: A History in Maps and Images* (New York: Monacelli Press, 2004).

4. Peter Charles L'Enfant to President George Washington, June 22, 1791, quoted in "L'Enfant's Reports to President Washington, Bearing Dates of March 26, June 22, and August 19, 1791," *Records of the Columbia Historical Society, Washington, D.C.* 2 (1899): 36.
5. *Alexandria Expositor*, March 16, 1803; *National Intelligencer*, April 22, 1803. Van Ness listed the total cost of the theatre at $11,468.65; Van Ness–Philip Family Papers, courtesy of the New-York Historical Society.
6. *National Intelligencer*, July 15, 1803.
7. Lewis Hallam and David Douglass built theatres in colonial New York and Philadelphia, and Thomas Wade West built several theatres in Virginia in the 1790s. Boston's Federal Street Theatre, Philadelphia's Chestnut Street Theatre, and Baltimore's Holiday Street Theatre were financed by shareholders and leased to performing companies. See William Dunlap, *A History of the American Theatre from Its Origins to 1832* (New York: J. and J. Harper, 1832); Journals of William Warren, Channing Pollock Theatre Collection, Howard University, Washington, D.C.; Heather Nathans, *Early American Theatre from the Revolution to Thomas Jefferson: Into the Hands of the People*, Cambridge Studies in American Theatre and Drama, ed. Don B. Wilmeth (New York: Cambridge University Press, 2003); and Lucy Blandford Pilkinton, "Theatre in Norfolk, Virginia, 1788–1812" (PhD diss., University of Michigan, 1993).
8. Theatre Committee, Washington, to John Bernard, Fredericksburg, September 24, 1803, Van Ness–Philip Family Papers.
9. Women and African Americans did attend plays at the Washington Theatre but were not part of the planning and did not own shares.
10. According to Van Ness, subscriptions of labor and materials totaled $2316.31½, while cash subscriptions came to $2625. Van Ness–Philip Family Papers.
11. The theatre committee did not indicate a preference for a particular plot of land; however, the majority of the lots apportioned to the federal government for "public" buildings were along the main corridor of the city plan, between the President's House and the Capitol Building. Thomas Munroe, Washington, to Thomas Jefferson, Monticello, March 14, 1803, Thomas Jefferson Papers, Library of Congress.
12. Members of the theatre committee also backed many other civic development projects including bank branches, an orphanage, several charities, and a penitentiary.
13. Thomas Jefferson, Monticello, to Thomas Munroe, Washington, March 21, 1803, Thomas Jefferson Papers.

14. The Washington Canal was yet another capital city project that began with a great idea that was difficult to translate into reality. Its history is chronicled in Cornelius W. Heine's "The Washington City Canal," *Records of the Columbia Historical Society, Washington, D.C.* 53 (1953): 1–27.
15. After the selection of Van Ness's lot, Carroll was no longer associated with the theatre project, perhaps unhappy with the location choice.
16. Marvin Carlson, *Places of Performance: The Semiotics of Theatre Architecture* (New York: Cornell University Press, 1989), 88.
17. *Alexandria Expositor*, June 8, 1803; *National Intelligencer*, June 1, 1803.
18. Van Ness–Philip Family Papers.
19. There is no mention of the exact size of the Washington Theatre in contemporaneous accounts; however, the second playhouse built in Washington could seat approximately seven hundred people and was described as significantly larger than the first.
20. *National Intelligencer*, September 11, 1805.
21. My descriptions of the theatre exterior and interior are pieced together from several sources. Van Ness's records, although incomplete, contain bills for various materials, including brick, lime, and sand, and for services such as painting and plastering. Advertisements in the *National Intelligencer* request plastering services on October 24, 1804. Audience reviews of performances printed in the newspapers frequently reference the uncomfortable benches and drab decor. When the committee took bids to finish the interior, it requested "finishing in a plain style" (*National Intelligencer*, June 25, 1804). The advertisements for performance evenings list prices for box and pit seating, although the number of boxes is unknown as no detailed records of ticket sales survive.
22. Bruce A. McConachie, "American Theatre in Context," in *The Cambridge History of American Theatre: Vol. 1, Beginnings to 1870*, ed. Don B. Wilmeth and Christopher Bigsby (New York: Cambridge University Press, 1998), 164.
23. Nicholas King to John P. Van Ness, September 18, 1803, Van Ness–Philip Family Papers.
24. Ibid.
25. *National Intelligencer*, July 30, 1804.
26. Ibid., September 9, 1805.
27. Van Ness–Philip Family Papers.
28. In Van Ness's account of the playhouse expenses, he lists the bank loan and the additional debts in a document he titled "Amt. of Expense or Cost of Theatre." It is unclear when this tally was made and Van Ness's records are far from detailed; however, his notes reveal a great deal about

the theatre committee's financial dealings. Van Ness's records indicate that the committee members relied heavily on their personal and professional networks rather than on a system of more formal contact, making it extremely difficult to keep track of subscribers' accounts. He does not name the bank that supplied the loan or detail the additional debt; Van Ness–Philip Family Papers.

29. Kenneth R. Bowling, *The Creation of Washington, D.C.: The Idea and Location of the American Capital* (Fairfax, Va.: George Mason University Press, 1991), 1–2.
30. *National Intelligencer*, June 1, 1803.
31. Ibid., April 20, 1804; reprinted from *New York Morning Chronicle*, April 19, 1804.
32. *National Intelligencer*, June 30, 1804.
33. Ibid., September 9, 1805.
34. John Tayloe to John P. Van Ness, April 10, 1804, Van Ness–Philip Family Papers.
35. *National Intelligencer*, August 4, 1804.
36. Ibid., October 5, 1804.
37. Ibid., November 21, 1804.
38. *Washington Federalist*, December 15, 1804.
39. Journals of William Warren, vol. 1, September 3, 1808, and August 1, 1809; *National Intelligencer*, July 31, 1809.
40. James Fennell, *Apology for the Life of James Fennell* (Philadelphia: Moses Thomas, 1814), 413.
41. Ibid.
42. *National Intelligencer*, September 9, 1805.
43. For a full chart of performances held in the Washington Theatre from its opening until its destruction by fire in 1820, see the appendix in AnnMarie T. Saunders, "'To the Advantage of the City': Playgoing, Patriotism, and the First Washington Theatres, 1800–1836" (PhD diss., University of Maryland, 2012); *Washington Federalist*, October 28, 1807.
44. Jacques-François Blondel, *Cours d'architecture* (1771), quoted in Carlson, *Places of Performance*, 78.

11. Labor, Theatre, and the Dream of the White City

Rosemarie K. Bank

Historians have long been aware that the "White City," erected in Chicago for the Columbian Exposition in 1893, offered a myth of American prosperity, papering over actual economic dislocation and decline. With this contrast between prosperity and decline in mind, it is time to examine how the Exposition simultaneously valorized and erased work, offering in the place of labor a vision of unified capitalist expansion and social progress. In order to consider how culture constructed such a myth in the midst of so much evidence to the contrary, this essay focuses on cultural workers—performers, but also those who produced and built cultural work—during the span extending from the explosion at the Haymarket in Chicago in 1886 to the Pullman strike of 1894 on the city's border.

I bracket the Columbian Exposition with the Haymarket affair and the Pullman strike for several reasons, none of which intends to imply a causal relationship. Haymarket and Pullman, like the Exposition, were Chicago events. Focusing upon Chicago helps decenter the New York bias in end-of-the-century theatre historical accounts. Further, Haymarket and Pullman, as will be explained, were both labor actions, the first centering upon immigrant and the second upon native workers. The Exposition made use of both labor pools and had to negotiate its own labor issues. Only by contextualizing more broadly do we begin to see the connections between labor and the view of culture writ large that the Exposition hoped to further. Typically, theatre historical accounts focus upon performers, places of performance, and audiences, with little attention given to performers as workers, performance as work, or audiences as members of societies with recoverable views of the place of workers and work in their culture as a whole. The Columbian Exposition provides a rich opportunity to examine how labor and culture interact.

In 1985, historian Richard Slotkin offered a metaphor useful to exploring the connection between labor and culture. In his book *The Fatal Environment: The Myth of the Frontier in the Age of Industrialization*, Slotkin suggests that the whole of the American nineteenth century was an age during which striking workers were equated with savages, an absorption of the myth of the frontier into discussions of labor that was common to public considerations of workers, especially strikers and labor organizers, by the time of the Columbian Exposition in Chicago in 1893. As the contemporaneous historian Henry Adams saw it, for example, the Chicago Exposition, for the first time, asked "the question whether the American people knew where they were driving." In Adams's view, the Exposition also answered that question, simultaneously providing "the first expression of American thought as a unity." Taking Adams and Slotkin together, the unifying thought can be seen to express the idea that workers (as well as Amerindians, immigrants, and others) were "savages," an idea that erases the celebration of what work (and America) had accomplished and that the Columbian "White City" sought to represent. The conflicts between valorization and erasure, civilized and savage, and progress and regress have given the 1890s a peculiar stamp, one that historian Alan Trachtenberg characterizes as reflecting "the incorporation of America," which he sees as the "unifying idea" that has shaped our perception of workers and of American cultural identity in the nineteenth century, and in our own times.[1]

* * *

While Henry Adams believed he perceived the first iteration of a unified American thought (about progress and identity), and while Slotkin sees that unified thought as a migration of the idea of "Amerindians as savages" to "workers as savages," Trachtenberg offers a way to see progress, labor, civilization, and savagery expressed in American history (in newspapers, political speeches, philosophy, letters, and so on) through the lens of "the incorporation of America," both in the production of goods and in the production of American culture. The Haymarket affair and the Pullman strike are examples of what the forces behind incorporation sought to achieve with respect to industrial production, but the proximity of these labor actions to 1893 and their location in the same city (Chicago) also serve as reminders that the Columbian Exposition was itself a performance of labor. By this, I mean that labor was performed in building the Exposition, though the "White City" had no workers' exhibit—"no place for workers," as James Gilbert has put it—save for a model "Workingman's Home" erected at the beginning of the Midway, intended to demonstrate the lodgings that could be rented or built on an income of $500 a year. Clearly, however, as Eugene V. Debs, leader of the American Railway Union, saw it, the Exposition was "a tribute to labor" in its celebration, as the fair's subtitle suggested, of "the work of all nations."[2]

The sundering of work from workers underscores Trachtenberg's point that "incorporation" stole focus at the fair, centering the spectator's attention upon the work of big business (Krupp, Pullman, Singer) rather than upon the labor of workers. The labor of performers, whose work has been considered as entertainment, social statement, and exploitation but rarely as labor, occurred at several fair sites. Three were directly connected to the Columbian Exposition: the fairground, the Exposition's Midway, and Buffalo Bill's Wild West next to the fairground. These sites emphasized ethno-performance. There were other entertainments on the Exposition's periphery—for example, Steele MacKaye's "Spectatorium" on the fair's northern boundary, envisioned as home to a Columbian drama called *The World Finder* but reduced by the depression of 1893 to a "Scenitorium" of special effects. Downtown in Chicago, Imre Kiralfy's spectacle *America* ran for months at the Auditorium Theatre, and there were numerous entertainments with nothing much to do with the Columbian Exposition—from Lillian Russell in comic opera to Eugen Sandow, the strongman—that played beside Chicago's many ethnic theatres and music halls. While material remnants of the Exhibition can still be found in Chicago, performance labor has vanished into the performances themselves.[3]

Although the Columbian Exposition actively erased the worker, the Haymarket affair and the Pullman strike drew public attention to the precariousness of both the performance of labor and the laborer. The Haymarket affair (or "massacre" or "riot") took place May 4, 1886, when a rally in support of workers striking the McCormick Harvesting Machine Company for an eight-hour day, called for Haymarket Square (at Randolph and DesPlaines Streets), resulted in a bomb blast and gunfire that killed eight policemen and four workers and wounded sixty officers and an unknown number of civilians.[4] Eight men connected to the rally, most born in Germany, were charged with the murder of a policeman killed by a pipe bomb, and seven of them were sentenced to death. Appeals extended to 1887. Of the seven convictions, two sentences were commuted to life in prison, one of the condemned committed suicide in his cell, and the remaining four men were hanged November 11, 1887.[5]

The significance of the Haymarket events to Chicago and U.S. history often draws attention from the gathering issues for the rally, which were the eight-hour day and the killing of two strikers on May 3, the day before the rally, by McCormick's Pinkerton guards. Obscured as well in the pro-management, anti-union rhetoric of the era was the amount of public support articulated for an eight-hour day and labor organizing. This support was often expressed on the stages of Chicago's many German *vereins* or fellowship buildings, with their small theatre-like assembly halls, or via fund-raising performances at ethnic-language theatres and concert saloons. Public support of protests against unfair labor practices was still evident at the time of the Pullman strike in 1894, a year after the Columbian Exposition closed. Pullman, Illinois, was a company town flanking Chicago whose Pullman Palace Car employees staged a strike May 11, 1894, when wages were cut 25 percent and sixteen-hour workdays continued. At the same time, rents in the town of Pullman ran 20 to 25 percent higher than normal for the area, and the prices of goods sold there were kept high. The American Railway Union, led by Eugene V. Debs, supported the Pullman strike and launched a national boycott against running Pullman cars. Labor actions at the Chicago site resulted in the deaths of at least thirteen strikers and the wounding of fifty-seven others and in the use of twelve thousand federal troops between July 3 and July 7, 1894, under General Nelson Miles and at the order of President Grover Cleveland, to break the strike.[6]

The importance of Pullman as the first national strike, the first use of a federal injunction against organized labor, and the first use of federal troops to fire on U.S. citizens against the wishes of a state should not obscure the judgment of the 1894 national commission investigating the matter that held George M. Pullman himself responsible for the strike; indeed, an 1898 Illinois Supreme Court ruling forced his company to divest itself of ownership in the town, now a part of Chicago. No less a Brahmin than Mrs. Potter Palmer, an intimate of Mrs. Pullman and the organizing force behind the Women's Building at the Columbian Exposition, wrote to Ralph Easley of the Chicago Civic Federation (August 1894) asking Easley to correct the misapprehension that Pullman had "'saved the country, as it were, from anarchy and future aggression from labor organizations'" and reveal "how unfairly Pullman had treated his workers." Though much worse in the number of deaths and the unrest it caused, the Pullman strike generated less cultural outcry in Chicago (Mrs. Palmer notwithstanding) than had the Haymarket affair. Perhaps the decline of public support derived from Pullman's national ("native"), rather than local ("immigrant"), nature as a labor action, but certainly some of that decline was due to the economic depression that had descended upon Chicago, and the nation, at the close of the Columbian Exposition, fueling the idea that laboring men and women should be grateful for any work American business provided.[7]

The union movement in the later nineteenth century was both a national movement and a movement across industries. Stagehands, for example, had begun to organize locally in the United States in 1886, the same year as the Haymarket events, and these locals were united into a national union in 1893, the year the Columbian Exposition was opened to the public. As a result, unionized stagehands were working theatre venues in Chicago when the Exposition opened. Actors organized a society in 1896, two years after federal troops broke the Pullman strike, but actors did not achieve recognition until, as Actors' Equity, they struck in New York in 1919. Their gains at that time—a minimum wage, paid rehearsals, eight performances a week, Sundays off, compensation for travel expenses, and other reasonable protections—suggest the reverse of the conditions under which actors were working in Chicago in 1893. While performers of all kinds continued to work under adverse or even dangerous or dishonest circumstances through the balance of the nineteenth century, ethno-performers fared less well than their white peers (for example, they were exploited by government agencies that often expected them to perform without compensation, or by agents who paid them badly or failed to keep contracted promises). Among these performers, Amerindians who worked for Buffalo Bill's Wild West, as I have noted elsewhere, seem to have done as well as comparable performers who were not Indians. These performers were, of course, seasoned professionals—"show Indians," as the Bureau of Indian Affairs called them—and more able to bargain in the pre-union 1890s than were amateur performers on the fairgrounds or ethno-acts on the Midway. Amerindians, African Americans, Hispanic Americans, and Mexicans and other foreign nationals also served as "stage hands" and animal handlers for Buffalo Bill's Wild West at salaries comparable to those paid to white employees for similar work, though none of these workers was unionized.[8]

Ethno-performers and particularly show Indians remind us that the relationship of all show workers to bosses was perceived as a dependency relationship, in the same way McCormick and Pullman saw their workers' interests as subservient to their own corporate interests. In this context, the "White City" of the Columbian Exposition demonstrated "the notion that in culture alone resides a power to enforce obedience, to teach acquiescence and consent," as Alan Trachtenberg has put it. In this view, the "White City" signified "the alliance and incorporation of business, politics, industry, and culture. The spectacle proclaimed order, unity, coherence—and mutuality [...] in the form of hierarchy." Confessing itself to be an illusion, the "White City represented itself *as* a representation," Trachtenberg observes, a sham offering "a truer vision of the real than did the troubled world sprawling beyond its gates."[9]

While it seems to me likely that those who made and toured the Columbian Exposition in the main recognized it as a representation, the "White City" summarized a century-long migration toward cultural division. As Richard Slotkin documents, during the Civil War, bellicose rhetoric equated the word "savage" not with the wild but with the barbaric. In this vein, northern war reports described southern soldiers as savages, just as Indians were called savages in newspaper reports of the Dakota Wars in 1862. Subsequently, and in the same sense, a social survey published in 1872 likened New York's child paupers to savages, and after the battle of the Little Big Horn in 1876, "the last stand" was often used metaphorically to describe the battles between labor and management, with workers as the savages. For the balance of the nineteenth century, as labor strife continued, newspapers repeatedly referred to both workers and immigrants as savages, surely not terminology intended to favorably depict them or their causes.[10]

In case the use of culture in this divisive way seems wholly on the bosses' side, workers also divided against their own interests to side with order, unity, and security, however temporary. Walter Wyckoff, for example, a Princeton graduate, decided to tramp the country in the 1890s in order to learn what life was like from a worker's perspective. One of the jobs he had in 1892, after an unemployed winter on the streets of Chicago, was as a "road builder" on the fairgrounds. There, he lived in a temporary "hotel" on the site of the future "Court of Honor" with four hundred other workers, who were fed as well as housed there. To prevent theft and keep labor organizers out, sentries patrolled the barricaded worksite and restricted the laborers' movements. Even so, Wyckoff records a sense of security, fueled, no doubt, by regular meals and a certain payday, despite the number of strikes that delayed construction.[11]

Though Wyckoff's education helped him serve as historian of a worker's life during the savage times for labor between Haymarket and Pullman, he was not alone in valuing security over worker solidarity. Many of the men with whom he worked constructing the Columbian Exposition, thrown out of work once the Exposition was finished and into the deepening depression of 1894, served as scab labor at the time of the Pullman strike. Divided from Pullman's striking workers, the Columbian laborers bought their temporary security at some cost. Schooled at the Pullman strike by the U.S. Army, the Chicago police soon became "the most effective of all the agencies involved" in putting down labor actions, as they subsequently demonstrated at the meat packing, teamster, and garment worker strikes of 1904, 1906, 1910, and 1915, where they protected goon squads and scabs and beat up and arrested only strikers. (As police historian Sidney Harring observes, "The scale of police anti-strike activity in Chicago during the early twentieth century is probably without parallel in American labor history.") In this kind of climate for labor, the Exposition's laborers could choose scabbing or striking. In either case, Adams's unified American thought and the celebration of "the work of all nations" were equally erased.[12]

Henry Adams captured the mythology and ideology of work at the Columbian Exposition, seeing in it the visualization of a long-developing idea. As Adams put it, "For a hundred years, between 1793 and 1893, the American people had hesitated, vacillated, swayed forward and back, between two forces, one simply industrial, the other capitalistic, centralizing, and mechanical. In 1893, [. . .] the majority at last declared itself, once for all, in favor of the capitalistic system with all its necessary machinery." Nothing surprised Adams more "than the ease with which he and his [. . .] friends slipped across the chasm, and alighted on the [. . .] capitalistic system."[13] In the same way that the Exposition simultaneously valorized and erased work, offering in the place of labor a "White City" of unified capitalist expansion and social progress, Adams understood that the progressive and libertarian vision that had characterized his privileged class for much of the postbellum era had, in fact, ended.

* * *

The Columbian Exposition was changed by (and changed) aspects of labor history as much as the Haymarket affair and the Pullman strike did, only the Exposition did so in cultural terms. What was visible at Chicago was consolidation and the illusion of unity. The prison work-gang labor format Walter Wykoff experienced (and enjoyed) offered a level of control similar to that found in company towns like Pullman, while workmen residing in Chicago enjoyed hardly more freedom in an environment where willing workers were a dime a dozen and labor organizers were barred from work sites. In Chicago and at the Exposition, performers, absent unions, bargained independently for what they could get, as in 1894, when Buffalo Bill's Wild West, instead of signing one contract for a hundred show Indians, as it had in the past, "signed one hundred contracts with one hundred Indians."[14]

The Columbian Exposition defined Chicago in 1893. The city had risen from the ashes of the Great Chicago Fire of 1871 and become not only a manufacturing but also a cultural capital. The imprint of that time remains visible today. The Berghoff murals, the Art Institute, the remains of the fair near the Museum of Science and Industry (itself once a fair building)—the lagoon, the tea house, the statue of Columbia/the Republic—are all triumphalist announcements and reminders of the arrival of Chicago, Daniel C. Burnham's "Paris of the prairie." Just as, in its disappearance, the Exposition erased the work that its appearance celebrated, so it defined performance in Chicago in multiple ways. In one sphere, there was a diverse theatre with clear cultural and populist tendencies that celebrated work of all kinds, from imperiled but plucky working heroines in melodramas to popular local songs. In another sphere, cultural hierarchy was celebrated, a "leveling up" through cultural work, such as the classical style of "White City" architecture or the self-improvement represented by offering the public lectures and concerts. In yet another, and simultaneous, sphere, the performance of work itself, from Haymarket to Pullman and through the Columbian Exposition, gave Chicago a shared history and local culture that was, for good and ill, distinct, a culture not afraid to be "savage." This vision of the city was captured most forcefully by Carl Sandburg's celebration of the raw American energy and effort of Chicago, "Hog Butcher," "Tool Maker," "Stacker of Wheat," "Player with Railroads," and "the Nation's Freight Handler," "stormy," " husky," "brawling," "City of the Big Shoulders," toiling, "piling job on job," and "cunning as a savage pitted against the wilderness."[15]

There was, however, another aspect to that history. In 1894, a year after the fair closed and mysteriously burned to the ground, incinerating the material history of the work of thousands, Eugene V. Debs's lawyer, Clarence Darrow, unsuccessfully appealed before the U.S. Supreme Court to overturn Debs's conviction for violating a federal injunction against boycotts. In his argument, Darrow drew the lesson of Pullman and of the numerous labor disputes of that era it summarized. Not only were corporations and the state pitted against workers, he said, but there was a clash of cultures. On the one side lay the illusion of substance represented by Pullman's view of Pullman's workers (and the creators of the White City's representation of "order, unity, [and] coherence"), and on the other side stood the monumental indifference exercised by the culture of plenty against those who created substance in sympathy with each other. The difference between philosophies was fundamental. Alan Trachtenberg reports that, according to Clarence Darrow, the members of the American Railway Union

> "doubtless believed that their fellow laborers were unjustly treated, and did not desire to handle the cars of a corporation that was unjustly treating their brothers who were engaged in a struggle with this company." It was the very right to consider each other "brothers" that Darrow insisted upon [. . .] for "the theory on which all labor organizations are based [Darrow said] is that workingmen have a common interest, and that an injury to one is the concern of all."

A more complex reading of the Columbian Exposition than one that sees only the binary tension between utopia and dystopia creates room for disagreement within "the common interest of all."[16] If labor is that common interest, given that all production "makes" something, what is produced by work can be recognized as culture. Culture can embrace a diversity that incorporation/unity/agreement cannot, one flexible enough to embrace savagery *and* civilization, illusion *and* production, as the "White City" and its workers did in practice.

In November 2011, the voters of the state of Ohio went to the polls and soundly rebuked the state legislature and governor by repealing a law denying the public workers of Ohio the right to collectively bargain. The number of votes against this legislation was greater than that which had elected the governor (who had stumped the state campaigning against the law's repeal) and far greater than the whole of the public workers in the state, including the members of their families old enough to vote. The illusion of substance represented by the Columbian Exposition reminds us that there is also a reality to illusion, and where cultural work is concerned (whether that of teachers, firemen, police, social workers, and the like today, or of performers, construction, and industrial workers in the 1890s), a little "savagery" is often necessary to see the "brotherhood" in the mythology, ideology, and practice of work that joins eras (and people) to each other.

Notes

1. Richard Slotkin, *The Fatal Environment: The Myth of the Frontier in the Age of Industrialization* (New York: Atheneum, 1985); Henry Adams, *The Education of Henry Adams* (1907; Boston: Houghton Mifflin, 1974), 343. Adams's unitary idea was not, of course, savagery. Alan Trachtenberg, *The Incorporation of America: Culture and Society in the Gilded Age* (New York: Hill and Wang, 1982).
2. See James Gilbert, *Perfect Cities: Chicago's Utopias of 1893* (Chicago: University of Chicago Press, 1991), 117, for more on "the Workingman's Home." Parallels between views of workers and views of race and racism at fairs are drawn in Robert W. Rydell, *All the World's a Fair: Visions of Empire at American International Expositions, 1876–1916* (Chicago: University of Chicago Press, 1984). For Debs, see Trachtenberg, *Incorporation*, 218.
3. Ethno-performing involving Indians is traced in L. G. Moses, *Wild West Shows and the Images of American Indians, 1883–1933* (Albuquerque: University of New Mexico Press, 1996), 138. Recent histories dealing with Buffalo Bill and wild west shows include Joy S. Kasson, *Buffalo Bill's Wild West: Celebrity, Memory, and Popular History* (New York: Hill and Wang, 2000), and Louis S. Warren, *Buffalo Bill's America: William Cody and the Wild West Show* (New York: Alfred A. Knopf, 2005). Performances

by other groups at the Columbian Exposition, domestic and foreign, are traced in Rydell, *All the World's a Fair.* For Steele MacKaye, see Barnard Hewitt, *Theatre U.S.A.: 1665 to 1957* (New York: McGraw-Hill, 1959), 265–68. For Kiralfy's spectacle, see Angelo Venanzi, *Imre Kiralfy's Grand Historical Spectacle "America": In Four Acts and Seventeen Scenes* (Chicago: Imre Kiralfy, 1893). For downtown entertainments generally, see Stanley Appelbaum, *The Chicago World's Fair of 1893: A Photographic Record* (New York: Dover, 1980), 103.

4. The rally (called by union organizers in support of the striking/McCormick workers)—normally a peaceful affair—resulted in a bomb blast and gunfire. It is still not known who set off the bomb; the gunfire was police, those killed were caught in the crossfire. My intention here is to avoid creating a causal connection between the rally and the violence that followed that has never been proven and would blame the workers.
5. Among many sources, see Paul Avrich, *The Haymarket Tragedy* (Princeton: Princeton University Press, 1984); and James Green, *Death in the Haymarket: A Story of Chicago, the First Labor Movement, and the Bombing That Divided Gilded Age America* (New York: Anchor Books, 2007). Those executed in connection with the Haymarket events were buried in Waldheim Cemetery, now Forest Home Cemetery, in Forest Park, just outside Chicago, where a memorial now marks their graves. The date, May 4, 1886, is exactly eighty-four years before a similarly described "massacre" or "riot" at Kent State University. The persistence of the contesting language is worth noting.
6. Concerning the Pullman strike, see (among others) J. Anthony Lucas, *Big Trouble: A Murder in a Small Western Town Sets Off a Struggle for the Soul of America* (New York: Simon and Schuster, 1998); David R. Papke, *The Pullman Case: The Clash of Labor and Capitalism in Industrial America* (Lawrence: University Press of Kansas, 1999); and Carl Smith, *Urban Disorder and the Shape of Belief: The Great Chicago Fire, the Haymarket Bomb, and the Model Town of Pullman* (Chicago: University of Chicago Press, 1995).
7. For Bertha Honoré Palmer, see Gilbert, *Perfect Cities*, 163.
8. For theatrical unions, see Hewitt, *Theatre U.S.A.*, 237, 329. For the term "show Indian," see Moses, *Wild West Shows*, and see Moses and the other sources cited in note 3 for workers at Buffalo Bill's Wild West generally. For my own considerations of Cody's show, see "Representing History: Performing the Columbian Exposition," *Theatre Journal* 54, no. 4 (December 2002): 589–606 (reprinted in *Critical Theory and Performance* [rev. ed.], ed. Janelle G. Reinelt and Joseph R. Roach [Ann Arbor: University of

Michigan Press, 2007], 223–44); "Telling a Spatial History of the Columbian Exposition of 1893," *Modern Drama* 47, no. 3 (Fall 2004): 349–66; and "'Show Indians'/Showing Indians: Buffalo Bill's Wild West, the Bureau of Indian Affairs, and American Anthropology," *Journal of Dramatic Theory and Criticism* 26, no. 1 (Fall 2011): 149–58.

9. Trachtenberg, *Incorporation*, 225, 230, 231.
10. Slotkin, *Fatal Environment*, 305 for southern soldiers, 311 for child paupers, 463–78 and 512–15 for the last stand, and 480–96 for laborers and immigrants.
11. Wyckoff's experiences were serialized for Scribner's and then issued (in 1899) as a two-volume account called *The Workers*. His motives were investigative and reportorial, part of the "muckraking" movement in popular writing characteristic of Upton Sinclair and Ida Tarbell. See Trachtenberg, *Incorporation*, 210–11, for some of Wyckoff's reflections.
12. For the Chicago police, see Sidney L. Harring, *Policing a Class Society: The Experience of American Cities, 1865–1915* (New Brunswick, N.J.: Rutgers University Press, 1983), 119, 122–26, 127. It is deeply ironic that the public workers' unions, particularly the police, are now among the strongest in Chicago.
13. Adams, *Education*, 344. Adams writes his autobiography in the third person, referring to "he" or "Henry Adams" instead of to "I" or "me."
14. Moses, *Wild West Shows*, 134–35, 138. Significantly, Cody's individual contracts meant the Bureau of Indian Affairs had gone out of the "show" business. Performing was now a kind of work like any other. The government might oversee the enforcement of contract terms, but individual Amerindian performers were responsible for what they signed; thus, the nature (and stipulated salary) of the contract indicated, as earlier, whether the performer was a contract player, featured performer, or star.
15. Carl Sandburg, "Chicago," *Poetry Magazine*, March 1914, 191–92.
16. Trachtenberg, *Incorporation*, 232–34.

Part Four

The Creative Work / The Work of Creation

Centering on the challenges of the creative process, this section returns to a consideration of the creative work itself and the work that creation requires. How might transformation be an inherent part of the creatvive process, for both individuals and communities? How might the physical labor of creation manifest in that creation? What are the personal and public repercussions for artistic failure? How does the work of art—the "product" of labor—or the intangible, inspired "stuff" of art-making factor into mythology, ideology, or practice? The essays by Melissa Rynn Porterfield, Tracey Elaine Chessum, and Jonathan Chambers explore different facets of these questions. Porterfield and Chessum delve into aspects of the creative process through their respective examinations of marketing and intellectual property. As Porterfield shows, the Three Rivers Shakespeare Festival's marketing plan played with perceptions of working-class identity in Pittsburgh, while Chessum's work on the iconic John Philip Sousa identifies the sacrifices that composers and lyricists make when copyright law fails to protect the working artist. The final essay in this collection, written by Jonathan Chambers, draws many of this volume's themes together—Rinde Eckert's work on *And God Created Great Whales* portrays both the creative work and the worker battling against nearly impossible odds to create art.

12. Blue-Collar Bard: Recalling Shakespeare through the Rhetoric of Labor

Melissa Rynn Porterfield

"Shakespeare?!? In Pittsburgh?!?" That was the incredulous response that Attilio "Buck" Favorini received at nearly every turn in 1979, when he first began to seek funding to start a Shakespeare festival in the once-thriving steel city. Favorini, a New York City native, had been eager to find a local outlet for his passion for the Bard since he relocated to take a theatre faculty position at the University of Pittsburgh in 1969. But the significant resistance he initially met from those in the city's philanthropic community put his passion to the test. Pittsburgh, they insisted, was a decidedly blue-collar town with little interest in trappings of elitist culture. In the "Steel City," labor, not art, was the prevailing ethos, uniting a racially and ethnically diverse population under one hard hat. It was a working man's town where professional sports was the preferred form of entertainment, beer was the preferred beverage, and the works of a four-hundred-year-old English poet were preferred only by elderly high school English teachers.[1] Pittsburgh, it seemed, was no place for Shakespeare. But despite the odds, five years later, Favorini would prove them all wrong when his fledgling company, the Three Rivers Shakespeare Festival (TRSF), became the sixth largest Shakespeare festival in the United States.[2]

If, as sociologist Maurice Halbwachs writes, "[e]very collective memory requires the support of a group delineated in space and time," then Favorini's challenge would be finding the particular aspects of Shakespeare's personal and professional history that would convince Pittsburghers that Shakespeare was theirs to recall.[3] This essay explores some of the rhetorical strategies used by the TRSF in its marketing materials as it worked to appeal to Pittsburgh's largely blue-collar audience base. The festival's particular remembrance of

Shakespeare sought to reconstruct the city's collective memory of the distant literary icon in a manner that was both congenial to its own institutional goals and reflective of the characteristics and values of the citizens of Pittsburgh.[4] Its attempts to resituate the collective memory of the classical English literary figure within the active cultural milieu of Pittsburgh effectively amounted to a kind of rebranding of the Bard, reconstructing Shakespeare to reflect the down-to-earth tastes and prevailing values of work, commerce, and physical prowess of the self-proclaimed "City of Champions." The festival's marketing materials sought to leverage Shakespeare's inherent cultural cachet in a way that simultaneously asserted its own legitimacy as a company and assisted the city's larger effort to improve Pittsburgh's identity on a national level. Finally, the TRSF took advantage of the inherently communal aspects of its "festival" format in order to strengthen the cultural community and reputation of Pittsburgh and to engage in a series of commemorative acts aimed largely at supporting its congenially constructed remembrance of Shakespeare.

The resistance Favorini first encountered can, in part, be traced to the city's long history of supposed antitheatrical sentiment, which has often been attributed to the puritanical ideals of its Quaker and Scots-Irish founding fathers. William Penn himself set the standard in 1682 when he declared playgoing to be "an offense against God [which incited] people to Rudeness, Cruelty, Looseness and Irreligion."[5] This early prohibition against entertainments, compounded by the traditional Scots-Irish, Presbyterian distaste for idleness, impelled early inhabitants to develop a strong work ethic as their most defining civil characteristic.[6] As early as the first decade of the 1800s, its citizens had begun to articulate the deeply felt connection between the city and the ethos of work. Pittsburgh's first bookseller, Zadok Cramer, wrote, "The character of the people is that of enterprising and persevering industry; everyman to his business is the prevailing maxim, there is therefore little time devoted to amusements or to the cultivation of refined social pleasures."[7] In an early promotional piece on the TRSF, local theatre writer Jim Davidson chronicled some of the earliest appearances of Shakespeare's works on Pittsburgh stages, including an account of one of the city's first Shakespeare festivals, produced in the 1833–34 season by a touring company. That festival boasted a season of six Shakespeare plays interspersed by a series of short original plays featuring a performing monkey that was, arguably, the company's largest draw. Very little information on the reception of the early festival's work exists, prompting Davidson to wryly note, "No one knows whether the monkey attempted Shakespeare, but it could scarcely have lowered the rock-bottom reputation of theatre in the hard-working Presbyterian town of Pittsburgh."[8] Despite the number of Shakespearean productions that graced the boards of Pittsburgh stages in the eighteenth and early nineteenth centuries, it was not until the rise of variety theatre, vaudeville, and minstrel shows that the city began to see lasting development in its professional theatre offerings, possibly because these traditions incorporated a wide-swinging mix of highbrow and lowbrow entertainments.[9] Still, the city's embrace of these popular theatre traditions notwithstanding, Pittsburgh could not shake its antitheatrical reputation, and by the end of World War II, theatrical offerings began to wane.

In her local theatre history, *Pittsburgh in Stages*, Lynne Conner identifies the 1950s as the city's most significant commercial theatre decline. She attributes the rapid deterioration to a number of factors: economic changes in the theatrical touring industry that eliminated Pittsburgh as an out-of-town tryout city; significant drops in commercial airfares, which allowed wealthy patrons the option of traveling to New York for a weekend of theatregoing; and the working class's attraction to a new crop of movie houses, local social halls, and little theatres that had begun to pop up in their own neighborhoods.[10] In spite of a thriving community theatre scene, Pittsburgh's perceived—though perhaps undeserved—reputation on a national level as a working-class city with working-class tastes persisted. Audience members were described as emotionally restrained with a tendency to "sit on their hands" during performances.[11] The city's professional theatre scene was dealt another crushing blow when the decline of the steel industry decimated Pittsburgh's economy, degrading its reputation nationally and making it a favorite punch line on late-night television. During the economic recession of 1981–82, more than 153,000 workers were laid off from Pittsburgh mills, the ripple effect of which prompted the closing of railroads, mines, and other local manufacturing factories.[12]

Through thick and thin, however, Pittsburgh citizens were heartened by the accomplishments of their professional sports teams. By 1979 the city had cultivated the nickname "The City of Champions," prompted by the Pittsburgh Steelers' unprecedented four National Football League championships in six seasons, the 1976 and 1980 national football championship wins by the University of Pittsburgh Panthers, and two Major League Baseball World Series wins by the Pittsburgh Pirates in 1971 and 1979.[13] The dual victories in 1979 were particularly noteworthy because, in addition to the championship wins, all four MLB hitting awards and the NFL MVP that year went to Pittsburgh players. Billboards, bumper stickers, and all manner of sports paraphernalia boasted of the city's new source of civic pride.[14] The nickname gained national recognition when *Sports Illustrated* featured Steeler

Terry Bradshaw and Pirate Willie Stargell on the cover of its December 24, 1979, issue with an accompanying article, "Two Champs from the City of Champions." The name solidified Pittsburgh's emerging identity as a major sports town and gave residents a new source of Pittsburgh pride.

In 1979, when Favorini began to lay plans for his new Shakespeare festival, he suggested that the key to combating what he referred to as the city's self-imposed cultural "inferiority complex" was to invigorate its collective memory of the Bard, who, Favorini believed, could in turn help pave the way for improving Pittsburgh's reputation on a national level. As a result, many of the marketing tactics employed by the festival were intended to create among its potential audience a familiarity with—even an ownership of—the historically and geographically distant theatrical icon. Favorini began his efforts to convert Pittsburghers to his brand of Shakespeare by stressing that, in contrast to other drier, more academic productions, the offerings of the TRSF would be "plain-spoken, vigorous, lively and unpretentious."[15] In a letter soliciting potential board members for the festival, Favorini articulated his proletariat-minded mission: "I am convinced that if Shakespeare is produced in a down-to-earth, unintimidating manner, people from all walks of life will come to enjoy and be enriched by him. After all, Shakespeare's original audience consisted of as many laborers as lords; there's no real reason that that can't be the case again."[16] Likewise, in appeals to local philanthropic organizations, Favorini took great pains to ensure that his festival would not cater to the cultural elite or the overeducated, offering the Bard's own working-class audience members as proof that "Shakespeare's plays are far more available and accessible to the average person than most of us would imagine. Shakespeare's own audience was composed of people from all walks of life, with workingmen and small businessmen predominating. There is no law that says that you need a Ph.D. to enjoy Shakespeare."[17]

In an attempt to attract Pittsburgh's proletariat, one of the festival's first marketing campaigns played heavily on the city's reputation as the "City of Champions" by leveraging the city's world-class athletes in an effort to construct Shakespeare as another one of Pittsburgh's greats. The campaign's slogan, "Pittsburgh's Other Willie," encouraged citizens to imagine Shakespeare, not within the dusty, academic context commonly associated with the playwright, but as a pop culture icon with the same power and prowess as local baseball hero Willie Stargell. In the company's first national press profile, *Wall Street Journal* reporter Carol Hymowitz wrote:

> Everybody around here knows who Willie is. Willie Stargell is captain and first baseman of the World Series champion Pittsburgh Pirates. The

> problem of the moment is how to whip up interest in "Pittsburgh's Other Willie": William Shakespeare. [. . .] So the local Shakespeare promoters are playing to local tastes [. . . and] urging the bleacher denizens to "celebrate summer with Pittsburgh's other Willie."[18]

The campaign included a television commercial in which Favorini, dressed as Shakespeare in full Elizabethan garb, bows graciously to two younger men as he leads a pack of runners in the Great Race, Pittsburgh's local marathon, accompanied by the campaign's tagline, "Shakespeare running here." The punning ad graphically reinforced the notion that Shakespeare commanded a large and devoted following and presented him as one of Pittsburgh's own champions, worthy of civic pride. The overwhelming success of the campaign seems to be due in no small part to the fact that Pittsburgh locals were thrilled to be in on a cultural joke—especially one that might have been lost on a more traditionally culturally savvy audience. Local reporter Bruce Steele's take on the marketing campaign not only praised its originality but noted that its unpretentious tone melded with the festival's recollection of Shakespeare himself: "Actually, the Willie slogan epitomizes the Three Rivers Shakespeare Festival's unworshipful approach to history's most gifted hack writer."[19]

Another of the TRSF's most popular marketing campaigns featured a comic book character named Super Bard, a tights-and-cape-clad depiction of Shakespeare drawn by festival actor Tim Hartman (figure 12.1). Introduced to the Pittsburgh public in 1989, the festival mailed over eighty thousand copies of a twelve-page comic book titled *The Amazing Adventures of Super Bard* to members of its mailing list. The comic book tells the story of literary caped crusader Super Bard, bent on restoring the public's belief in Shakespeare's accessibility; Super Bard eventually frees Pittsburgh from a shape-shifting supervillain called "Malaise" and his attempts to create a "Summer of Terror" in the city. Along the way, the hero impresses such Pittsburgh notables as Mayor Masloff, sportscaster Myron Cope, and local television personalities Paul Long and Joe DiNardo as he valiantly fights to save Steeler Franco Harris from certain malaise. The spring 1989 edition of the TRSF's newsletter, *Folio*, featured a photograph of Favorini and Harris at the festival's unveiling ceremony for the Super Bard marketing campaign, which, due in no small part to Harris's involvement, was subsequently reprinted by several local newspapers. In the *Folio* article, Favorini explained that Super Bard was a reflection of the festival's ongoing mission "to give people a new way of looking at Shakespeare [. . .] to assail the idea that he's some dried up old relic from the past."[20] The extremely successful campaign became the cornerstone for the TRSF's tenth anniversary marketing campaign and was featured in a series of local radio and print ads, as well as in a series of national print ads that ran in the *Wall Street Journal*, the *New York Times*, and the *London Daily News*. In many ways, Super Bard was a personification of the enduring traits that characterize the spirit and ideals of Pittsburgh. An original, artistic product of the city, he evoked notions of athleticism, vigor, and invincibility. His materially powerful persona counteracted the potentially off-putting, heady, and overly academic connotations often associated with the study of Shakespeare.

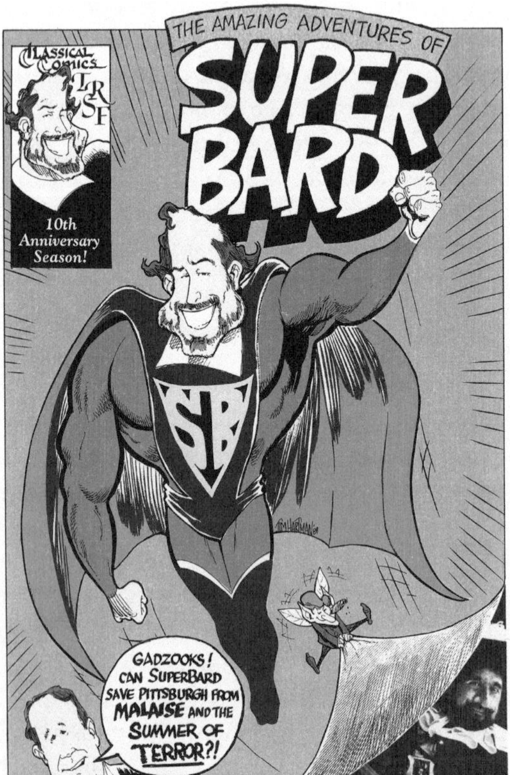

Fig. 12.1. Cover image of the comic book *The Amazing Adventures of Super Bard*. Illustrated by Tim Hartman; produced, printed, and distributed by the Three Rivers Shakespeare Festival (1989). Courtesy of Three Rivers Shakespeare Festival Records, 1980–95, CTC 24, Curtis Theatre Collection, Special Collections Department, University of Pittsburgh.

While many of the TRSF's artistic, aesthetic, and marketing choices sought to emphasize Shakespeare's identity as a populist entertainer, other decisions represented a desire to remain connected to the traditional Shakespeare industry. One such example of these conflicting impulses can be seen in the coordination of the festival's inaugural season with the Folger Shakespeare Museum Exhibit Tour of 1980. The tour was drawn to Pittsburgh, in part, by funding from the city's Renaissance II program, a multifaceted civic effort dedicated to improving Pittsburgh's national reputation by stimulating economic and cultural growth. When Favorini learned that the Folger had selected Pittsburgh as one of its tour stops, he resolved that, "by hook or by crook, we're starting the festival this summer."[21] By coordinating its opening with the Folger tour, the TRSF was able to capitalize on the marketing efforts of the established Shakespeare institution in order to stimulate public and media interest in its own fledgling organization. Interestingly, tour planners were keenly aware that even with the reputation and financial backing of the Folger, the exhibit's rare manuscripts, diaries, and copies of the First Folio would not likely be enough to draw the predominantly blue-collar workers of Pittsburgh to a museum. As Donald Adams, coordinator of the exhibit, admitted, Pittsburgh was challenging because "Pittsburgh is a town of steelworkers who labor hard by day and spend their midsummer nights rooting for the Pirates, not at the theater. We can't exactly walk into steelworker bars and say, 'Hey guys, let's hear it for Middle England!'"[22] In response, the Pittsburgh sponsors of the tour "augmented those documents with some homemade entertainment—puppet shows, Elizabethan musicals and dances, even fencing matches" by local artists and performers in an attempt to attract a broader spectrum of the city's population to the Carnegie Museum. The plan to include more popular entertainments paid off: the exhibit drew "about 3,000 visitors a week, including a broader mix of viewers than on previous stops in Kansas City and San Francisco. A recent poll of 100 visitors here showed that almost 40% of them hadn't been to the museum in a year."[23] By maximizing cross-marketing strategies with the Folger and the Carnegie and by offering deep discounts to their performances, the TRSF was able to draw much of the audience from the museum exhibit to the theatre conveniently located right across the street.

While development materials produced by the TRSF frequently championed the traditionally held opinion that Shakespeare was an important part of improving the cultural and theatrical reputation of Pittsburgh nationally, they did so, as Jen Harvie suggests, in ways that "simultaneously indicate[d] the importance of other principles of social organization" around which the city was organized.[24] In other words, the marketing strategy reinforced

Pittsburgh's prevailing dedication to work and industry even as it advocated the cultural importance of Shakespeare to the community. To maintain its place in Pittsburgh's labor-centered culture, the TRSF frequently highlighted its identity as a "fully professional" theatre company. Early press and marketing materials from the TRSF stressed that even though the festival was associated with and housed at the University of Pittsburgh, the company was "not college theatre" but a "union-affiliated" organization that hired "more local professionals than any theatre in town."[25] A brochure aimed at raising local corporate funding clearly illustrates the TRSF's rhetorical strategy to characterize its importance to the city in the language of work. The brochure opens to reveal a shot of the city's downtown skyline accompanied by text emphasizing the festival's mission to make "Shakespeare accessible to all people" by keeping ticket prices low and providing free performances through "a contract with the City Department of Parks and Recreation."[26] The brochure then lays out a brief description of the festival's history and guiding principles. Tellingly, this information is divided by section headings written to engage with the city's predilection for labor and commerce: "Dollars & Cents," "Jobs," "Help," and "Intern."[27] Likewise, a copy of the TRSF's 1983 Company Profile contains a paragraph stressing the many local workers associated with the festival. "The Festival is staffed by professionals whose careers are based in Pittsburgh, by the finest graduates and faculty members from local theatre training schools, and by guest artists. [. . . It] operates under a letter of agreement from the Actors' Equity Association."[28]

Further, the TRSF emphasized its importance to the overall economic success of the city by assuring readers that, unlike other Shakespeare festivals in the United States that staffed their theatres with itinerant artists who were in residence only for a few months each year, the TRSF was "entirely a Pittsburgh project." In his fund-raising efforts, Favorini boasted that the TRSF had not "hired high-priced actors from New York to come here for a week and then go home. Rather we have sought and found the finest talent Pittsburgh has to offer."[29] The TRSF's promotional materials stressed its down-home identity, employing a sports metaphor to highlight its continued dedication to reflect the "true colors of the Three Rivers Area":

> The [hiring] policy represents neither parochialism nor regional chauvinism, but is rooted in practicality and cultural philosophy. Practically, the Pittsburgh area is rich in students and graduates of first-rate theatre-training schools. There are more and more local professionals performing full- or part-time. Finally, there is a growing number of performers originating from Pittsburgh who have relocated

> elsewhere for professional reasons. These groups constitute the Festival's "first-round picks" for its staff. We trust this policy makes sense to you, as well, in a more profound way, conveying to the public that Pittsburgh can produce and encourage its own artists and culture, rather than being merely the recipient of cultural "packages" put together elsewhere.[30]

The strategy was a sound one; it was rhetorically in line with the work-based ethos of the city and reflected Pittsburgh's Renaissance II campaign goal to retain recent college graduates in the local workforce. The TRSF's focus on such policies not only reassured local theatre talent that it was possible to stay and work locally but also reinforced the idea that Pittsburgh didn't need to outsource its cultural needs.

In order to appeal to its Pittsburgh audience, one of the TRSF's signature aesthetic choices was a focus on the physical vigor and violence frequently found in Shakespeare's plays; this emphasis reflected the tough, competitive spirit of the "City of Champions." The festival received extensive critical praise for its combat choreography, much of which was devised by University of Pittsburgh faculty member W. Stephen Coleman, who served as both a director and fight choreographer and acted in several productions for the festival.[31] However, despite the festival's critical success in the staging of fights, audience responses to the TRSF's first production of *The Taming of the Shrew* (1980) varied. Local Shakespeare "purists" were upset by what they perceived as an unnecessarily vigorous staging and complained that the actors "roll and leap across the stage [. . .] with such fury [. . .] that the audience becomes exhausted."[32] Others, like retired steelworker Fred Gertenschlager, "loved the production precisely because it was 'so lively'" and vowed to return to see the festival's other productions based on *Shrew*'s rough-and-tumble feel.[33] The festival's emphasis on the earthier, more violent, and physically vigorous aspects of the plays was part of its broader desire to create what Favorini has referred to as a "visually lush production aesthetic" that would encourage audience members to fully immerse themselves in the world of the play and would thereby combat any anxiety the uninitiated audience members might experience.[34]

Another of the TRSF's signature production aesthetics was its frequent use of original songs and musical scores composed by festival member Christine Frezza.[35] Favorini recalls that her compositions were "invaluable" to the festival's attempts to create a truly immersive experience for its audiences.[36] In promotional interviews, Frezza focused her recollections of Shakespeare on the rich pageantry found in his plays: "[Shakespeare] knew people in the audience didn't want to limit themselves to words. They wanted music, they wanted pageantry, they wanted everything they didn't have in their everyday life."[37] While Frezza demonstrated a vast breadth of musical knowledge, the popularity of her work came not from her expertise in orchestrating and arranging historically accurate compositions but from her ability to craft simple, appealing, and memorable tunes that appealed to Pittsburgh audiences and stuck with them as they left the theatre. Actor Martin Merritt, who played Orlando in *As You Like It*, speculated that the popularity of "Who Killed the Deer," one of the show's original tunes, was due to the fact that it "sounds like a beer song," adding that "it's the kind of song you're humming a few scenes later."[38]

Finally, the TRSF's insistence on maintaining a true festival environment, through preshow events, meals, and other entertainments, created an atmosphere in which Pittsburghers were able to take a direct role in the work of commemorating Shakespeare. The idea that festival entertainments are capable of creating and supporting communities is articulated by social anthropologist Alessandro Falassi, who defines the word "festival" as a "periodically recurrent social occasion," participated in either "directly or indirectly and to various degrees" by members of a community "united by ethnic, linguistic, religious, historical bonds, and sharing a world view. Both the social function and the symbolic meaning of the festival are closely related to a series of overt values that the community recognizes as essential to its ideology and world view, to its social identity, its historical continuity, and to its physical survival, which is ultimately what festival celebrates."[39] Like rituals, festivals confirm and reinforce the identity of their membership through their emphasis on shared, lived experience, making them a particularly apt tool for commemoration.[40] The TRSF's festive offerings allowed Pittsburghers the ability to see their integral place in the communal recollection of Shakespeare and in building and celebrating their own local community.

As part of his research into the operations at other Shakespeare companies, Favorini travelled to Stratford, Ontario, in 1979 and secured a meeting with John Hirsh, then associate artistic director at the Stratford Festival, to solicit advice about starting his own Shakespeare company. Favorini recalls Hirsh likening the Shakespeare business to "the movies, where the profit margin was in the popcorn, not the ticket price of the movie. [. . .] Creating the festival atmosphere was the most important thing."[41] In addition to being an integral part of the festival's financial viability, these offerings helped to imbue the city's collective memory of Shakespeare with a spirit of fun and playfulness often unassociated with more stuffy, academic recollections of the Renaissance dramatist. In the first few years of operations, these offerings were sparse; the Good Companions, a group of festival actors, performed a series of musical numbers and period dances outside the theatre in a preshow that culminated in a fanfare of trumpets to open the house. But in 1983, the TRSF expanded these offerings into a "Renaissance Fair" in honor of the city's Renaissance II campaign. Over the years, as the burden of planning and staffing these activities grew, the festival invited other local groups and artists to take part; preshow entertainments began as much as three hours before showtime and included jugglers, sword fights, a roving company of fools, face painting, children's shows, craft booths, a souvenir "Shakespeare Shoppe," and even a jousting exhibition. In addition to promoting community building, the TRSF's decision to remain focused on its ancillary festival offerings had two additional benefits: institutional financial viability and the ability to imbue the city's collective memory of Shakespeare with a spirit of fun and playfulness often disassociated from more stuffy, academic recollections of the Renaissance dramatist.

Even when the logistics of feeding audiences became a nightmare for the TRSF organizers, Favorini insisted the festival continue because of the ability these shared meals had to create a sense of community among audience members.[42] And, rather predictably, Pittsburghers were quite vocal in their feedback regarding the menu. Initially the TRSF strove to provide authentic "Elizabethan" food, but it quickly revised this strategy when feedback indicated that the meals were not to the consumers' liking and instead arranged for gourmet catering companies to provide meals and snacks. But these offerings, too, proved to be too unfamiliar for Pittsburgh tastes. Favorini remembers the situation as being ridiculously difficult. "I mean we tried all kinds of things [. . .]. But the things that really worked best were the most ordinary, down-home Pittsburgh meals [. . .] rigatoni, pierogies, green salads."[43] These audience demands for meal offerings more in line with local tastes uphold Falassi's assertion that "festivals are ultimately community affairs. Indeed, they provide the occasion whereby a community may call attention to itself and, perhaps more important in our time, its willingness to display itself openly. It is the ultimate public activity."[44] Favorini insists that the idea was not to try and create an authentic Elizabethan cultural experience but rather to present a variety of approachable entertainments that would allow contemporary audience members—who would later spend two to three hours sitting more or less passively in the dark, listening to others—an opportunity to build active, personal memories of their experience of "Shakespeare." For Favorini, the festive atmosphere of the TRSF's preshow offerings supported his often-quoted belief "in the humanizing magic of the theatre, [and] of its powers to bring people together in an awareness of what it means to live fully."[45]

But perhaps, as Falassi suggests, for the citizens of Pittsburgh, the festive atmosphere of the TRSF encouraged a break from their traditional preoccupation with work and offered an opportunity to embrace the opposite impulse: play. Festival employees often attempted to battle against the academic connotations that accompanied the mention of Shakespeare by emphasizing the "fun" that audiences would experience with its brand of Shakespeare. In an interview for the *Tribune-Review*, Favorini tried to allay audience concerns that seeing Shakespeare might be "difficult":

> The most important thing to know about the Shakespeare Festival is that it's great fun. [. . .] We have entertainment outside, jugglers, musicians to get you started, the theatre itself is interesting architecturally; it's a national historical landmark. [. . .] We try to bring our audience into Shakespeare's world. [. . . The TRSF] opens up a new world and creates a sense of discovery. That's what makes the festival so much fun.[46]

Ultimately, by reconstructing the collective memory of Shakespeare among the city's inhabitants and presenting his works in an unpretentious manner that reflected the most fundamental values of its blue-collar citizens, the festival was able to begin to combat the city's cultural inferiority complex. And while in its time the TRSF may not have converted every audience member to lifelong love of the Bard, it is certain that its acceptance by average Pittsburghers helped pave the way for the theatrical renaissance that began in the late 1990s and continues to this day.[47]

Notes

1. Attilio Favorini, interview by Melissa Rynn Porterfield, June 28, 2011 (hereafter Favorini interview). In his interview, Favorini detailed the resistance he received in his initial fund-raising attempts. His recollections are upheld by local theatre press of the time. See also George Anderson, "Shakespeare Festival Here's No Midsummer Night's Dream," *Pittsburgh Post-Gazette*, May 2, 1979, Three Rivers Shakespeare Festival Collection, 1980–1995, CTC 24, Curtis Theatre Collection, University of Pittsburgh (hereafter TRSF Collection).
2. Yvonne Steele, "Booking the Bard," *Pittsburgh Arts* 2, no. 4 (1984): 2, TRSF Collection.
3. Maurice Halbwachs, *On Collective Memory*, translated, edited, and introduction by Lewis A. Cosner (Chicago: University of Chicago Press, 1992), 84.
4. For more on the term "collective memory" and the possibility of a socially reconstructed memory of the past, see ibid., 21, 28, 46, 51.

5. Quoted in Lynne Conner, *Pittsburgh in Stages: Two Hundred Years of Theatre* (Pittsburgh: University of Pittsburgh Press, 2007), 16.
6. Ibid., 16.
7. Zadok Cramer, *The Navigator: Containing Directions for Navigating the Ohio, and Mississippi Rivers. . . .* 8th ed. (1801; repr., Pittsburgh: Cramer and Spear, Franklin Head Bookstore, 1814), 4.
8. Jim Davidson, "Pittsburgh's a Stage for 3 from the Bard," *Pittsburgh Press*, June 16, 1983, TRSF Collection.
9. Conner's *Pittsburgh in Stages* gives the most comprehensive historical account of the theatrical life of the city during the eighteenth and nineteenth centuries. Her thorough examination of the popularity of vaudeville in Pittsburgh is explored in chapter 4, "Theater as Big Business: 1897 to 1915."
10. Ibid., 21.
11. Beatrice Lewis, "Pittsburgh's a Poor Road Town, but Just Needs Encouragement," *New York Times Herald Tribune*, July 6, 1941, TRSF Collection.
12. John Hoerr, *And the Wolf Finally Came: The Decline and Fall of the American Steel Industry* (Pittsburgh: University of Pittsburgh Press, 1988), 689.
13. Also of note during this era was Steeler fullback Franco Harris's role in the now famous "Immaculate Reception" play, which resulted in a controversial win for the Steelers in the final minutes of the 1972 AFC Division playoff game against the Oakland Raiders.
14. The "City of Champions" nickname experienced a more recent revival in 2009, when the Pittsburgh Penguins won the NHL's Stanley Cup and the Steelers captured their sixth NFL championship (tying them for the team with the most championships), resulting in the *Sporting News* declaring it the "Best Sports City" of the year.
15. Attilio Favorini to Robert Kavanaugh, December 16, 1982, TRSF Collection.
16. Ibid., December 16, 1982.
17. Attilio Favorini to Sandra Collier, May 21, 1980, TRSF Collection.
18. Carol Hymowitz, "Another Willie Makes It Big in Steel City," *Wall Street Journal*, August 7, 1980, TRSF Collection.
19. Bruce Steele, "Pittsburgh's Other Willie," *Pittsburgh New Sun*, June 26, 1980, TRSF Collection.
20. "Superhero Makes Rare Appearance at Press Conference," *Folio*, Spring 1989, 1, TRSF Collection.
21. Quoted in Steele, "Pittsburgh's Other Willie."
22. Quoted in Hymowitz, "Another Willie Makes It Big in Steel City."
23. Ibid.
24. Jen Harvie, *Theatre and the City* (New York: Palgrave Macmillan, 2009), 14.
25. Attilio Favorini to Robert Kavanaugh, December 16, 1982, TRSF Collection.

26. Development Mailer, Three Rivers Shakespeare Festival, 1983, TRSF Collection.
27. Ibid.
28. Company Profile, Three Rivers Shakespeare Festival, 1983, TRSF Collection.
29. Attilio Favorini to Sandra S. Collier, May 21, 1980, TRSF Collection.
30. Fourth Season Souvenir Program, Three Rivers Shakespeare Festival, 1983, 22, TRSF Collection.
31. Coleman used the stage name "Alex Coleman," a reference to his grandmother's maiden name, for professional acting credits. Coleman also served as interim executive director of TRSF during 1986 when Favorini was on sabbatical.
32. George Anderson quoted in Hymowitz, "Another Willie Makes It Big in Steel City."
33. Ibid.
34. Favorini interview.
35. Currently an associate professor of theatre arts at Southern Utah University, Frezza has written over three hundred scores and served as the director of music for the Utah Shakespeare Festival for twenty-two years.
36. Favorini interview.
37. Quoted in Davidson, "Bard Liked It with Pageantry," *Pittsburgh Press*, July 30, 1981, TRSF Collection.
38. Ibid.
39. Alessandro Falassi, *Time Out of Time: Essays on the Festival* (Albuquerque: University of New Mexico Press, 1987), 2.
40. Ibid., 176; Paul Connerton, *How Societies Remember* (New York: Cambridge University Press, 1989); Edward Casey, *Remembering: A Phenomenological Study* (Bloomington: Indiana University Press, 1987), 218–19, 235–41.
41. Favorini interview.
42. Company meeting minutes from 1985 on reveal that the planning and staffing of these meals was the source of endless conflict between festival representatives and local food purveyors.
43. Favorini interview.
44. Falassi, *Time Out of Time*, 181.
45. Attilio Favorini to Gov. Richard L. Thornburgh, March 13, 1979, TRSF Collection.
46. David Zuchowski, "Pittsburgh . . .Stratford on the Mon," *Pittsburgh Tribune-Review*, May 28, 1988, TRSF Collection.
47. Favorini stepped down as producing director of the TRSF in 1992 due in part to conflicts between the University of Pittsburgh and the festival. Three years later, the economically crippled festival folded.

13. Songs of Salaried Warriors: Copyright, Intellectual Property, and John Philip Sousa's *The Free Lance*

Tracey Elaine Chessum

John Philip Sousa, self-proclaimed "Salesman of Americanism" and perhaps the most widely known American musician in the world during his time, was not a "fan" of the new recording technology that began to take commercial hold at the start of the twentieth century. While the phonograph captivated the country and other bands rushed to get their names on recorded discs, the Sousa Band was uncharacteristically silent and unrepresented. The reasons for Sousa's reluctance to record his famous band were varied, but the primary reason stemmed from the fact that record companies were selling recordings of Sousa marches by other bands and Sousa never saw one cent from these sales. Recording companies were making money from his music, and he was not. Sousa found this practice downright un-American.

Copyright protections in the United States, prior to the 1909 United States Copyright Act, were extended only to works that could be published in print, like books and sheet music. The most recent Copyright Act of 1831 did not anticipate the widespread sale of recordings of music in its construction, and therefore the manufacturers of sound recordings and player-piano rolls were not obligated to offer any compensation to composers of the recorded works. While recordings were made from copyrighted print music, composers of the period found it unfair that they were paid once (in the form of sheet music sales) for a recording that was sold tens of thousands of times over.[1]

In response to the growing outrage from composers (and a host of other writers, speakers, and performers whose works could not be copyrighted and were, therefore, recorded and sold without any remuneration), the Library of Congress held a series of conferences in 1905 aimed at creating formal language to extend copyright protection beyond reproductions that could be physically seen with the eyes to those reproductions meant for the ear.[2] Artists and other interested parties, including recording companies, used these hearings to push for a new copyright act that would give to artists and record companies "divisible copyrights" for multiple forms of reproduction. These divisible copyrights would provide not only copyright protections to publish music in print but also separate protections to record a work or perform that work (in any way).[3] This would provide protection and remuneration to composers, artists, and recording companies—whose recordings could also not be copyrighted under the 1831 Copyright Act—for their contributions to a recording, ensuring that everyone would be compensated accordingly.

Composers knew that the act would not pass easily because the American public, as well as many in congressional leadership, were unwilling to limit the nature of a progressive, new recording technology and its products. Many in Congress, including the chair of the House Committee on Patents, Representative Frank Currier (R-NH), were skeptical of copyright expansion due to the ultimate public benefit that recordings could provide. Reasoning that recordings could offer millions across the country access to a wealth of information in a new and dynamic way, they believed these recordings should be freely accessible and were wary of designating them as a new form of "property."[4]

Therefore, Sousa, along with other popular advocates of copyright expansion, was asked to become a warrior for the protection of intellectual property—a warrior who was tasked with changing the country's perception of the copyright argument in order to expand copyright protection to include both print and aural forms of creation. Consequently, Sousa took his message about copyright abuses to the American people in the form of a comic opera titled *The Free Lance*. With this comic opera, Sousa attempted to use his iconic, celebrity status and persuasive hold over conceptions of American identity to persuade audiences that true Americans paid workers in full for all their work—that they stood for intellectual property rights. The message of *The Free Lance* not only championed the protection of intellectual property but also illustrated the fate of governments that turned a blind eye to the unauthorized use of the work of their citizens.[5] While Sousa's name, music, and comic operas had been co-opted by others—including members of the U.S. government—to support political or ideological stances, *The Free Lance* represents the first time that Sousa himself used his celebrity sway to influence public opinion for his own personal gain and to criticize a government with whom he had long collaborated.

Sousa was an American cultural icon in his own time, a representative symbol of American life and culture both at home and around the world.[6]

He styled himself as the "Salesman of Americanism," and newspapers hailed him as the "Pied Piper of Patriotism." He was such an important part of American life that by 1898 the *Musical Courier* could declare, "It is Sousa in the band, Sousa in the orchestra, Sousa in the phonograph, Sousa in the hand organ, Sousa in the music box, Sousa everywhere. The American composer is the man, not of the hour or of the day, but of the time!"[7] He seemed to embody the achievement of all that America as a democratic nation promised.

As the battle to change American perception of expanded copyright protections got underway, it was Sousa's "American" celebrity that made him an ideal spokesman. The beloved American composer lamented to the public:

> Do they [members of Congress] not realize that if the accredited composers, who have come into vogue by reason of merit and labor, are refused a just reward for their efforts, a condition is almost sure to arise where all incentive to further creative work is lacking, and compositions will no longer flow from their pens; or where they will be compelled to refrain from publishing their compositions at all, and control them in manuscript? What, then, of the playing and talking machines?[8]

Sousa's intention was most likely to concern the public with the reality of no more rousing Sousa marches; however, his logic exemplifies the interesting nineteenth-century connection between a man's work and American identity. For Sousa, his success was attributed to his own "merit and labor"—his work, not his talent. Work created a man's identity; therefore, a man's work, whether artistic, intellectual, or physical, had to be rewarded—especially in a nation that extolled the virtues of the self-made man. If Sousa, the quintessential American, was being denied access to an aspect of what would one day be termed the "American Dream," what would happen to the average American man?[9]

This was powerful rhetoric for the time. Sousa's turn-of-the-century society was in constant flux, navigating the social, political, and cultural transformations attributed to rapid industrialization, searching for options on the best way to deal with new societal paradigms. Even as the reforms and social movements of the Progressive Era sought to recapture and redefine America as the land of opportunity, the national worry was that America was now a nation of unsatisfied dreams.[10] As such, equal access to the pursuit of economic and social advancement—the ability to become a self-made man—became a decisive battleground.[11]

The societal shift away from an eighteenth-century communal context to an industrial world that stressed the importance of the individual created a notion of American manhood that was decidedly focused on a man's work and individual achievements. This was the focal point of a man's identity. Work in this era gave a man the "power of social creation"—the power to make himself and his family, to raise their social position, to pursue the American Dream as far as his own ingenuity would allow— and the ability to "exercise [. . .] manliness through dominance" in industry, sport, or, in Sousa's case, artistic prowess.[12] A man's work, therefore, was his only means of an earned sense of economic and social mobility—to deny him payment for his work was emasculating.

In Sousa's opinion, recording companies were gaining monetary wealth by proxy: they were stealing his intellectual property and accumulating their wealth through his labor, depriving him of the monetary gain that would have been garnered by his artistic output.[13] Sousa argued that this kind of intellectual theft stripped the nation's workers of their intellectual and creative vitality and would hinder their ability to participate in the capitalist system as equals. It would destroy a worker's ability to become a self-made man. While recordings did not stop Sousa from performing his work, he argued that it stopped him from reaping the full social rewards and benefits of his work. Without payment, he was denied the rise in social position that additional capital would provide his family. It stopped him from fully exhibiting his American manhood.

Sousa believed that if the hard work that resulted in an "original product of his brain" was not respected, he had a right and a duty as a great American to use everything at his disposal to challenge the policies that were, in his view, emasculating not only him but the rest of the nation as well.[14] In his arguments for the expansion of copyright, Sousa can be construed as both fighting for his own piece of the American capitalistic pie and railing against the fact that his own manliness, as well as the manliness of all American men, was being challenged in this battle.

In composing his public advocacy case, Sousa drew upon specific nationalist rhetoric surrounding the self-made man and the anxiety around shifting nineteenth-century ideas of American manhood. The fears that the self-made man was no longer a possibility for all and that American manhood was therefore in jeopardy were powerful motivators—and Sousa used this to his advantage. In order to persuade the country that new copyright protections were needed, Sousa—the quintessentially American self-made man—used his own name and story to bolster his arguments. Sousa had risen to the upper echelons of American society. He began life as a child of immigrants, and through his talent, hard work, and keen business sense he raised himself from humble Marine Band musician to international celebrity.[15]

This celebrity status provided him with the access to government officials, presidents, kings, and queens that few other Americans enjoyed. Sousa's name had come to be identified with those characteristics that Americans of the period prized as part of a distinctly "American" identity: honesty, patriotism, talent, and plain hard work. He offered to the public an expression that encompassed a passionate love of one's country, meticulous social order, and Judeo-Christian moral values—all while being a self-made man *and* a child of immigrants![16] Gradually, this ideal image became intertwined with more crudely capitalistic ventures, and Sousa's name and reputation were used to hawk everything from bicycles to cigars. Sousa's image as an American man became a carefully constructed brand used to sell tickets, music, and, at times, ideology.[17]

In and of itself, the name "Sousa" held the power of persuasion due to the man's iconic stature. During his time, to invoke the name, image, or music of Sousa became a way to establish a stated rhetoric as the "American Perspective" or the perspective of the mythic "good American." Sousa initially watched from the sidelines as concert promoters, producers, and U.S. government officials used this mythology to propagate new social and political ideas both through his band concerts and, more thoroughly, through his many works of musical theatre.

Sousa's comic operas, which enjoyed tremendous popularity with audiences as well as a great deal of critical and commercial success, harnessed his iconic status and were constructed to play a role in how American identity was manufactured and disseminated between 1898 and 1907. These operettas reflected new definitions of the "American" from the stage and circulated this new character nationally and internationally.[18] Sousa's comic operas can be cast as *cultural ambassadors* for social and political ideas—as musical theatre works attempting to redefine American identity in the eyes of audiences on both sides of the Atlantic. Due to his position as a cultural icon, Sousa's musical theatre works held exceptional power to persuade audiences about which identity markers they should embody, both within the United States and abroad. These comic operas established their perspective as Sousa's perspective, and therefore as the "good American" perspective, manipulating audiences into conflating rhetoric with their own conceptions of identity.

Promoters, producers, and government officials alike would rework or at times blatantly rewrite Sousa's comic operas to advance their own ideas and to meet their own needs. For example, tour producers reworked Sousa's most popular production, *El Capitan*, to Other the Spanish after the sinking of the USS *Maine* in the Havana harbor. This retooled production presented audiences with a picture of the "American" that was in favor of war with

Spain and of the protection of American interests abroad, and encouraged audience members to stand and show themselves to be Americans by their support for these ideas. *The Charlatan* was revised by its leading man (and good friend of the current American ambassador to Britain) in 1900 to aid the ambassador's agenda of convincing both Britons and Americans that an alliance between their two countries was in everyone's best interest. In the British production, the American character presented with friendly "hands [from] across the sea," one who shared in English history and the "white man's burden." This American was no longer a separatist misfit but a sympathetic pro-imperialism ally in a time when Britain and the United States enjoyed no formal alliance at all.[19] Additionally, *Chris and the Wonderful Lamp*, premiering on Broadway January 1, 1900, marketed consumer products to American audiences. The producers of this production cast the representative American as a zealous collector of consumer goods.

The musical theatre production—particularly on tour—served as one of the first forms of mass popular entertainment that could be used to political and social advantage. Sousa's comic operas, like *El Capitan* and *The Charlatan*, with their cross-country and transcontinental tours, provided a picture of how the musical stage could be used for the dissemination of information. As seen in the preceding examples, these cultural ambassadors were powerful agents advocating political and social change and intervening in debates about national identity, race, foreign policy, and now copyright and labor. Ironically, Sousa does not seem to have minded the rewriting of his operettas because it served to keep the productions relevant, which favorably affected his bottom line. However, that did not mean that he was not keeping a watchful eye on the proceedings.

The use of his operettas to sell ideology taught Sousa that his own agendas could be effectively integrated into musical theatre offerings and be devastatingly effective. Sousa was famous for using his name—his personal brand—to hawk products for local shops or business partners or to support ideology that he felt benefited the American public.[20] He often used his band concerts and his favorite medium, the rural press interview, to share his views on what would make America a better nation. However, as the debate over copyright began in earnest, Sousa was touring Europe with the Sousa Band and needed another vehicle to bring the Sousa/American perspective to the nation.

While on tour, Sousa was in the midst of writing a new comic opera with established librettist Harry B. Smith, which would eventually become *The Free Lance*.[21] They had begun collaborating in the fall of 1904; however, as copyright discussions were being held in 1905, they scrapped their earlier drafts of *The Free Lance* (which dealt with the Mexican-American War at one point and a character named Lillian Lamoor at another). The two rewrote and then rechristened the comic opera to become a voice for composers' rights, creating a new libretto that extolled the virtues of the nineteenth-century relationship between work and American manhood in turn-of-the-century culture and served to propagate expanded intellectual property rights during a time of musical piracy and copyright infringement by what Sousa termed "the menace of mechanical music."[22]

The newly refashioned production scrapped the formerly realistic setting of the Mexican-American War and replaced it with the fictional countries of Braggadocia and Graftiana.[23] Braggadocia is a country of hard-working artisans. In the musical drama, this artistic kingdom goes bankrupt because its emperor steals the artistic property of his subjects and claims it as his own, thereby depriving them of any ability to make money. This throws the nation's people into despair and plunges their country into debt.[24] The emperor congratulates himself for being a master of art "by proxy." Audiences are first introduced to the emperor with his opening solo:

> I grant that there are people who have talents rather various
> Quite capable and clever
> In some few fields of endeavor;
> But I opine my genius is as much more multifarious
> My general Proficience
> Is the next thing to omniscience
> Of course there may be others with a little stray ability;
> But I'm the sole monopolist of wholesale versatility
> There's not an art or science of which anyone may tell
> In which I do not perfectly excel.
>
> But I do it all by proxy!
> By proxy! By proxy!
> I hire a clever chap to represent me, don't you see.
> I think it's rather foxy
> It certainly is foxy.
> Another fellow does the work. The credit comes to me.[25]

The emperor is cast as a lovable but greedy thief who tries to marry off his only daughter to the prince of the neighboring Graftiana, hoping to receive a loan to bail his country, and himself, out of debt. What the emperor does not know is that the duke of Graftiana is also deeply in debt and seeks a loan from the emperor. The princess and prince object to being part of this financial transaction and flee, forcing their fathers to conscript two common laborers, Griselda and Sigmund Lump, into impersonating their royal children. When the sham marriage is exposed, the kingdoms go to war.

Ironically Sigmund Lump, the "Free Lance" of the title, was an independent war hero from times past, and both kingdoms spend much of the musical searching for him in an effort to win his assistance, not realizing that he is already in their midst. When it is revealed that he is not merely a common laborer but the war hero that both kingdoms desire, Lump admits that he cannot fight for either kingdom "by proxy." Like the emasculated biblical Samson, Lump's battle prowess left him when he lost his hair. Lump was, therefore, forced to return to the kingdom and raise goats, taking for himself the name "Philemon" (itself a reference to the New Testament slaveholder who is asked to forgive the past transgressions of the slave Onesimus and treat him as a brother for the public benefit of the Colossian church). Following this revelation, Lump happens upon a witch looking for her long-lost daughter who can be identified only "by the usual copyrighted signs," and he correctly recognizes and restores the daughter to her mother. The witch repays him by regrowing his hair, allowing Lump to regain his battle skills, and he subsequently vanquishes both armies. When neither government can pay him for his work, he exclaims, "What!!! Do you mean to say that after my fighting like a demon, on both sides I can't collect what's coming to me?"[26]

As payment, Lump assumes the crowns of both countries, all the while reminding the audience that there must be a financial reward for one's work. He sings:

> I am a salaried warrior
> And I do not fight for fame;
> For I'm a regular business man
> And the cash is all I claim.
> O glory may be all right enough
> But it pays no bills you see;
> So when a victory grand I win
> My terms are C.O.D.[27]

The free lance goes on to reference his suspicion of "trusts," his policy to refuse services unless full payment is expected, and the physical and social security that comes from a paycheck. This narrative, simplified for the purposes of this essay, mirrors Sousa's ideas about intellectual property: work must be rewarded financially, those who recognize and return the property of others are rewarded, and those who gain by proxy, or allow others to gain by proxy, will be swiftly taken out of power.[28]

For Sousa and Smith, the emperor of Braggadocia represented recording companies, greedily gaining credit "by proxy," while the duke of Graftiana signified U.S. government officials colluding with recording companies to strip artisans of their right to fair payment. These two entities "married" their ideas and sold their moral compasses down the river by authorizing the theft of intellectual property. The resulting war between Braggadocia and Graftiana paralleled the upcoming congressional hearings, where money and the impact on commerce, not the morality of intellectual theft, occupied the center of the discussion.

The character of Sigmund Lump stands as the representative "good American," as well as a theatrical embodiment of Sousa himself. Lump is bumbling and unmanly as Philemon (the man who used to own property, only to see that property be reconstituted as free and to be forced to accept it as an equal exchange), severed from his ability to fight by the shaving of his hair and thereby stripped of his physical process and the expression of his manhood. Congressional committees asked composers to accept the freedom of their work without remuneration, and this similarly severed them from their ability to reap the financial rewards needed to pursue the status of a self-made man. However, as the free lance, Lump pursues his work valiantly after his hair and strength have been returned to him and thus is entitled to respect and payment.[29] Therefore, the true public benefit is not gained through the free exchange of property but through the restoration of property to the worker and thus manhood to the American. When the free lance did not receive respect and payment, he took what was rightfully his—the power to rule the kingdoms, restore order, and promote fair play. Lump's performance of manhood through the physical action of work can be viewed as an extension of Sousa's performance of American national manhood through the defense of his intellectual property.

Sousa announced in January 1906 that *The Free Lance* was complete and would be premiering in March.[30] In the following months, reports began to surface that the opening of *The Free Lance*, now with a new director, Herbert Gresham, had been moved to the Court Square Theatre in Springfield, Massachusetts, and set for March 26, 1906.[31] Sousa was touring with the Sousa Band and did not attend opening night; however, the *New York Telegraph* reported that the show "scored an instant success. It was difficult to realize that it was a 'first night,' so smoothly did it run."[32]

After a series of out-of-town tryouts, *The Free Lance* completed its run in Philadelphia with a "Professional Matinee" for composer/performer George M. Cohan and the George Washington Jr. Company on April 12, 1906.[33] Response from audiences had been so overwhelmingly positive that the piano-vocal arrangements were already being sold—with copyright protection.[34] *The Free Lance* opened to a full Broadway house at the New Amsterdam Theatre on April 16, 1906, and garnered Sousa the best press he had ever received for his comic operas.[35]

In May and June 1906, shortly after *The Free Lance* opened on Broadway, Congress held its first hearings on the need for a new copyright act. Sousa served as the celebrity spokesman and testified on behalf of composers, authors, and publishers. In the hearings, Sousa argued that musical compositions, in their aural form, were an extension of the "writings" granted protection under section 8, clause 8, of the Constitution (which allows Congress to set up the system of copyrights) and that allowing recording producers to purchase one set of music for thousands of copies was morally inequitable. When these two arguments failed to sway the hearing in his favor, Sousa suggested that further growth of mechanical music would mean the demise of the amateur musician and of American music as a whole.[36]

At the end of the hearings, Sousa did not think he had persuaded the congressmen because they had voted to reconvene the hearings in December 1906 instead of determining to move forward with a new copyright act. Therefore, Sousa took yet another argument to the people.[37] As *The Free Lance* began its national tour in August 1906, Sousa began writing an essay titled "The Menace of Mechanical Music." The article appeared in *Appleton's Magazine*, a celebrity essay publication, in the fall of 1906.[38] In it, Sousa declared that mechanical music was like "the English sparrow, which, introduced and welcomed in all innocence, lost no time in multiplying itself to the dignity of a pest, to the destruction of numberless native song birds, and the invariable regret of those who did not stop to think in time."[39] Sousa intimated that mechanical music would tear apart the fabric of "native" society by stripping it of its intellectual and creative vitality and would lead to the demise of American patriotism, saying, "Then what of the national throat? Will it not weaken? What of the national chest? Will it not shrink?"[40]

With "The Menace of Mechanical Music," Sousa further exemplifies the anxieties that led him to become involved in the copyright debate. The demise of the self-made man, the right to full access to capitalistic venture, and the right to exercise his American manliness were inextricably bound up in this debate. Without comprehensive copyright laws—laws that protected American artistic workers from intellectual theft and allowed them to benefit from the work of their creative brains—the national throat would weaken and the national chest would indeed shrink, if only by a reduction in American creative output. A man's creative work could not garner him only glory and could not only benefit the public good, for it "pays no bills you see."

After closing on Broadway in July 1906, *The Free Lance* embarked on a forty-week national tour. However, in a departure from the established routes of Sousa productions along the touring circuit, the show was routed to Washington, D.C., in December of that year—the same week that the congressional hearings on copyright were set to resume. Congressmen, therefore, had to continue their hearings against the backdrop of *The Free Lance*, where those who gain "by proxy" and support those who gain "by proxy" are taken out of power.

Sousa's work, along with the work of others, was ultimately successful in changing public opinion, as the bill he fought for was made law on March 4, 1909. The American Society of Composers, Authors, and Publishers was founded in 1914 to collect the royalties from the Copyright Act of 1909.[41] This change in public opinion was accomplished not by a single action but by a series of persuasive arguments. *The Free Lance* was one way Sousa brought his message on copyright to the American people, using it as a cultural ambassador to tell audiences around the nation that all men, even composers, should be *salaried* warriors—whose terms are COD.

Notes

1. Patrick Warfield, "John Philip Sousa and 'The Menace of Mechanical Music,'" *Journal for the Society for American Music* 3, no. 4 (2009): 446.
2. Alex Sayf Cummings, *Democracy of Sound: Music Piracy and the Remaking of American Copyright in the Twentieth Century* (New York: Oxford University Press, 2013), 21–22.
3. Ibid., 19–20. In *White-Smith vs. Apollo*, the Supreme Court ruled that a piano roll for a player piano was not infringement on existing sheet music copyrights because it could not be "read" by a human being.
4. Ibid., 23–24.
5. For further information, see Tracey Elaine Chessum, "(Musical) Sales Pitches from the Salesman of Americanism: The Comic Operas of John Philip Sousa" (PhD diss., University of Maryland, 2012).
6. Douglas B. Holt, *How Brands Become Icons: The Principles of Cultural Branding*, dig. ed. (Boston, Mass.: Harvard Business School Press, 2004), 20. Using Holt's theories of cultural icon formation, Sousa emerged as an American cultural icon around 1898, one that embodied identity myths that became "consensus expressions of particular values held dear by some members of society."
7. "The Era of Sousa," *Musical Courier* 37 (July 4, 1898), as quoted in Patrick Warfield, "The March as Musical Drama and the Spectacle of John Philip Sousa," *Journal of the American Musicological Society* 64, no. 2 (Summer 2011): 294.

8. John Philip Sousa, "The Menace of Mechanical Music," *Appleton's Magazine* 8 (1906): 284.
9. While the American Dream exudes different meanings over the life of the American nation, in the 1890s, the idea of American promise gave men access to social and economic mobility through their work. While notable women including Elizabeth Cady Stanton, Lucretia Mott, Lucy Stone, Susan B. Anthony, and more had argued in favor of women's rights since the mid-nineteenth century, the concept of the "self-made man" still referred predominantly to men in this period. See Jim Cullen, *The American Dream: A Short History of an Idea That Shaped a Nation* (New York: Oxford University Press, 2003); Lawrence R. Samuel, *The American Dream: A Cultural History* (Syracuse: Syracuse University Press, 2012); and Calvin C. Jillson, *Pursuing the American Dream: Opportunity and Exclusion over Four Centuries* (Lawrence: University of Kansas Press, 2004).
10. See Robert H. Wiebe, *The Search for Order: 1877–1920* (Westport, Conn.: Greenwood Press, 1967).
11. See Michael Kimmel, *Manhood in America: A Cultural History* (New York: Free Press, 1996); Gail Bederman, *Manliness and Civilization: A Cultural History of Gender and Race in the United States, 1880–1917* (Chicago: University of Chicago Press, 1995); and E. Anthony Rotundo, *American Manhood* (New York: Basic Books, 1993).
12. Rotundo, *American Manhood*, 176. See also chapters 8 and 9.
13. Sousa, with his capitalistic perspective, was an outspoken critic of the labor movement.
14. Sousa, "Menace of Mechanical Music," 282.
15. Paul E. Bierley, *John Philip Sousa: American Phenomenon* (Van Nuys, Calif.: Alfred Publishing, 2001), 10, 14; Warfield, "March as Musical Drama," 294; Patrick Warfield, "Salesman of Americanism, Globetrotter, and Musician: The Nineteenth-Century John Philip Sousa, 1854–1893" (PhD diss., Indiana University, 2003), 3.
16. Paul E. Bierley, *The Works of John Philip Sousa* (Westerville, Ohio: Integrity Press, 1984), 8–9. Sousa's father emigrated from Spain and his mother from Bavaria.
17. For further information, see my discussion of the mythmaking process in chapter 1 of "(Musical) Sales Pitches from the Salesman of Americanism."
18. Sousa saw nine comic operas and one musical comedy produced between 1879 and 1913; most embarked on successful tours, including *El Capitan* and *The Charlatan*.
19. English poet Byron Webber's "Hands across the Sea" can be traced to the nineteenth century. The *New York Times* indicates that the phrase suggests

"a venturesome metaphor indicating the obstacles which common blood and common ideals would overcome." "Hands across the Sea," *New York Times*, February 24, 1908, 6; "Choate on the Boer War," *New York Times*, December 1, 1899, 3. Rudyard Kipling's *The White Man's Burden* (subtitled *The United States and the Philippine Islands)* sought to remind the United States that imperialism was the highest of callings, though it came at a high cost. According to the poem, it was essentially the United States' duty to colonize the Philippines. Rudyard Kipling, "The White Man's Burden," *McClure's Magazine*, February 1899, 290–91; "Thanksgiving Day Banquet," p. 17, container 25, Joseph Hodges Choate Papers, Manuscript Division, Library of Congress, Washington, D.C.

20. While modern marketing and advertising theories of branding are dependent upon the existence of a mass market, it is an appropriate designation for Sousa's marketing strategies because he began operating during the emergence of the modern mass market (via newspapers and magazines) and because his travels around the world allowed him to circulate his own personal celebrity brand internationally in a way other brands could not during a time of print media. Douglas B. Holt, *How Brands Become Icons: The Principles of Cultural Branding*, digital ed. (Boston, Mass.: Harvard Business School Press, 2004), 19; Matthew Thomson, "Human Brands: Investigating Antecedents to Consumers' Strong Attachments to Celebrities," *Journal of Marketing* 70, no. 3 (July 2006): 104–5.
21. Sousa and Smith discussed two distinctly different operettas prior to this moment. "Sousa Back Home, Writes New Opera," University of Illinois, Center for American Music and Sousa Archives, Paul Bierley Collection (hereafter Bierley Collection), Series 7: Press Book 22.1; "Sousa-Smith Opera," Summer 1905, Bierley Collection, Series 7: Press Book 21.1.
22. Sousa, "Menace of Mechanical Music."
23. "'The Free Lance' Hit Comic Opera Bullseye," *New York Press*, April 17, 1906, Bierley Collection, Series 7: Press Book 26.
24. The title of the *King of Braggadocia* was changed to the *Emperor of Braggadocia* during out-of-town tryouts; however, published and unpublished versions of the script use these two titles interchangeably.
25. Punctuation reproduced as in the original. *The Free Lance*, p. 12, Harry B. Smith Papers, City Museum of New York.
26. Ibid., 35.
27. Ibid., 33. For a complete summary of *The Free Lance*, see Bierley, *Works of John Philip Sousa*, 27–28.
28. Though the connection between Sousa's copyright issues and his operetta may seem obvious, it was not. At the end of February, Klaw and Erlanger

changed the title of the piece from *The Free Lance* to *King for a Day*. When Sousa learned his producers had changed the title, he protested. The title was significant and deliberately chosen, he argued—a free lance was a medieval mercenary, but Sousa was also a freelance musician—and the substitution detracted from the show's intended message: free lances should be paid for their work. The title was immediately restored; the official story reported by the *New York Morning Telegraph* was that Sousa was "superstitious" of the new title and that it gave him "the spooks." Clipping labeled *Philadelphia Telegraph*, February 24, 1906, Bierley Collection, Series 7: Press Book 80; "Superstitious Sousa Has Title Changed," *New York Morning Telegraph*, March 9, 1906, ibid.

29. This parallel between Philemon, the runaway slave, and Sousa is problematic on several levels, especially considering that slavery had been abolished in the United States a mere forty years before. However, it does exemplify some of the entanglements of the issue and the frustration of composers.
30. On January 10, 1906, Sousa released the title of *The Free Lance* and said that he had completed the work "10 days ago." He sold the production "on royalty" to Klaw and Erlanger. Unlabeled clipping, January, Bierley Collection, Series 7: Press Book 80; "Sousa Writes Comic Opera to Come Out Soon," *Hartford (Conn.) Post*, January 10, 1906, ibid.
31. "King for a Day," *Musical America* (New York), March 3, 1906, Bierley Collection, Series 7: Press Book 80.
32. "Sousa's Latest Opera Produced," *New York Telegraph*, March 27, 1906, Bierley Collection, Series 7: Press Book 26.
33. "Professional Matinee To-day," *Philadelphia Record*, April 12, 1906, Bierley Collection, Series 7: Press Book 80.
34. *Music and Musicians* 24, Bierley Collection, Series 7: Press Book 80.
35. "'The Free Lance' Hit Comic Opera Bullseye," *New York Press*, April 17, 1906, Bierley Collection, Series 7: Press Book 26.
36. Warfield, "John Philip Sousa and 'The Menace of Mechanical Music,'" 451.
37. Ibid.
38. Frank Luther Mott, *A History of American Magazines, Vol. V, 1905–1930, Part 2* (Cambridge, Mass.: Belknap Press of Harvard University, 1968), 27–33.
39. Sousa, "Menace of Mechanical Music," 278.
40. Ibid., 281.
41. Warfield, "John Philip Sousa and 'The Menace of Mechanical Music,'" 456.

14. Working on a Masterpiece: Rinde Eckert's *And God Created Great Whales*

Jonathan Chambers

For more than thirty years, Rinde Eckert has engaged in writing, composing, and performing works for the stage that are deeply philosophical and categorically theatrical.[1] With his "new music-theatre" piece, *And God Created Great Whales*—workshopped at PS 122 in New York City in the late 1990s, first performed at the Foundry Theatre, also in New York City in 2000, and subsequently revived nationally and internationally—Eckert takes as his point of departure Herman Melville's masterpiece, *Moby-Dick*.[2] Regarding his work's connection to its iconic source material, Eckert has remarked, "I'm not interested in doing *Moby-Dick*. Melville did that very well."[3] Instead, as with many of Eckert's other pieces, such as *The Gardening of Thomas D.*, *Orpheus X*, and *Ulysses Highway*, and their circumlocutory connections to the *Divine Comedy*, the myth of Orpheus and Eurydice, and *The Odyssey* respectively, *And God Created Great Whales*' relation to *Moby-Dick* is more thematic, metaphoric, and complex than it is a literal reiteration of the major plot points from Melville's narrative. In this way, Eckert's piece is perhaps best thought of as a *Moby-Dick*-inspired rumination that "stands in clear relation to [Melville's] epic but ramifies it in completely different ways."[4] More precisely, Eckert transforms Captain Ahab's concentrated fixation on the pursuit of the great white whale into a meditation on loss, revelation, death, consciousness, and the mysterious, obsessive, and tortured nature of artistic creation. While I am interested in all of these thematic threads and will touch on each in the course of this essay, the latter serves as my through-line. To that end, I will consider specifically the ways in which Melville's tale "of one man's obsession with a large white whale" becomes in the hands of Eckert an analogue for the vexed, compulsive, and glorious process of generating creative work.[5]

While its primary organizing principle is largely thematic, *And God Created Great Whales* does have a narrative thread. In sum, Nathan, played by Eckert, is a piano tuner and composer who anxiously and obsessively works to finish an opera based on Melville's masterpiece before his failing memory vanishes forever. From the moment of his first entrance during the preshow—wearing a crumpled gray suit that bears the marks of having been lived in for a very long time—until the final moments, when a storm of amnesia overtakes his mind, Nathan attempts to create, all the while struggling against the inescapability of memory loss that make it increasingly difficult to do so. Thus, Nathan's disintegrating consciousness—a condition that progressively worsens as the eighty-minute performance pushes forward—and its effect on his obsessive pursuit of art are counterpart to the physical challenges Melville's Ahab faces in his all-engrossing pursuit of the white whale. Just as Melville characterizes Ahab's chase of his quarry as an act that is both transcendent and tortured, Eckert represents Nathan's artistic labor as simultaneously sublime and grueling. In both pieces, then, human beings use work to rise above the mundane in an effort to glimpse the divine.

To compensate for his condition, Nathan uses a collection of color-coded tape recorders marked for particular functions: blue is the "master tape," green is for "incidental notes," red is the "working tape," orange is "to record anything [he] remember[s] from the past," and yellow is for "miscellaneous philosophical ruminations."[6] These tape recorders are scattered pell-mell about the playing space. He also wears a white tape recorder, tied around his neck with rope and secured with thread-worn duct tape to his waist. When Nathan pushes play on this tape recorder in the first moments of the performance, several things are revealed:

> Your name is Nathan. You are suffering memory loss. You are listening to a set of instructions you put together to help you continue. Do not take the tape out of the machine for any reason. Do not take this tape recorder from around your neck.
>
> You many stop this tape and rewind whenever your memory proves capable, whenever you can anticipate the instructions. Until then, let the tape play.
>
> Today you will continue to work on your opera. *Moby-Dick*.[7]

Thus, the white tape recorder, hanging from Nathan's neck, secured to his body, and dictating his artistic labor, is an analogue to the white whale that burdens and controls Ahab's entire existence; it, along with the other tape recorders, serves not only as Nathan's substitute mind but also as a regulating, balancing, and compelling weight or ballast.[8] Though the voice on the tapes is that of Nathan (that is, Eckert), recorded at a time when he was still lucid and aware of his condition, it is never made clear how this system of recording was created, what caused his condition in the first place, how long it has been going on, or how much time passes during the action of the performance. Eckert's refusal—or perhaps, more accurately, lack of interest—in providing answers to these questions is just one of the ways that he escapes the burden of narrative and instead invests *And God Created Great Whales* with a sense of swirl and churn.

This sense of swirl and churn is key to Eckert's attempt to create a multilayered dramaturgy, which simultaneously evokes not only the cluttered state of Nathan's failing mind and the ever-present churning sea that dominates Melville's epic but also the chaotic, unpredictable nature of artistic creation. To be sure, while the locus of the action is, in a literal sense, Nathan's apartment/studio, the piece is located even more so in the mind of Nathan, a space where the action is interior, where thoughts instead of events emerge and recede outside of any normative sense, and where time is indeterminate. In other words, as a replacement for a physical locale and linear unfolding of event, the action of *Whales* takes place entirely (save for the brief coda) in the realm of his darting consciousness, and the focus is on Nathan battling his fading memory, struggling to finish his great work of art, all the while simultaneously inspired and overwhelmed by the cultural weight of Melville.

Eckert's endeavor to hold all of these thematic and narrative threads before his audience concurrently not only captures the oftentimes darting and leaping quality of the mind in the throes of artistic creation but is also an apt tribute to the complexity of Melville's art, which defies singular genre classification. To be sure, the discursive range manifest in *Moby-Dick*—including "short story, drama, travelogue, romance, quest, adventure, sermon, tall tale, folklore, and myth, as well as economic, historical, and other expository information about the American industry of whaling and biological data about the cellular structure or cetology of whales"[9]—has been aptly termed a "symphony" and a study in the "multiplicity of perspective."[10] The simultaneity of thematic and narrative threads is, perhaps, the most readily apparent way that Eckert endows *And God Created Great Whales* with a sense of multiplicity; yet monolithic, linear, and rational structures are troubled in other ways as well. For instance, in the course of the performance Eckert draws on a vast range of musical styles, from aria to spiritual and from sea chant to discordant sound. His borrowing and blending of these musical traditions is sometimes faithful and sometimes not, creating musical hybrids that defy tradition and reason. The cacophony of musical sounds corresponds with the collage of words spoken: Melville's prose is nestled against text authored by Eckert. In this regard, then, the composite of spoken word and musical sounds not only matches the convolution of genres contained in Melville's novel but also captures the sense of disquiet that haunts the mind of the obsessed artist at work.

The setting is similarly layered and multiple. As noted above, the mise-en-scène is, in a literal sense, Nathan's apartment/studio, and yet it is something more as well. Dominating the stage is a baby grand piano, wrapped with sailing line that evokes the rigging of Melville's whaling ship, the *Pequod*.[11] Two ends of the sailing line extend vertically into a triangle to suggest the sail of a ship. Surrounding the piano-boat are bits of scrap paper, flashcards, Post-it notes, items torn from magazines and books, cassette tapes, and snapshot-sized pictures. The purpose of these items is ambiguous: they may be the strewn source material left in the wake of the harried artist at work and/or the tools used as Nathan attempts to recall and "prime the memory" and/or perhaps the detritus and debris floating in the sea surrounding the *Pequod*. Also scattered about the playing space are musical instruments: a ukulele, a frame drum, a tambourine. A few packing crates are set below the piano-boat as well as in the upstage-left corner. Upstage-right is a large mast-like structure, extending upward beyond the sightline. Attached to it is more sailing line, which intersects the space horizontally and vertically, and upon which some of the tape recorders hang. Thus, the entire mise-en-scène is a merging and blurring of Nathan's studio/mind and Ahab's whaling ship. To be sure, the setting conveys powerfully the simultaneous presence of times, worlds, and events—real, literary, and imagined—all caught in an eddy. It conveys as well the notion that the world surrounding the obsessed artist at work is transformed by the art created.

This sense of indeterminate swirl and churn is borne out in characterization as well. Sharing the stage with Nathan throughout is a protean figure, referred to as the Muse, played in 2000 and again in the various revival productions by mezzo-soprano Nora Cole. At the beginning of the piece, the Muse is discovered upstage-left, dressed in a striking red dress, sitting on the perch of packing crates, "softly plucking a ukulele," while Nathan sleeps at the piano. When his hand falls on the keys, Nathan is jarred awake; he stands, stumbles, looks inquisitively at the piano and his unfinished musical chart, and seems at a loss. This moment of disorientation is interrupted and calmed when the Muse gently but firmly instructs him to "push play."[12] After receiving the reminder of his condition and the description of his task noted above, the voice on the tape directs Nathan:

> Look around the room.
>
> There is a woman. She is a product of your imagination. She will be helping you. She is infallible, so listen to anything she has to say about music, or art, or the dark night of the soul, or whatever. But do not follow her advice on cooking or any other thing related to the physical world.[13]

The Muse thus calms Nathan and works to keep him on task. Beyond this, the introduction of the Muse immediately brings to the fore, in the form of one of the main characters, the primary theme in the performance: though clearly vested with considerable power and knowledge, the Muse that guides the artist's work is nonetheless an apparition whose evanescent presence is uncertain and mysterious. In this regard, she embodies the inexplicable nature of artistic creation (figure 14.1).

While the Muse is the most recurrent of the personas Cole assumes, she also conjures into being many of the characters from *Moby-Dick*. In the course of the performance, Pip, Queequeg, Starbuck, Ishmael, and Ahab (to name a few) are channeled through dialogue, song, and dance by Cole and Eckert into brief and fleeting existence. In all cases, however, the lines between Nathan and the Muse and other figures drawn into their world are blurred, as if filtered through the prism of Nathan's weakening mind or

Fig. 14.1. Nora Cole (the Muse) and Rinde Eckert (Nathan) in *And God Created Great Whales*. Photo: Caleb Wertenbaker.

the rippling haze of moving water. The most significant of the other figures the Muse conjures is Olivia, who (of course) is not drawn from Melville's narrative. Olivia both is and is not the Muse. When first introduced, Olivia is described as a former opera diva who would like Nathan to write a part for her. But as the piece unfolds, the truth of this biography becomes less certain; instead, it becomes conceivable that Nathan has endowed someone named Olivia, who might just be a client who wants her piano tuned, with the persona of a former opera diva. Or maybe Olivia is both a former opera diva and a client who wants her piano tuned. As is Nathan's memory of *Moby-Dick*, the details regarding Olivia and his relationship with her, while initially appearing somewhat clear, are increasingly fuzzy; fleeting moments of lucidity (that is, a flash of a particular memory on occasion that may or may not be true) are abruptly unsettled, never complete, and in no way grounded in certainty.

Olivia is often called into being when Nathan plays messages, voiced by Cole, which she has left for him on his answering machine, hence adding to the sense of indeterminacy. In his extended review of the 2000 production published in *Postmodern Culture*, Jeffrey Insko persuasively argues that the very presence of the Muse/Olivia introduces into Melville's hypermasculine world the heretofore-repressed feminine. Cole, an African American female, displays remarkable range as she embodies many of Melville's most famous male characters of various ethnicities and in so doing invokes notions of "gender performativity and racial fluidity." As with narrative structures, sounds, and words, Melville's iconic characters emerge, merge, and recede, displacing traditional gender and racial expectations. While Eckert clearly seems to be interested in throwing light on the "gender exclusivity" of both *Moby-Dick* and, by extension, "the culture that produced it," Insko convincingly contends that such criticism (in typical postmodern fashion) is never overdetermined.[14] Indeed, instead of being pulled to the fore, this critique is just one of the many impulses that advance and retreat, swirl and churn, as does the sea for Ahab or the unsettled mind of Nathan.

The sense of incessant and unsettled movement as the primary organizing principle for characterization is compellingly evident when the Muse (speaking as Olivia) recalls one of the phone messages Olivia left for Nathan. She begins: "No part for me then. Perhaps you'd consider putting in something."[15] On the one hand, the request made in these two sentences—which in bits and pieces recurs throughout the performance—may be construed as Olivia, as client, asking her piano tuner for a part for her piano; on the other, it could be Olivia, as former opera diva, asking for a part in Nathan's opera, in so doing calling attention to the absence of the feminine voice in Melville's work. Or, perhaps it is some merging of these two scenarios in Nathan's failing mind. Notably, it is the second scenario that apparently wins the day, overriding the initial ambiguity, as is evidenced by the specificity of the balance of the line. The Muse, conceivably still conjuring Olivia, continues: "Perhaps Ahab could have a vision. A dark woman appears to bring him a promise or a warning. Or maybe some heavenly creature at the end descending over Ishmael floating on his coffin. She could look just like me. Hanging there on a celestial wire, singing of redemption or love."[16] While the Olivia-as-former-opera-diva scenario seems to be verified at this moment, because of the indeterminacy and blurring of the Muse and Olivia at this point and throughout, as well as the recurring nature of bits and pieces of this line at other points in the performance, it is also possible to see the scenario as yet another instance where the promise of certainty is, on second glance, not certain at all. In this regard, it is as if the compelling promise of completing the opera overtakes and rewrites even the most mundane of conversations and interactions that haunt Nathan's memory. All interactions are drawn into his swirling consciousness, obsessed with completing his masterwork.

Olivia, an uncertain character played by the ephemeral Muse, amplifies indeterminacy in other ways as well. For example, neither the operatic part Olivia requests nor the scene she describes in her phone message are in *Moby-Dick*. To be sure, at the end of the novel the great whale destroys the *Pequod* and its crew is pulled into the swirling vortex created as it sinks into the sea. It is only in the short epilogue that it is revealed that Ishmael alone survived, when he was pulled from the sea by a passing ship, the *Rachel*. Olivia's imagined scene might be a call for Nathan, the artist, to exercise poetic license by anthropomorphizing the *Rachel* into a role suitable for the former opera diva, Olivia. Nathan's inability and refusal to comply with the request—perhaps driven by his fear of letting go of the certainty of Melville's narrative that continues to stick in his failing memory—eventually leads to an argument between Nathan and the Muse regarding the artist's responsibility when dealing with a source text. While the subject of fidelity to one's source is the initial point of discussion in the heated exchange, more knotty issues quickly bubble to the surface, including the role of inspiration in creation, the often-reactionary representational politics of opera, the masculinist ideology frequently marshaled in great art, and the restrained, ignored, and forgotten place of women in the narrative of the United States.

MUSE. It's a cameo. Something feminine—a ballast for all that monomaniacal striving. It's a good idea. I like it.

NATHAN. It's a star turn. It's an exaggeration. She doesn't belong. It's a whaling ship, for God's sake.

MUSE. It's an opera, for God's sake. Exaggeration is its lifeblood. [. . .]

NATHAN. It doesn't work. It's not a magical place. It's a bloody business. There are no comforting visions. There is the ship and the whalebones and the harpoons and the stuck whale, lanced and bleeding running from these rancorous creatures, then the towing of the carcass, the slaughter, the men high on the kill, the water white with frenzied sharks tearing at the wounded obliging flesh. There are no visitations, no sculpted women appearing in the dark with prayers and promises.

MUSE. Are you telling me I'm wrong? Are you telling me I don't know what I'm doing? Listen to the tape, Nathan. It says "infallible." It says, "Listen to everything she has to say about the dark night of the soul."

NATHAN. It also says "product of my imagination."

MUSE. Is that a threat? Are you threatening me? Don't you dare. I'm the only thing that stands between you and a completely blank mind, so don't you dare.[17]

As he does with other parts of the piece, Eckert refuses to offer an easy or pat resolution to the issues brought to the surface in this dispute between Nathan and the Muse. Instead, the issues eddy with bits and pieces of Melville's narrative and inconclusive information regarding Olivia and her history with and relation to Nathan. In sum, then, Olivia is as nebulous as the Muse, invoking in powerful ways the sense of swirl and churn. In so doing, Eckert puts on stage the complexity of artistic creation; he shows inspiration as vexed, the expectations of the past as burdensome, and the creative process as frequently torturous.

While the fleeting and irresolute nature of Nathan's memory is vital to the thematic and narrative structures of *And God Created Great Whales*, the very conception of memory and its connection to the task of artistic creation is also a strong undercurrent. As did Ishmael, Nathan records his memories of the attempt to land the great work of his life, seeking to ensure posterity. However, whereas Ishmael's recollection of the *Pequod*'s fateful excursion was indisputably certain and his memory was positioned before his audience of readers as a faithful recapitulation of events, Eckert provides neither Nathan nor his audience with any such certitude. Indeed, when Nathan remembers events or facts, it is repeatedly left unclear if the memory is true or grounded. Thus, departing from the securely anchored narrative of *Moby-Dick* in which memory was stable, in *And God Created Great Whales* Eckert conceives of memory not only as variable but also as constructed at the moment of recall as an entirely new mental experience. Of course, the grand irony of all this is that while Eckert drew on a work of literature that assumes memory is reliable, he nevertheless exposes the labyrinth-like conception of memory that troubles such sureness. In so doing, he leads his audience to reflect on what memory is and to think deeply about what role it plays in the process of artistic creation. Moreover, he creates an audience experience that parallels that of Nathan's: whereas Nathan works to remember and, in turn, to create, Eckert's audiences must work to make sense of the process they see unfolding before them.

At the end of *Moby-Dick*, Ahab's hubris leads him to sacrifice himself to the great cause of his life. Likewise, near the end of *And God Created Great Whales*, madness overtakes Nathan's mind. Standing center stage, with all the tape recorders hanging around his neck playing simultaneously (recalling the frenetic moments at the end of *Moby-Dick* when the harpoon line wraps around Ahab's neck and he is pulled into the sea by the fast-retreating whale), Nathan is pulled under, his noble artistic venture left incomplete. The first part of the coda to the performance adds little hope: Nathan is discovered sitting stage right, gazing blankly offstage. The flicker of a television image is projected on his face, matched with the faintly playing sound from the 1956 movie *Moby-Dick*, starring Gregory Peck. At this moment, there is a sense that without memory, Nathan is nothing. The only hope in this moment is that his composition, like the source material it is based upon, will be pulled from oblivion years after he is gone.

All that said, while Nathan seems doomed to end in void and his effort to land his whale (that is, complete his opera) is never clearly resolved, his attempt at creation is compellingly beautiful. Nearing the halfway point of the performance, the/his voice on the white tape recorder around his neck declares, "If you are still listening, your disease has progressed. You may need to exercise or prime the memory, before starting your day."[18] This warning is immediately followed by a moment when Nathan "primes" his memory with flash cards: at one point, he evocatively holds up a picture of the "ocean," represented by a scrawled swirl or vortex, while at the same time he holds a picture of a "mind," represented by a strikingly similar image.[19] The jump-start attempt works and Nathan's "memory kicks in." The representation of creation in the moments that follow is shown as glorious. The pace quickens. Ideas and laughter flow. The artist and his Muse revel in the glory brought about by the obsessive pursuit of art. This optimism and glory is offset, however, when, near the end of the piece, the voice on the tape recorder around Nathan's neck observes, "If you have not rewound by now, this means your disease has progressed to a critical stage."[20] The voice then instructs him to take his materials and place them in a box, attach an already-addressed envelope to it, and put it in the mailbox outside his door.

The second part of the coda suggests that Nathan was successful in following these directions. The Muse enters (or is it Olivia?), now dressed in a brilliant white dress, and finds the catatonic Nathan sitting in front of the television and the half-packed box that contains his work on the piano. After momentarily reading the incomplete chart and libretto, she pushes play on one of the tape recorders. Hearing the sound of his in-process opera fill the air, Nathan stirs and is drawn back into the world (momentarily?); as the lights fade, the Muse takes Nathan's hand, helps him to his feet, and leads him downstage (evoking the rescue of Ishmael by the crew of the *Rachel*, as narrated in the epilogue of Melville's epic, as well as the part in Nathan's opera as requested by Olivia) while singing the stirring strains from his *Moby-Dick* opera. While this moment is unquestionably beautiful and is shot through with a sense of the profound energy required for artistic creation and the moments of ecstasy it can bring, it also calls to mind the high cost / low reward and precarious nature of that activity. Indeed, while the Muse and Nathan will share this moment of beauty, it is never made clear if the masterpiece that consumed the artist will exist beyond this one moment.

Beyond the multilayered dramaturgy used to explore the complicated process of artistic creation, *And God Created Great Whales* swirls and churns on the topic of artistic creation in one other, perhaps more metatextual, way. In short, of the many ironies that bubble to the surface in the piece, one of the more striking is how Eckert poeticizes the claim of Melville scholar Thomas Inge:

> Millions of Americans who have never read a line by Melville know the names of Moby-Dick [and] Captain Ahab. [. . .] *Moby-Dick* is the great-unread American novel [. . . It is] a challenge which many undertake but few finish, yet probably the most revered work of fiction by anyone who cares about writing and American culture. [. . .] So widely known is the basic plot structure of *Moby-Dick* and so frequently has it been adapted to the media that there are people who think they have read the novel without having gone near the actual text.[21]

Building on this observation, I would like to suggest that Nathan's inability to recall the plot of Melville's masterpiece is a sort of joke shared with many in Eckert's audience: as with Nathan, they either have never read it or, in a best-case scenario, wish to forget that they were forced to read it in high school or college.[22] Thus, Nathan's failure to remember—or his ability to remember only the most widely circulated highpoints—is conterminous with the public's relationship to Melville's text: we all know it (or think we do), but do we really know it at all? A line spoken by the Muse near the end of the piece echoes this sentiment. Noting that she does not exist beyond the limits of Nathan's mind, she conflates her status with that of Melville's text: "Meanwhile my publisher puts out this ragtag paperback. I'm like the pulp edition. Dramatic picture on a glossy cover: the whale breaching like an angry loaf of bread, the boiling sea, the swamped ship."[23]

While the subtext of this lament remains layered and multiple, part of what is invoked is the frequent preoccupation American culture has had with *Moby-Dick* for nearly eighty years. Since being "discovered" in the 1920s by the likes of D. H. Lawrence, championed as the literary embodiment of the American spirit, and thrust to the fore of national consciousness by mid-century critics and canon-makers like Lionel Trilling and F. O. Matthiessen, Melville's masterpiece has been "one of great ongoing cultural productions"[24] in the United States, which makes the fact that it is "the great-unread American novel" all the more ironic. Countless culture makers—from numerous avant-garde, mainstream, and popular artists who draw upon and critique its themes, to politicians who laud it as exemplar of the adventurous (or is it obsessive?) American spirit—have and continue to respond to, abuse, revise, and appropriate the text. Eckert seems keenly aware of the enormous and varied collection of meanings within which Melville's text circulates. Where *And God Created Great Whales* separates itself from those other endeavors is in the way it manages to tap into the spirit of obsession that rests at the thematic core of Melville's novel and offers a moving rumination on the ways in which that same kind of obsession haunts the swirling and churning labor of artistic creation.

Notes

1. A variety of terms have been applied to Eckert's work, including new music-theatre, performance art, new dance, new opera, chamber opera, and postmodern theatre. In his work he draws widely from theatre, dance, and music traditions, as well as from historical, literary, and philosophical texts.

2. The spring 2000 Foundry Theatre production, directed by David Schweiser, received uniformly positive reviews. It received an Obie and was nominated for a Drama Desk Award. The piece was remounted in September 2000, and again from November 2001 through January 2002, by the Culture Project. That production was remounted in various locations, nationally and internationally. A revival production was first workshopped at the University of Southern California in 2009 and in turn staged at REDCAT (Roy and Edna Disney / CalArts Theatre) in Los Angeles in early 2012. This revival production was subsequently staged in New York by the Culture Project in February and March 2012. My review of the revival production appeared in the March 2013 issue of *Theatre Journal*. Some of the ideas and observations made in this essay are included in that review as well as in the introduction I authored to the collection *Orpheus X and Other Plays* by Rinde Eckert (South Gate, Calif.: NoPassport Press, 2012), 4–13.
3. Don Shewey, "Rinde Eckert: 'Not *Moby-Dick* but Whale-ish,'" *New York Times*, June 11, 2000, AR4.
4. Ibid.
5. Rinde Eckert, *And God Created Great Whales*, in *Orpheus X and Other Plays* (South Gate, Calif.: NoPassport Press, 2012), 84.
6. Ibid., 84, 99. My reading of the script is supplemented through multiple viewings of the DVD recording of the 2009 revival, recorded at the University of Southern California (unpublished), as well as by my seeing the piece performed live at the Bleecker Street Theatre in New York on February 29, 2012. Also informing my analysis are the reviews of Tom Seller, "Amazing Grace: Rinde Eckert's *And God Created Great Whales* and *An Idiot Divine*," *Theatre* 31, no. 2 (2001): 116–18; and Jeffrey Insko, "Art after Ahab: Review of *And God Created Great Whales*," *Postmodern Culture* 12, no. 1 (2001).
7. Eckert, *And God Created Great Whales*, 84.
8. Insko, "Art after Ahab."
9. Sharon Talley, *The Student Companion to Herman Melville* (Westport, Conn.: Greenwood Press, 2007), 49.
10. Robert K. Martin, *Hero, Captain, and Stranger: Male Friendship, Social Critique, and Literary Form in the Sea Novels of Herman Melville* (Chapel Hill: University of North Carolina Press, 1987), 67; Shelia Post-Lauria, *Correspondent Colorings: Melville and the Marketplace* (Amherst: University of Massachusetts Press, 1996), 117.
11. My description of the setting is based on my observations of the 2012 revival production, designed by John Torres and Caleb Wertenbaker, and based on original designs by Kevin Abrams.

12. Eckert, *And God Created Great Whales*, 83.
13. Ibid., 84.
14. Insko, "Art after Ahab."
15. Eckert, *And God Created Great Whales*, 92.
16. Ibid., 92.
17. Ibid., 117–18.
18. Ibid., 99.
19. Ibid., 102.
20. Ibid., 124.
21. Thomas Inge, "Melville and Popular Culture," in *A Companion to Melville Studies*, ed. John Bryant (Westport, Conn.: Greenwood Press, 1986), 695–96. Insko also briefly explicates Eckert's work via Inge.
22. Insko, "Art after Ahab."
23. Eckert, *And God Created Great Whales*, 122.
24. Insko, "Art after Ahab."

Conclusion: Waiting in the Wings—Work

Elizabeth A. Osborne

In the fall of 1937, Susan Glaspell asked playwright Arnold Sundgaard to write a play about syphilis for the Federal Theatre Project (FTP). The resulting play, *Spirochete*, would serve as the FTP's poster child for a national campaign against the nefarious venereal disease. But for Sundgaard and Glaspell, *Spirochete* became emblematic of a very different battle—this one over intellectual property and workers' rights. Commissioned by Glaspell in her role as director of the FTP's Midwestern Play Bureau, Sundgaard researched and wrote *Spirochete* almost entirely on his own time rather than in the course of his employment, which he believed meant that he owned the rights to the play. The FTP disagreed. Glaspell advocated tirelessly for Sundgaard and writers' rights, drawing the Dramatists Guild into the fight and ultimately threatening to resign from the FTP. While she and Sundgaard eventually prevailed, the victory was hollow. Glaspell's relationship with the FTP was irreparably damaged and she resigned soon after. Ironically, the victory cost Sundgaard his job with the FTP as well; the royalties that he earned from *Spirochete* made his income—briefly—high enough that he was no longer eligible for government relief. And so, while Glaspell and Sundgaard argued successfully for Sundgaard's rights, the cost of that triumph was the loss of their gainful employment at the height of the Great Depression—in spite of the fact that their employer had been founded precisely to put unemployed theatre workers back to work.[1]

This sobering tale shines light on the hard truths that often surround worker advocacy. It also recalls the many traumas that happen in the process of bringing a theatrical work to life beyond the limelight that is visible to the audience. *Spirochete* did, after all, become part of the legend of the FTP, but it did so through the play's larger effect on the public awareness and discourse surrounding syphilis nationwide. As the May 4, 1938, issue of *Variety* argued, "In Spirochete the Federal Theatre finds its best argument for its existence; delivering a play of real social importance."[2] Nowhere did the *Variety* article list the challenges that Glaspell and Sundgaard faced in fighting for Sundgaard's rights as the writer, and future articles ignored the departures of Glaspell and Sundgaard from their FTP employment. Those stories quietly disappeared from view, replaced by a focus on the play's public good.

This volume has attempted to resurrect such stories and to lay a foundation for scholarly work that intentionally and systematically strives to pull back the curtain so as to reveal theatrical work and workers in their many facets. Taken together, these essays span a range of questions about workers, working conditions, and the erasure of certain workers from written memory and raise larger questions about the "work of the public mind" and acts of creation. Operating at various intersections of theatre, history, and performance, they defy preconceived notions of theatrical work and workers and delve into previously forgotten theatrical labor of the past. They remind scholars that the lives of workers outside the theatre—intimate partnerships, day jobs, and the multiple activities that occupy theatre workers' time away from work—can be just as revealing to the historical record as focused studies of plays, performers, and technicians. And they challenge theatre and performance scholars to expand how they think and write about work, contending that theatre itself could be one way of accessing the "work of the public mind" in the making and remaking of popular ideology. The many perspectives and approaches shown by these scholars suggest that this field of study is ripe for further research, and it is the collective hope of the authors that theatre and performance scholars will take up this cry for continued, deep, and theoretically informed discourse.

While initially inspired by the economic downturn that began with the bursting of the housing bubble in 2007 and continued through the writing of this book, this dual inquiry into theatre and work is timeless. Whether the U.S. economy is in the midst of a boom or a bust is immaterial. In a capitalistic society, economics will always play a vital role in understanding the culture, the people, and the hidden relationships that drive individuals to act. Yet this important facet often goes ignored in theatrical research. Instead, scholarship constellates around those historical moments when economics play such an enormous role in the lives of a people that they simply cannot be ignored. Certainly, the workers' theatre movements of the Great Depression are worthy of attention—and, as such, are represented in this volume—but connections between marketing and the building of a new Shakespeare festival or the reverberations of intellectual property law in the comic operas of John Philip Sousa reveal creative new ways of thinking about theatre history.

As noted in the introduction and in the individual section overviews, this volume considers theatre from act to artifact so as to reveal and interrogate the many ways that work resonates within the theatre. As the essays have demonstrated—to borrow an important theme from Sara Freeman's essay—work and theatre have a long, complex, and intimate partnership. While we have divided this volume into engaging thematic sections that we hope are helpful to those readers planning to teach courses on labor and performance, we also recognize that these categories are also, in some ways, artificially imposed and that other themes beg for further exploration. Yet the essays in this volume address many of these questions as well. How, for example, might the process of collaboration shape creative works? Sara Freeman's focus on the long-term influence of intimate partnerships on creative work provides fertile ground for such study, as does her own work establishing potential historiographical approaches for scholars interested in exploring creative partnerships, collective creation, devised productions, or other established alliances.

Numerous essays in this volume also raise important questions about the virtues and costs of artistic creation; whether intellectual, emotional, physical, social, or economic, what cost does creativity exact from creators? Jonathan Chambers and Max Shulman both study the costs that creative works exact on workers' bodies. In Chambers's essay, the lead character tumbles toward madness even as he struggles to finish his final creative work. Shulman's essay shows the performers' bodies literally becoming the canvas that displays their entertainment prowess; beaten, battered, bruised, or permanently deformed, these popular entertainers could never escape their work. Christine Woodworth's essay returns to the economic facts of life: theatrical workers must also survive in the real world of rent, food, and utility bills, and the jobs that they take to pay those bills have a real impact on the theatre they create. Rosemarie K. Bank examines another phenomenon—cultural workers who build a landscape that literally erases the worker from the idealized city of the future. As these scholars suggest with their research, it is time to publicly interrogate the long-held stereotype of the starving artist who survives on ramen noodles, a friend's threadbare sofa, and the irrepressible drive to create art.

Work in the theatre often revolves around issues of credit as well, an issue that our title—*Working in the Wings*—begins to address. The *Under the Gaslight* anecdote with which we opened this collection is often overlooked in favor of the high-profile, international court battle between Augustin Daly and Dion Boucicault over which artist owned the rights to the train effect and could secure fees for its use onstage. More recently, in the famous 1996 battle over the rights that dramaturg Lynn M. Thomson could gain from her work on Jonathan Larson's *Rent*, the issues of credit and remuneration became paramount concerns.[3] Tracey Elaine Chessum peers into John Philip Sousa's personal campaign for the protection of composers' intellectual property, reminding readers and audiences that the creative work is indeed the culmination of an extraordinary amount of labor and that workers deserve credit and payment for that work. Tom Robson's recovery of the nineteenth-century theatre technician offers another approach to this issue, as the workers he strives to recover are those who are habitually and often intentionally relegated to the theatrical wings so as to maintain the magic of the theatre. So, too, does Jerry Dickey's work on the African American waiters who also danced the cakewalk in resort hotels during the early twentieth century attempt to recover these hidden workers. Chessum, Robson, and Dickey pursue innovative ways to track and think about such questions, challenging the scholar to seek out new archives and new ways of thinking about old archives. What methodologies might encourage further recoveries of the artists, technicians, stage managers, designers, and other hidden theatrical workers of the past? What insights might such recoveries lead to in contemporary scholarship?

Another vital set of questions emerges when considering the work of the theatre. Elizabeth Reitz Mullenix in her essay conceives of theatre as "the work of the public mind," and this way of thinking about how theatre influences, reflects, and reimagines public and national identity offers intriguing possibilities. AnnMarie T. Saunders similarly incorporates the idea of theatre as one of the elements that helped formulate a more uniform national identity during the United States' early formative years. Melissa Rynn Porterfield's work on the rise of the Three Rivers Shakespeare Festival in Pittsburgh follows a parallel trajectory; in founding the festival and developing the marketing program that would make it a success, Attilio Favorini played to the city's own identity—tweaked with an infusion of the illustrious Bard. How does the work of the theatre permeate popular culture? How might these ideas of nation formation, public identity, and theatrical performance play into discussions of the function of theatre in the twenty-first century? How, too, might they help scholars to reimagine strategies for theatre and social change?

At the same time, the power of theatre as an instrument for social empowerment can be seen in its myriad popular entertainments and the audiences that love them. As Chrystyna Dail, Elizabeth A. Osborne, and Dorothy Chansky demonstrate, even the most frequently sown historical intersections of theatrical performance and labor can reveal hidden gems when carefully and methodically probed. Dail's work on the UAW Union Theatre, for example, yields the surprising portrait of the Union Theatre using performance to encourage antidiscriminatory thought and practice in its membership. Osborne's essay on the Federal Theatre Project's Caravan Theatre reminds us of the enormous potential audience for theatrical works and of the possibilities inherent in a national theatre designed to serve the working class. Aimed less at a widespread, popular audience, Chansky's work comparing two radically different approaches to women's work in the domestic sphere suggests that theatre offers a way of processing and challenging social expectations. Each of these essays effectively rediscovers something, whether reimagining the concerns of union or worker theatres, offering new ways of thinking about a long-established theatre organization, or tasking readers with rethinking their preconceived notions about domestic work for women. How, then, might contemporary theatre and performance scholars use economics to reread those histories that appear to be already thoroughly written?

While they may at first glance appear less glamorous than the thrilling performances that happen onstage or the intriguing process of writing or directing a play, the details of funding, marketing, audience development, working conditions, salaries, and more are perilous to ignore. Early 2014 saw a resurgence of labor activism as Actors' Equity members protested pay inequities for performers on national tours who often received less than actors playing the same roles in Broadway theatres.[4] At the same time, the hit immersive-theatre production *Sleep No More* has raised concerns about the hours, tasks, and physical toll required when producers use unpaid interns rather than hire paid employees.[5] In each of these examples, fiscal matters are interwoven with ethical concerns for producers, laborers, and audiences.

In a world that seems increasingly interested in science, technology, engineering, and mathematics (STEM), largely at the expense of the arts and humanities, it behooves theatre practitioners and scholars to find ways of making connections between the STEM fields and the arts. The essays in this volume serve as one collective foray into that perceived gap. After all, the work of stage technicians who build and create specialized stage machinery depends on engineering. Marketing analysis relies on advances in statistics in order to target and appeal to ideal donors and audience members. Writers interested in receiving royalties must confront contracts and sales figures. Productions as diverse as Tom Stoppard's *Arcadia*, Caryl

Churchill's *A Number*, David Auburn's *Proof*, and Michael Frayn's *Copenhagen* confront the challenges, traumas, joys, confusion, and laughter that result from collisions of theatre and science. And perhaps most interesting of all, small educational companies such as Fusion Science Theatre (Madison, Wisconsin) and Michigan State University's Science Theatre (Lansing) use performance to teach kids about the wonders of chemistry and physics, and the excitement of data collection. As Fusion Science Theatre's website states, the company's approach "combine[s] best practices from science teaching with theatre techniques to produce shows that are investigative, interactive, multi-modal, and verifiably educational."[6] Certainly, questions of work, workers, and the many intersections with theatre, performance, and history that have framed this book concern themselves only peripherally with these ideas, but it is our hope that they dare more theatre and performance scholars to leap into productive conversations across disciplines. We invite social scientists to consider the rich terrain at which the essays in this volume hint and encourage theatre scholars to explore how alternative methodologies might offer ways of thinking about material that our own frames can only partially address. How might theatre and theatre history thrive in this social, cultural, and political atmosphere?

Working in the Wings has set out to bring theatrical work—and workers—out of the wings and into the scholarly spotlight. By delving into histories that reveal hidden work and workers, working conditions, behind-the-scenes work made intentionally invisible, the processes of creating theatrical work, and the many ways that themes of work reverberate through popular culture in the United States, this volume collects a few of the many histories that need to be told. How might these methodologies, themes, and topics be extended to theatre history in other times and places? What might they reveal about the national identities of Greece, Russia, or China, or about communities in South Africa, Argentina, or Australia? How might questions about extratheatrical employment, pay equity, or intimate partnerships inform discussions of community theatres, the Free Theatres of Europe, or the Little Theatre Movement? What other questions about the intersection of theatre, labor, and history require further research? In many ways, *Working in the Wings: New Perspectives on Theatre History and Labor* is about the processes that serve as the foundation for creative work and for scholarship; as theatre and performance scholars, we strive to recover, reveal, and remember those acts.

Notes

1. Arnold Sundgaard, interview by John O'Connor, September 5, 1976, Boston, Mass., WPA Oral Histories Collection, Special Collections and Archives,

George Mason University, Fairfax, Va. The debate over Sundgaard's authorial rights is also documented in a series of letters exchanged between Susan Glaspell, Hallie Flanagan, and Harry Minturn (acting assistant director of the FTP). Of particular note is Glaspell's letter to Flanagan dated April 18, 1938. Glaspell sent carbon copies to multiple high-ranking WPA officials and threatened to bring the Dramatists Guild into the disagreement unless Flanagan capitulated. NARA, RG 69, E839, box 13, "Spirochete—Living Newspaper, Syphilis."

2. Formatting preserved from source. Gold, "*Spirochete*," *Variety*, May 4, 1938, 56.
3. Jesse McKinley, "Family of 'Rent' Creator Settles Suit over Authorship: Dramaturge Gets Money and Playbill Credit," *New York Times*, September 10, 1998, B3. For a detailed response to the issues raised in the lawsuit by thirty-five major late twentieth-century playwrights, see August Baker, Neena Beber, Deborah Baley Brevoort, and Carlyle Brown, et al., "An Author Is an Author Is an Author," *American Theatre* 15, no. 6 (July/August 1998): 6–7.
4. Patrick Healy, "Actors Jam Meeting to Seek Higher Pay for Tours," *New York Times*, January 12, 2014, http://www.nytimes.com/2014/01/13/theater/actors-jam-meeting-to-seek-higher-pay-for-tours.html (accessed February 6, 2014).
5. Christopher Zara, "Former 'Sleep No More' Interns Say Immersive NYC Megahit Offers Little Educational Benefit," *International Business Times*, December 7, 2013, http://www.ibtimes.com/former-sleep-no-more-interns-say-immersive-nyc-megahit-offers-little-educational-benefit-1499418 (accessed February 6, 2014).
6. "Method Workshops," Fusion Science Theatre, http://www.fusionsciencetheater.org/method-workshops/ (accessed January 25, 2014). For more on Science Theatre at Michigan State University, see http://www.pa.msu.edu/sci_theatre/.

Contributors

Rosemarie K. Bank is the author of *Theatre Culture in America, 1825–1860*, and is currently preparing *Staging the Native, 1792–1892*. A member of the College of Fellows of the American Theatre and a Fellow of the Mid-America Theatre Conference, she was the editor of *Theatre Survey* from 2000 to 2003. Several times a fellow of the National Endowment for the Humanities, Bank is a professor of theatre at Kent State University.

Jonathan Chambers is a professor of theatre at Bowling Green State University. He is the author of the book *Messiah of the New Technique: John Howard Lawson, Communism, and American Theatre, 1923–1937* and of the introduction to *Orpheus X and Other Plays* by Rinde Eckert. He has served as the editor of *Theatre Topics*, the president of the American Theatre and Drama Society, and the vice president for research and publication for the Association for Theatre in Higher Education.

Dorothy Chansky is the author of *Composing Ourselves: The Little Theatre Movement and the American Audience*. Her work has appeared in *TDR*, *Theatre Journal*, the *Journal of American Drama and Theatre*, and *Text and Performance Quarterly*. She is the editor of *Theatre Annual* and writes criticism for *New York Theatre Wire*. She heads the history/theory/criticism track in the Department of Theatre and Dance at Texas Tech University.

Tracey Elaine Chessum is an assistant professor of theatre at Ball State University and is a founding artistic director of the Pallas Theatre Collective in Washington, D.C. Her scholarship focuses on musical theatre between 1880 and the First World War.

Chrystyna Dail is an assistant professor of theatre history at Ithaca College. Her research interests include social activist performance, the intersection of race and politics in performance, twentieth-century Ukrainian theatre, and witchcraft on the U.S. stage. She has published articles in the *Journal of American Drama and Theatre*, *Theatre History Studies*, the *Arthur Miller Journal*, and *Performing Arts Resources*.

Jerry Dickey currently serves as a professor in and the director of the University of Florida School of Theatre and Dance. He is a coauthor of *Susan Glaspell and Sophie Treadwell* (with Barbara Ozieblo), a coeditor of *Broadway's Bravest Woman: Selected Writings of Sophie Treadwell* (with Miriam Lopez-Rodriguez), and the author of *Sophie Treadwell: A Research and Production Sourcebook*. His essays have appeared in numerous books and journals.

Sara Freeman is an associate professor of theatre arts at the University of Puget Sound. In 2007 she received the Gerald Kahan Award for the best essay in theatre studies by a younger scholar from the American Society for Theatre Research. She is a coeditor of *Public Theatres and Theatre Publics* and *International Dramaturgy: Translation and Transformations in the Theatre of Timberlake Wertenbaker.*

Elizabeth Reitz Mullenix is the dean of the College of Creative Arts and a professor of theatre at Miami University. She is the author of *Wearing the Breeches: Gender on the Antebellum Stage*. Her second monograph, *Upon a Conspicuous Stage: Civil War Theatre and the Performance of Nationhood*, is currently in progress.

Elizabeth A. Osborne is an associate professor in theatre studies at Florida State University. The author of *Staging the People: Community and Identity in the Federal Theatre Project* and a coeditor of *Working in the Wings*, her new research delves into the role performances play in the making and remaking of memory and history over time.

Melissa Rynn Porterfield teaches at the Carnegie Mellon School of Drama. She has presented her work at the Comparative Drama Conference, the Mid-America Theatre Conference, and the American Society for Theatre Research and published her chapter "Srbljanovic's Ugly American: Simultaneously Constructing Serbian and American Identities" in *Portrayals of Americans on the World Stage*.

Tom Robson is an assistant professor of theatre and dance at Millikin University. His work has been published in *Theatre History Studies*, *Ecumenica*, and the film journal *Jump Cut*. His research primarily focuses on American theatre of the latter part of the nineteenth century and the early part of the twentieth, particularly African American performance.

AnnMarie T. Saunders is the department chair of the Performing and Visual Arts magnet program at Annapolis High School. She is a former assistant editor for *Theatre Journal* and a peer reviewer for the *Journal of American Drama and Theatre* and *Dramaturgy Protocol*. Saunders works as a director, an actor, and a dramaturg in professional and academic theatres in the Washington, D.C., area.

Max Shulman is a doctoral candidate at Tufts University and is presently a lecturer at Rutgers University. Shulman's forthcoming dissertation, "America Menaced: Drug Addiction in Popular Entertainment, 1890–1940," traces the representation of the drug addict in melodrama, variety, jazz acts, and early film.

Christine Woodworth is an assistant professor of theatre at Hobart and William Smith Colleges. Her work has appeared in *Theatre Symposium*, *Theatre History Studies*, *Theatre Annual*, *Text and Presentation*, and a number of edited collections. Woodworth is a coeditor of *Working in the Wings*. She is a past participant in the Mellon School of Theater and Performance Research at Harvard University.

Index

Page numbers in italics indicate illustrations.

Theater in the Americas

The goal of the series is to publish a wide range of scholarship on theater and performance, defining theater in its broadest terms and including subjects that encompass all of the Americas.

The series focuses on the performance and production of theater and theater artists and practitioners but welcomes studies of dramatic literature as well. Meant to be inclusive, the series invites studies of traditional, experimental, and ethnic forms of theater; celebrations, festivals, and rituals that perform culture; and acts of civil disobedience that are performative in nature. We publish studies of theater and performance activities of all cultural groups within the Americas, including biographies of individuals, histories of theater companies, studies of cultural traditions, and collections of plays.

Queries and Submissions
Scott Magelssen, Editor
magelss@uw.edu

Robert A. Schanke, Founder and Editor, 2000–2014

Other Books in the Theater in the Americas Series

Shadowed Cocktails: The Plays of Philip Barry from "Paris Bound" to "The Philadelphia Story"
Donald R. Anderson

A Gambler's Instinct: The Story of Broadway Producer Cheryl Crawford
Milly S. Barranger

Unfriendly Witnesses: Gender, Theater, and Film in the McCarthy Era
Milly S. Barranger

The Theatre of Sabina Berman: "The Agony of Ecstasy" and Other Plays
Translated by Adam Versényi
With an Essay by Jacqueline E. Bixler

Staging Social Justice: Collaborating to Create Activist Theatre
Edited by Norma Bowles and Daniel-Raymond Nadon

Messiah of the New Technique: John Howard Lawson, Communism, and American Theatre, 1923–1937
Jonathan L. Chambers

Composing Ourselves: The Little Theatre Movement and the American Audience
Dorothy Chansky

Ghost Light: An Introductory Handbook for Dramaturgy
Michael Mark Chemers

The Hanlon Brothers: From Daredevil Acrobatics to Spectacle Pantomime, 1833–1931
Mark Cosdon

Richard Barr: The Playwright's Producer
David A. Crespy

Women in Turmoil: Six Plays by Mercedes de Acosta
Edited and with an Introduction by Robert A. Schanke

Rediscovering Mordecai Gorelik: Scene Design and the American Theatre
Anne Fletcher

A Spectacle of Suffering: Clara Morris on the American Stage
Barbara Wallace Grossman

American Political Plays after 9/11
Edited by Allan Havis

Performing Loss: Rebuilding Community through Theater and Writing
Jodi Kanter

Unfinished Show Business: Broadway Musicals as Works-in-Process
Bruce Kirle

Staging America: Cornerstone and Community-Based Theater
Sonja Kuftinec

Words at Play: Creative Writing and Dramaturgy
Felicia Hardison Londré

Entertaining the Nation: American Drama in the Eighteenth and Nineteenth Centuries
Tice L. Miller

Documentary Trial Plays in Contemporary American Theater
Jacqueline O'Connor

Cuba Inside Out: Revolution and Contemporary Theatre
Yael Prizant

Stage, Page, Scandals, and Vandals: William E. Burton and Nineteenth-Century American Theatre
David L. Rinear

Contemporary Latina/o Theater: Wrighting Ethnicity
Jon D. Rossini

Angels in the American Theater: Patrons, Patronage, and Philanthropy
Edited and with an Introduction by Robert A. Schanke

"That Furious Lesbian": The Story of Mercedes de Acosta
Robert A. Schanke

Caffe Cino: The Birthplace of Off-Off-Broadway
Wendell C. Stone

Teaching Performance Studies
Edited by Nathan Stucky and Cynthia Wimmer
With a Foreword by Richard Schechner

Broadway's Bravest Woman: Selected Writings of Sophie Treadwell
Edited and with Introductions by Jerry Dickey and Miriam López-Rodríguez

The Humana Festival: The History of New Plays at Actors Theatre of Louisville
Jeffrey Ullom

Our Land Is Made of Courage and Glory: Nationalist Performance of Nicaragua and Guatemala
E. J. Westlake